WHAT WE
Believe
AND WHY

Volume 1
Third Edition

Lester Hutson

What We Believe and Why - Volume 1 (Third Edition)

Copyright © 2015 Lester Hutson

First Edition - December 1972
Expanded Edition - September 1975

All rights reserved, including the right to reproduce this book or portions thereof in any form without the permission of the author.

All scripture is from the King James and American Standard versions of the Bible, which are in the public domain. All quoted scripture is from the King James version unless otherwise noted.

ISBN: 978-0-9836802-8-4

www.lesterhutson.org

Table of Contents

	Foreword	i
1	The Importance of Studying the Word of God	1
2	How to Study the Word of God	6
3	Proof of Divine Inspiration of the Bible Through Facts, Bible Construction and Prophecies	12
4	The Biblical Claim to Divine Inspiration	20
5	Only the Bible Is Divinely Inspired	24
6	The Existence of a Triune God	28
7	The Father, the Son, and the Holy Spirit	32
8	How the Holy Spirit Convicts the Lost	37
9	The Nature of Man and the Devil	44
10	Blood Redemption, God's Method of Remitting Sins	48
11	Faith, God's Method for Appropriating Eternal Salvation	52
12	The Unpardonable Sin	57
13	In Christ We Have Eternal Security	64

14	The Fatherhood of God and the Brotherhood of Man	68
15	God's Threefold Salvation	74
16	The Difference Between Son-ship and Fellowship	83
17	The Truth About Romans 10:13	89
18	Prayer Is Exclusively for the Children of God	95
19	Under Discipline	101
20	Sanctification	107
21	Doubtful Things	111
22	Water Baptism: Every Believer Should Be Baptized	116
23	Water Baptism: Immersed by a New Testament Church	119
24	The Bible Does Not Teach Baptismal Regeneration	123
25	Baptized into the Body	134
26	Church Membership	139
27	Joining and Attending Church	143
28	The Completion of the Apostolic Ministry	147
29	The Purpose of the Apostolic Ministry	152

30	The Apostolic Ministry Was Limited to the Apostles and Those to Whom They Administered the Gifts	157
31	The Apostolic Ministry Ceased When It Served Its Purpose	162
32	Unknown Tongues	167
33	Miracle Healing	181
34	The Lord's Return	190
35	Resurrection and Judgment	194
36	Tribulation and Millennium	198
37	What a Church Is and When It Was Founded	201
38	The Lord's Church Is Local	206
39	Worshipping in the Church	210
40	Financing the Lord's Church	215
41	The Treatment and Office of the Pastor of the Church	220
42	The Testimony Shown by the Lord's Supper	230
43	Why We Use Wine in the Lord's Supper	236
44	God's Call for Unity in the Church Demands Closed Communion	240
45	The Church of Christ and the Body of Christ Are the Same	247

46	The Biblical Definition of the Word Church Answers Many Questions	252
47	The Make Up and Structure of an Autonomous Church	258
48	The Bible Churches Were Autonomous	263
49	No One Is at Liberty to Violate the God-Ordained Pattern for Church Organization and Operations	268
50	The Sin of Failing to Exactly Follow God's Pattern in Church Organization	273
51	The Lord's Church Should Be Missionary	277
52	The Authority to Carry out Missionary Work Rests in the Church	281

About the Author   286

Foreword

This book is not designed to be easy reading, as one would read a novel. Instead, it is a study book; hopefully, a compliment to the Bible. Effort has been made to present some of the fundamental doctrines of the Bible in a systematic, simple and logical way. I am only focusing on the major Bible doctrines that I consider to be very basic to the faith. It is my sincere desire that this book is studied and these truths mastered by every reader.

I am grateful to God for the response to this book over the years. Those familiar with the book know that there was an original edition followed by an expanded edition in which chapters were added. The *expanded edition* became known as *What We Believe and Why I*. A few years later it was followed by *What We Believe and Why II*. Both volumes have experienced widespread distribution; however, this first volume has seen the most consistent demand.

With this *"Third Edition"* comes a measure of editing; not a re-write, but an improvement in the grammar and wording. The content remains the same; hopefully, the truths contained herein are expressed more clearly and concisely. No chapters from *What We Believe and Why I* have been subtracted and no new chapters have been added. The spacing and layout has also been improved. I am happy to say that a new cover has been added.

Thanks to each one who has encouraged me to keep alive *What We Believe and Why I*. All existing copies have been exhausted. With the help and encouragement of dear friends, new and improved copies are now available. Again, I wish to express my appreciation for so much reader help with circulation; especially, the help of my fellow ministers. The Lord continues to use this book to advantages I never suspected.

Lester Hutson

Chapter 1

The Importance of Studying the Word of God

2 Timothy 2:15

The Bible is the Word of God, **2 Timothy 3:16**, and the Word of God is *"Truth,"* **John 17:17**. It is my firm conviction that every man has a right to **study the Bible** and should **diligently do so**. There's no other way to learn the truth except by study.

This lesson is designed to show why you should study the Bible.

SECTION ONE

THE WORD OF GOD TEACHES US TO STUDY

A. There are those who teach that the common man should not study the Bible.

  1. They contend it is too complicated for the ordinary man to understand.

  2. They say those who have had years of training in the Bible would have far superior knowledge than any layman.

3. Thus, they conclude that the average layman should not confuse himself by studying the Word for himself. He should just take the word of those educated in religion or those with high positions in the church.

B. Two things should be noted at this point:

1. A lot of education in the Scriptures does not necessarily produce a man with accurate understanding of the Scriptures. (As observed in Saul of Tarsus, **Philippians 3:4-6, Acts 22:3**).

2. Even a common man with little education can glean great gems of truth from the Scriptures. (Peter is a case in point, **Acts 4:13**).

C. Therefore, the Bible teaches every man to study it diligently.

1. The principle of diligent study is clearly set forth in the Old Testament, **Deuteronomy 6:7-9**.

2. The prophets practiced diligent study of the Scriptures, **1 Peter 1:10-11**.

3. Solomon said, *"The heart of the righteous studieth to answer,"* **Proverbs 15:28**.

4. Moses said, *"O that they were wise, that they understood this, that they would consider their latter end!"* **Deuteronomy 32:29**.

5. Timothy said to *"study"* God's Word, **2 Timothy 2:15**.

D. Failure to acquaint oneself with the truth is a serious offense against God.

1. First, failure here is direct disobedience and rebellion against God's commandments:

    a. He plainly says *"Study,"* **2 Timothy 2:15**.

    b. Rebellion before God *"is as the sin of witchcraft,"* **1 Samuel 15:22-23**.

2. Second, how could we ever perform the acts by which we are *"approved unto God,"* **2 Timothy 2:15**, if we don't even know what those acts are?

a. It is in His Word that He has revealed His wishes, **1 Corinthians 2:10**.

   b. Obviously, without study, a man remains ignorant of the truth and thus by willful ignorance becomes a violator of God's truths.

E. **2 Peter 3:5-7** quickly shows that God abhors willful ignorance.

   1. The Word of God is spiritual food for the soul, **Matthew 4:4**, and to grow in grace we must partake of it.

   a. Without it a man will be a dwarfed, spiritual weakling.

   b. Listen to the rebuke and exhortation given here, **Hebrews 5:12-14**.

   2. Great harm has been done to the cause of Christ by Christians who had more zeal than knowledge:

   a. Jesus said, *"If the blind lead the blind, both shall fall into the ditch,"* **Matthew 15:14**. That reality can be commonly witnessed in well-meaning people.

   b. Those who would serve God should equip themselves with knowledge from His Word. *"Be ready always to give an answer to every man that asketh you a reason of the hope that is in you with meekness and fear,"* **1 Peter 3:15**.

SECTION TWO

ONE OF THE MOST REWARDING THINGS A MAN CAN DO IS TO STUDY THE WORD OF GOD

A. Jesus said a man of the Word is like one who can bring old and new treasures out of a house, **Matthew 13:52**.

   1. The Bible is truly a treasury of rich and precious gems.

   2. *"O the depth of the riches both of the wisdom and knowledge of God! how unsearchable are his judgments, and his ways past finding out,"* **Romans 11:33**.

B. The Word of God is a lamp and light for us. It also produces wisdom: **Psalm 119:105**.

   1. It shows us life's pitfalls and where the safe ground is.

   2. This is truly a time when men need the light of wisdom found in God's Word. This is a day of deep spiritual darkness:

      a. The norms of this day include drug abuse, crumbling morals, lost values on life, marriage failures, wicked ideologies and a general uncertainty about everything, especially the future.

      b. At the same time, *"The foundation of God standeth sure,"* **2 Timothy 2:19**.

      c. It is good to study something that's sure and steadfast.

      d. David said, *"Thy word have I hid in mine heart, that I might not sin against thee,"* **Psalm 119:11**.

C. The more you master the Word of God, the richer and more rewarding your life will become:

   1. Your capacity for appreciation of fine things enlarges, **Isaiah 28:9**.

   2. Your life will be permeated with a richer, fuller meaning, **James 1:25**.

   3. Paul said *"consider what I say; and the Lord give the understanding in all things,"* **2 Timothy 2:7**.

   4. It is easy to see why David said, *"Thy testimonies have I taken as an heritage for ever: for they are the rejoicing of my heart,"* **Psalm 119:111**.

SECTION THREE

THERE IS A PROPER WAY TO STUDY GOD'S WORD

A. Notice that Paul speaks of *"rightly dividing the word of truth,"* **2 Timothy 2:15**.

The Importance of Studying the Word of God

1. No one is to misuse the Word of God to prove his points.

   a. We should gather our points from it; not misuse a passage to support our points.

   b. No one is at liberty to take Scriptures out of context and pervert meanings to say what he wants it to say.

2. The Word of God does not have to align with us; rather, we are to align with it.

   a. *"Knowing this first, that no prophecy of the scripture is of any private interpretation,"* **2 Peter 1:20**.

   b. The Bible levies stiff judgments for those who tamper with the Scriptures, **Ezra 6:11, Revelation 22:18-20**.

B. When you study God's Word, you must take all of it as it is.

   1. Scripture with Scripture will give the true context and meaning, **Isaiah 28:10**.

   2. Build your beliefs on book, chapter, and verse evidence.

   3. When you do that, you will not be as proverbial children tossed about with every wind of doctrine, **Ephesians 4:14**.

   4. The man who properly and diligently studies the Word of God will be like the mighty tree described by David in **Psalm 1:1-3**.

Chapter 2

How to Study the Word of God

2 Timothy 2:15

We have observed that a great percentage of those who would study God's Word do not know how. Many think Bible study consists of merely reading a few passages or consulting commentaries. Though these actions are often beneficial, they do not constitute good Bible study. The points set forth here by no means compose the last word in Bible study, but they will prove helpful to the earnest student of God's Word.

SECTION ONE

ONE SHOULD HAVE PROPER MOTIVES FOR STUDYING GOD'S WORD

A. We should study *"to show"* ourselves *"approved unto God."*

    1. Our studying should not be done just because we want to answer a Campbellite, Catholic, Jehovah Witness, or someone else about a Bible point. (Study may enable you to answer, but that should not be the motivation to study.)

    2. The motivation to study should not be a desire to become "smarter than someone else" or a "religious smart aleck."

Paul condemns those who are *"puffed up,"* **1 Corinthians 4:6, 18-19**. Seldom do you find folks more repulsive than those who are puffed up and proud of how much they know about the Bible.

3. Our love for our Lord should move us to study God's Word so that we may be APPROVED OF HIM.

   a. Paul said, *"For the love of Christ constraineth us,"* **2 Corinthians 5:14**.

   b. He also said, when love moves us to do what we do (and study would certainly be included), we will not be proud and boastful, for *"charity ... is not puffed up,"* **1 Corinthians 13:4**.

B. We should study that we may be *"a workman that needeth not to be ashamed."*

1. The Bible teaches us to *"earnestly contend for the faith which was once delivered unto the saints,"* **Jude 3**; but a great many of God's workmen scarcely know what *"the faith which was once delivered"* is, let alone how to contend for it. Many Christians have been members of a Bible church where they had access to the Word of God for many years. Too many of them did not take advantage of the Bible teaching that was offered to them nor studied the Bible for themselves. That is shameful.

2. Shouldn't a workman be ashamed before God when, after ample time to equip himself, he still can't tell his own friend or child how to be saved from the penalty of sin? Or what constitutes scriptural baptism? Or the difference between justification and sanctification?

3. Through study a man can avoid shame before God. If a man does not study, he is open to rebuke. *"Of whom we have many things to say, and hard to be uttered, seeing ye are dull of hearing. For when for the time ye ought to be teachers, ye have need that one teach you again which be the first principles of the oracles of God; and are become such as have need of milk, and not of strong meat. For every one that useth milk is unskilful in the word of righteousness: for he is a babe,"* **Hebrews 5:11-13**.

C. We should also study that we might *"rightly"* divide *"the Word of Truth."*

    1. Whole denominations are built on Scriptures wrongly divided.

    2. Such practices as wresting Scriptures from their context, using them in a sense never intended and applying texts which are directed to believers to alien sinners build false concepts and propagate error and heresy.

    3. There is a perfect harmony in the Scriptures, and honest study of the whole perspectives of God's Word will enable a student to rightly divide the Scriptures.

        a. As we have the Holy Word of God which compares *"spiritual things with spiritual,"* **1 Corinthians 2:13**, we should consider all of the comparisons. This necessitates our searching the Scripture to learn what all the various passages say on any given subject. Paul said, *"Consider what I say; and the Lord give thee understanding in all things,"* **2 Timothy 2:7**. But we cannot expect proper understanding until we *"consider"* all (not just an isolated segment) of what the Scriptures say on the subject.

        b. Isaiah stated it this way. *"Whom shall he teach knowledge? and whom shall he make to understand doctrine? them that are weaned from the milk, and drawn from the breasts. For precept must be upon precept, precept upon precept; line upon line, line upon line; here a little, and there a little,"* **Isaiah 28:9-10**.

        c. Since God's Word is not so arranged that all that is said upon one subject is said in the same chapter (or even the same book), it becomes necessary to consider chapter and verse with other chapters and verses. This often involves covering hundreds of places, all establishing a given truth.

        d. From these three points given in **2 Timothy 2:15**, one can see the three basic motives which should motivate us to study God's Word. The motives are to be approved of God, not be ashamed of God and His Word, and to rightly divide the Scriptures.

SECTION TWO

ONE SHOULD DEVELOP GOOD STUDY HABITS

A. If possible, you should have a certain time to study.

1. The Bereans of **Acts 17:11** searched the Word *"daily."* We need spiritual food every day just as much as we need physical food.

2. A Bible student will find great profit in setting aside a definite period of time every day for Bible study rather than just doing it at random whenever the urge or time may present itself.

3. Like any other study, it is more profitable if done when you are rested and alert.

4. And, you cannot "cram" or learn it all at one time. Solomon said, *"much study is a weariness of the flesh,"* **Ecclesiastes 12:12**. A reasonable amount every day does far more good than a "crash course" of several days, followed by no or sporadic study for a long period of time.

B. It is also profitable to have a definite place to study.

1. If possible, have a private place where you have proper lighting, quietness, a desk and surroundings of a comfortable nature.

2. It is also good to have a place where you can keep paper, pins, reference materials, etc.

C. Be scholarly and systematic during study.

1. Decide upon a particular subject.

    a. Don't just skim along grasping whatever may pass by; apply yourself to specifics, nail down a subject and dig out those truths.

    b. Don't select too broad a range of subject material. You can't learn it all at one time. As you grasp one truth, you can move to another; and slowly but surely your Scriptural knowledge will increase so that you'll be able to tackle larger and larger portions.

c. Learn to stick with the subject.

   (1) Take one at a time.

   (2) Don't switch from subject to subject and learn little about either.

2. All Scriptural knowledge is good, but organized material is more profitable.

   a. Use pencil and paper, and make notes.

   b. Notes are word pictures, and it is said that one picture equals many words.

   c. It has been proven that most people retain and learn much more by making notes as they study.

   d. If it was good for you when you first studied it, it will also be good for you when you later consider your notes.

3. Ask yourself questions about the subject.

   a. Who is doing the talking? To whom is he speaking? What is the subject? When did it happen? Where did it happen? Why did it happen? How did it happen? etc.

   b. If you can answer the questions "who," "what," "when," "why," "where," and "how," your Bible knowledge of the passage or subject will be helped.

4. Search the Scriptures.

   a. Remember to compare book, chapter, and verse, with book, chapter, and verse. No book is a better commentary on the Bible than the Bible itself, **Isaiah 28:9-10**.

   b. Next to the Bible a good, unabridged concordance is probably the best reference book there is.

   c. Other helps such as Bible dictionaries, commentaries, word studies, subject studies, etc., are helpful.

5. Once Bible material is dug out, organize it under definite headings.

6. Review your findings from time to time.

SECTION THREE

GOOD BIBLE STUDY REQUIRES MEDITATION

A. Meditation is reflection upon, consideration of, or intent observance of that which has been previously considered.

1. As the definition shows, it would be impossible to meditate upon that which has not been previously considered; therefore, meditation starts with the consideration of some point.

2. As **Joshua 1:8** exhorts, the truth of God's Word should be so stamped in our minds that we can recall it for reflection or meditation.

B. Meditation is a time for looking at the Scripture from as many different angles as possible.

1. Ask the "who," "what," "when," "why," "where," and "how" questions.

2. Is it a command to obey? Something for which to praise God? An example to follow? A promise to claim?

3. Are there any conditions attached?

4. Emphasize different words in the verse or text as in **Psalm 23:1**.

   a. The **LORD**.

   b. The LORD **is**.

   c. The LORD is **my**.

   d. The LORD is my **shepherd**.

5. Apply the truth to your own life.

6. How does the truth affect you? And why? And what are you going to do about it?

7. Pinpoint your shortcomings to the truth and determine to grow in grace.

Chapter 3

Proof of Divine Inspiration of the Bible Through Facts, Bible Construction and Prophecies

Malachi 3:10

I believe that the most fundamental of all doctrines is that the Bible is God's divinely inspired Word. If you do not accept the Bible, then you will also reject its teachings. If you think the Bible is merely the work of men, then you'll put no more confidence in it than you would in any other good book. You are wasting your time using the Bible to prove a point to a man who doesn't believe the Bible. In this chapter, we shall endeavor to prove that the Bible is God's Word without appealing to the statements it makes about its own authenticity. We use this text because you can prove the Bible is truly God's Holy Word.

SECTION ONE

EXAMINATION OF TWO ASPECTS OF THE BIBLE WILL SHOW YOU IT IS NOT MAN'S, BUT GOD'S BOOK

A. There are provable facts which show the Bible could not be man's product.

1. The circumstances under which the Bible came about are beyond human orchestration.

   a. Written by about 40 different men over a 1600 year period from B.C. 1492 to 100 A.D.

   b. The writers were from all walks of life.

      (1) Kings as David and Solomon.

      (2) Statesmen as Daniel and Nehemiah.

      (3) Priests as Ezra.

      (4) Educated men as Moses and Paul.

      (5) Uneducated men as Peter, James, and John.

      (6) A Herdsman named Amos.

      (7) A Tax collector named Matthew.

      (8) A Medical Doctor named Luke.

      (9) Mighty Seers as Isaiah, Jeremiah.

   c. These men were from different lands.

      (1) The wilderness of Sinai.

      (2) The cliffs of Arabia.

      (3) The hills and towns of Palestine.

      (4) Shushan in Persia.

      (5) The River Chebar in Babylonia.

      (6) The dungeons of Rome and Asia Minor

      (7) The lonely Isle of Patmos in the Aegean Sea.

   d. These men wrote with no intention of producing a part of a book as the Bible and were often not aware that others were writing.

e. Yet, in spite of these unusual circumstances, they wrote a book that is consistent with itself and has never been proven in error.

2. The construction of the Bible attests to its validity.

   a. The Bible is many books in one.

      (1) The Bible is actually composed of 66 separate and independent books in two divisions.

      (2) Each of these books has its own theme and analysis.

   b. Yet, each book is essential to the complete understanding of the Bible.

      (1) No book of the Bible may be thoroughly understood without all the others.

      (2) The Bible is so inter-related that every book, chapter, verse, and even punctuation is essential to understanding the whole.

   c. In spite of this arrangement, which would surely produce an incoherent mess, no other book is more harmonious than the Bible.

      (1) Like a great jigsaw puzzle; each piece fits into the whole.

      (2) The 66 books form one continuous story (humanity in relation to God).

      (3) The 66 books have one great theme (the person and work of Christ).

3. The scope of subject matter covered in the Bible makes it a book alone in a class of its own.

   a. No other book covers broad subjects with such detail.

      (1) The Bible is a history from eternity before the creation to eternity after time and all in between.

(2) The Bible tells the human story from beginning to ending.

(3) The Bible traces a nation (Israel) from beginning to ending.

(4) The Bible describes the earth from stem to stern.

(5) Only the Bible describes sin, Satan, God and the plan of redemption.

   b. All of this, plus much more, is found in the Bible, yet the Bible is a relatively small book.

(1) Many accounts of WWI alone far exceed the size of the Bible.

(2) And many larger books tell far less than the Bible.

4. When you look at the facts alone, it is obvious that the Bible is not a mere coincidence; nor could it have come to be the work that it is except that some great power (we believe God) directed the project.

B. The prophecies of the Bible are undeniable proof that the Bible is the work of God; not man.

  1. Let me show you that not every prediction is a prophecy. There are at least five requirements for legitimate prophecy.

    a. It must be made known prior to its fulfillment.

    b. It must be beyond all human foresight.

    c. It must give details; not be general and ambiguous.

    d. A sufficient time must elapse between its publication and its fulfillment to exclude the prophet or any interested party from fulfilling.

    e. There must be a clear and evident fulfillment of the prophecy.

  2. The Bible truly is a book of prophecy.

    a. Either by type, symbol, or direct statement, about 2/3 of all Scripture is prophetic.

    b. The Bible hazards the most unlikely predictions concerning the future and records their fulfillment when the centuries have brought about the appointed time.

3. Consistent accurate prophecy is beyond the ability of man.

    a. Man can hazard enough guesses and sooner or later he may get one or two right, but he certainly can never get all of them 100% right.

    b. Thus, when we find a book of prophecies all 100% right, we know that book had to be produced by somebody far greater than any man or group of men.

4. Let us now consider a small number of Bible prophecies.

    a. **Genesis 6:14-17** predicted a great flood would come and cover the whole earth. **Genesis 7:10-24** records the fulfillment. Science today admits that at one time, every inch of this earth was covered with water. (Consider the frozen remains of animals which have been discovered with grass in their stomachs and lungs.)

    b. **Genesis 17:2-6** gives unlikely prophecies of Abraham which have come true.

    c. **Genesis 50:24-26** says that Joseph's Bones would leave Egypt. **Exodus 12:31-40** fulfilled it.

    d. **Isaiah 44:28-45:4** spoke of Cyrus the Persian 200 years before he was born. Many intricate details were given. Compare **Daniel 6**.

    e. Jeremiah predicted that Zedekiah would see the King of Babylon, and that the Babylonian king would take him to Babylon as a captive; yet Zedekiak would never see Babylon, **Jeremiah 34:3**. See also **Ezekiel 12:13**. Only God could have known that his eyes would be put out before he reached Babylon, **2 Kings 25:6-7**.

f. The destruction of Tyre, **Isaiah 23:1-18,** is a historical fact.

g. Over 3500 years before the telescope, God said the stars are too many to number **Genesis 15:5**.

h. Over 2200 years before Columbus discovered America, God said the earth is a sphere in **Isaiah 40:22**. Who, but God, could have known?

i. The prophecies about Christ's first appearance alone are sufficient to show the Bible cannot be man's product.

   (1) In connection with the death, burial and resurrection of Jesus Christ, at least 25 specific predictions about Him were fulfilled.

   (a) Such specific occurrences as His betrayal for 30 pieces of silver, **Zechariah 11:12**, desertion by His disciples, **Zechariah 13:7**, none of His bones to be broken, **Psalm 34:20**, that He'd be buried in a rich man's tomb, **Isaiah 53:9**, etc., were foretold. They were foretold by numerous prophets over a period ending not less than 400 years before Christ's crucifixion.

   (b) To give you some idea of how slim the chances were that these predictions would all be fulfilled, consider...

   (I) If I predict an earth quake in Houston next year, by the law of compound probabilities, the chances are one in two that it will occur. If I say it will be on Easter, the chances are 1 in 4. Each time I add another detail, the chances against it double: 1 in 2, 1 in 4, 1 in 8, 1 in 16, etc.

   (II) Applying this mathematical principle to the day Christ died, the chances were 33,554,432 against 1 that the 25 prophecies would be fulfilled.

(2) During His lifetime, Christ fulfilled every prophecy concerning His first coming (a total of 109).

    (a) The chances were one in billions that He'd do it, yet He did.

    (b) Yet, there are skeptics who say man wrote these prophecies. Doesn't it stretch your imagination to believe that man did it?

5. If the chances are 1 in billions that the prophecies concerning Christ would be all fulfilled, what would be the chances that these, plus the hundreds of other prophecies which have been fulfilled, would all come true?

    a. If we could successfully prove one error in the Bible, it would be different. But we can't; not in the slightest way.

    b. When you consider that this is literally history written in advance, written with absolute accuracy and that man with all his technology cannot equal this, you must admit that the Bible truly is a book that cannot be explained apart from God.

SECTION TWO

COMPARE THESE FACTS AND FIGURES WITH MAN'S GREATEST INTELLECT

A. Suppose 40 men, some learned and some ignorant, in many different lands, from many walks of life, should unbeknown to each other, and with no one to initiate or co-ordinate the project, write 66 books over a 1600 year period.

    1. If all these books were compiled into one book, do you suppose there would be any sense to?

    2. If they were all of a medical nature, do you suppose you could doctor a sick cow (let alone a human) by it?

B. Suppose a group of our greatest intellects today should sit down to predict the events of the next 500 years.

1. Do you suppose they correctly could name coming countries, presidents, wars, etc.?

2. Do you suppose that if they made 100 predictions, they'd get even 10% absolutely correct?

C. If the Bible is such a simple book, and no more than other leading books, and we are so much smarter and civilized than the Bible writers were, then why don't some of our "brains" produce a work equal to the Bible?

D. By way of comparison we must admit that man today is nowhere near intelligent enough to produce a work equal to the Bible, nor is there another work on earth that can touch the hem of its garment.

SECTION THREE

WHAT THEN ARE THE ONLY LOGICAL CONCLUSIONS WHICH CAN BE DRAWN?

A. If man is at best nowhere near capable of producing a document similar to the Bible, then why think men produced the Bible?

1. How could man produce what he is incapable of producing?

2. If man couldn't produce it, it is safe to conclude he didn't.

B. If man didn't produce it, then who other than God of the Bible did?

1. By the laws of plain logic, what other conclusion could possibly be drawn?

2. Our conclusion is unequivocally that the Bible is the divinely inspired Word of almighty God.

Chapter 4

The Biblical Claim to Divine Inspiration

2 Timothy 3:16

From a logical standpoint, it is obvious that the Bible is true. Great factors, apart from its own statements of its truth, attest to it being the Holy Word of God. We will now consider its statements which vindicate it as being the inspired Word of God.

REPEATEDLY, THE BIBLE CLAIMS TO BE THE INFALLIBLE WORD OF GOD

A. Notice how the Bible writers claimed to be inspired of God and thus to write the mind of God, not man.

  1. Paul said, *"For I neither received it of man, neither was I taught it, but by the revelation of Jesus Christ,"* **Galatians 1:12**.

  2. He also said, *"For this cause also thank we God without ceasing, because, when ye received the word of God which ye heard of us, ye received it not as the word of men, but as it is in truth, the word of God, which effectually worketh also in you that believe,"* **1 Thessalonians 2:13**.

  3. David affirmed, *"The Spirit of the LORD spake by me, and his word was in my tongue,"* **2 Samuel 23:2**.

4. Listen to Paul's claim of revelation to himself and the other Bible prophets in **Ephesians 3:2-5**, *"If ye have heard of the dispensation of the grace of God which is given me to you-ward: How that by revelation he made known unto me the mystery; (as I wrote afore in few words, Whereby, when ye read, ye may understand my knowledge in the mystery of Christ) Which in other ages was not made known unto the sons of men, as it is now revealed unto his holy apostles and prophets by the Spirit."*

5. Many spoke of *"the Spirit of the LORD"* and *"the word of the LORD"* being upon them as in **Zechariah 4:6, Ezekiel 11:5, Isaiah 61:1, Jeremiah 25:3**.

6. Paul said *"We have the mind of Christ,"* **1 Corinthians 2:16**. In speaking about all of the Scriptures he said, *"God hath revealed them unto us by his Spirit,"* **1 Corinthians 2:10**.

7. Listen to **1 Corinthians 2:12-13** as Paul claims the apostles were told what to say by the *"Holy Ghost."* *"Now we have received, not the spirit of the world, but the spirit which is of God; that we might know the things that are freely given to us of God. Which things also we speak, not in the words which man's wisdom teacheth, but which the Holy Ghost teacheth; comparing spiritual things with spiritual."*

8. **Hebrews 1:1** affirms, *"God, who at sundry times and in divers manners spake in time past unto the fathers by the prophets."*

9. The apostles Peter and John stated, *"For we cannot but speak the things which we have seen and heard,"* **Acts 4:20**.

10. Peter asserted that the Holy Ghost inspired the Scriptures. *"Searching what, or what manner of time the Spirit of Christ which was in them did signify, when it testified beforehand the sufferings of Christ, and the glory that should follow. Unto whom it was revealed, that not unto themselves, but unto us they did minister the things, which are now reported unto you by them that have preached the gospel unto you with the Holy Ghost sent down from heaven; which things the angels desire to look into,"* **1 Peter 1:11-12**.

11. Peter stated, *"For the prophecy came not in old time by the will of man: but holy men of God spake as they were moved by the Holy Ghost,"* **2 Peter 1:21**.

B. Though Jesus Christ did not write any Scripture, He testified that it is true.

    1. He said of the Word of God, *"Thy Word is truth,"* **John 17:17.**

    2. He told the apostles that it would be the Spirit of God which would guide them. *"I have yet many things to say unto you, but ye cannot bear them now. Howbeit when he, the Spirit of truth, is come, he will guide you into all truth: for he shall not speak of himself; but whatsoever he shall hear, that shall he speak: and he will shew you things to come. He shall glorify me: for he shall receive of mine, and shall shew it unto you. All things that the Father hath are mine: therefore said I, that he shall take of mine, and shall shew it unto you,"* **John 16:12-15.**

C. It is not just a part but the whole Word of God which is said to be true.

    1. Notice the text, *"All scripture is given by inspiration of God,"* **2 Timothy 3:16.**

    2. **Revelation 19:9** says *"These are the true sayings of God."*

    3. John was told to *"Write: for these words are true and faithful,"* **Revelation 21:5.**

    4. **1 Corinthians 13:10** speaks of the completed writings as *"that which is perfect."*

    5. David said, *"I esteem all thy precepts concerning all things to be right,"* **Psalm 119:128.**

D. Since God said these things, they are true for God is always truthful.

    1. God *"cannot lie,"* **Titus 1:2.**

    2. God is *"full of grace and truth,"* **John 1:14.**

    3. *"And to the angel of the church in Philadelphia write; These things saith he that is holy, he that is true, he that hath the key of David, he that openeth, and no man shutteth; and shutteth, and no man openeth,"* **Revelation 3:7.**

    4. *"And unto the angel of the church of the Laodiceans write; These things saith the Amen, the faithful and true witness, the beginning of the creation of God,"* **Revelation 3:14.**

E. Since God told the Bible writers what to say, the Bible is said to be infallibly true.

    1. *"The word of the Lord endureth forever,"* **1 Peter 1:25.**

    2. *"For ever, O LORD, thy word is settled in heaven,"* **Psalm 119:89.**

    3. *"Nevertheless the foundation of God standeth sure,"* **2 Timothy 2:19.**

    4. Jesus said, *"Heaven and earth shall pass away, but my words shall not pass away,"* **Matthew 24:35.**

F. In view of these and other claims and proofs, I am not afraid or hesitant to affirm to you that the Bible is truly the Holy, Divine, and Infallible Word of God.

Chapter 5

Only the Bible Is Divinely Inspired

It is our firm conviction that the Bible is the only divinely inspired writing there is and that only the Bible writers can claim infallibility. We believe that it is a serious, damnable sin against God for men to claim infallibility today or make any writing equal to the Scriptures. Thus, adding to or taking from is a cursed act. This lesson is designed to give you the teaching of the Word of God upon the subject.

ONLY THE BIBLE WRITERS CAN LEGITIMATELY CLAIM INFALLIBILITY

A. Our previous chapter cited many Scriptures all showing that the Bible is indeed God's holy, divinely inspired Word.

    1. The questions now before us are, (1) "Were the Bible writers the only divinely inspired writers the world has seen?" and (2) "Is the Bible the world's only divinely inspired book?"

    2. Many religious sects say, "No."

        a. The Catholics, Mormons and Pentecostals are among those who say they have other writings which are also infallibly inspired.

        b. Especially the Pentecostals apply Jesus' promise of infallibility in **John 16:12-14** to themselves.

3. Our answer is "yes." The Bible is it: there is no other divinely inspired, infallible book; and no man today is inspired in the divine sense of the Bible.

B. Notice the difference in the way the apostles received Scriptural knowledge and in the way we receive it.

1. The apostles received it verbatim; directly of God in absolutely infallible form.

   a. The apostles were told to *"take no thought beforehand what ye shall speak, neither do ye premeditate: but whatsoever shall be given you in that hour, that speak ye: for it is not ye that speak, but the Holy Ghost,"* **Mark 13:11.**

   b. Paul said, *"For I neither received it of man, neither was I taught it, but by the revelation of Jesus Christ,"* **Galatians 1:12.**

   c. Jesus said, *"the Spirit"* would tell them *"all truth,"* **John 16:12-14.**

   d. **1 Corinthians 2:7-16** shows well that God simply opened their minds and gave them the truth, apart from study, a rare happening in all of history.

2. Our way of learning the truth is so different; we are only able to get it by study.

   a. **1 Timothy 4:13, 15** tells us to read and study.

   b. The Bible says *"Consider what I say; and the Lord give thee understanding in all things,"* **2 Timothy 2:7.**

   c. Listen to Paul, *"Hold fast the form of sound words, which thou hast heard of me,"* **2 Timothy 1:13.**

   d. **2 Timothy 2:15** tells us to *"study."*

3. It is quite evident that the apostles' way and our way of receiving truth is very different:

   a. It should be noted that the apostles did not get their truth by strange impulse and feelings as do so many of the modernists who apply divine inspiration to themselves.

   b. As the aforementioned Scriptures substantiate, these men clearly had it revealed to them of God.

C. It should be clear that the promise of infallibility as set forth in **John 16:13** applies only to the revelation of Scripture, not the interpreting of it.

   1. If the promise applied to interpretation, then all sincere, Spirit-led, Bible students would of necessity come to the same conclusions. (But they don't. They hold all sorts of conflicting views, yet all claim to be infallibly led of God.)

   2. If it is true that the Spirit today guides us into *"all truth,"* then surely some of us would have gotten there, for God is not the author of confusion, **1 Corinthians 14:32-33**.

   3. If God inspired all those who apply this text to themselves, then harmony would prevail among their words and writings even as it does in the Bible.

   4. Today, knowledge of God's mind is inseparable from study, meditation and consideration of God's Word and providence; and most of the problems we confront today are directly related to shallow misinterpretations given to the Scriptures. The problem is that men base their actions on how they feel, not on what God says about it.

D. The Bible warns against men misapplying infallibility to themselves. They produce writings and make statements which they claim to be absolutely true, but the fact is that such claims are simply not true. Only the Bible is the infallible Word of God.

   1. There are many Bible warnings of the coming of false teachers.

   a. Consider **1 Timothy 4:1-3, Matthew 24:11, 24, 1 John 4:1, 2 Peter 2:1-3.**

   b. Jesus warned, *"Beware of false prophets, which come to you in sheep's clothing,"* **Matthew 7:15.**

   2. Notice what a dangerous thing it is to add to or take away from the Bible.

   a. Deuteronomy 4:2 and **12:32** warns.

   "Ye shall not add unto the word which I command you, neither shall ye diminish ought from it, that ye may keep the

commandments of the Lord your God which I command you," **Deuteronomy 4:2.**

"What thing soever I command you, observe to do it: thou shalt not add thereto, nor diminish from it," **Deuteronomy 12:32.**

    b. **Ezra 6:11-12** also warns, *"Also I have made a decree, that whosoever shall alter this word, let timber be pulled down from his house, and being set up, let him be hanged thereon; and let his house be made a dunghill for this. And the God that hath caused his name to dwell there destroy all kings and people, that shall put to their hand to alter and to destroy this house of God which is at Jerusalem. I Darius have made a decree; let it be done with speed."*

    c. **Revelation 22:18-19** is also a case to illustrate, *"For I testify unto every man that heareth the words of the prophecy of this book, If any man shall add unto these things, God shall add unto him the plagues that are written in this book: And if any man shall take away from the words of the book of this prophecy, God shall take away his part out of the book of life, and out of the holy city, and from the things which are written in this book."*

E. The Bible is sufficient and we don't need another revelation.

    1. You can't improve that which is perfect, **1 Corinthians 13:10.**

    2. It furnishes us all we need, **2 Timothy 3:16-17.**

    3. Notice that God thinks it is sufficient.

        a. It's for time and eternity, **Isaiah 30:8.**

        b. Heaven and earth may pass, but *"the word of the Lord endureth forever,"* **1 Peter 1:25, Matthew 5:18, Matthew 24:35.**

F. Two inescapable conclusions:

    1. No man can legitimately apply infallibility to himself today.

    2. The Bible claims infallibility. All other supposedly infallible writings are fakes.

Chapter 6

The Existence of a Triune God

Genesis 1:1

We believe, beyond doubt, in the existence of one God who is of such infinite ability as to reveal Himself in limitless forms and ways all at the same time; but who has seen fit to reveal Himself chiefly in three distinct personalities ... namely the Father, Son, and Spirit. It is because of these three persons of God that we call Him a triune God.

SECTION ONE

THERE IS MASSIVE EVIDENCE PROVING GOD REALLY DOES EXIST

A. The existence of the universe testifies of God's existence.

    1. Almost everyone admits that the universe had to start somewhere (it has not existed forever.)

        a. The evolutionist says it evolved from heat and gases.

        b. Many look at it (most of the world) as having come about by chance without any guiding force.

c. It really takes quite an imagination to think that something as complex, intricate, sophisticated and gigantic as the universe could have accidently come into being out of absolutely nothing.

2. To the honest mind, the universe stands as a great testimony to the existence of the great God of the universe.

   a. **Romans 1:19-20** says the creation attests to God's existence and power.

   b. Every time you look at rocks, trees, weather, stars, fish, etc., you are looking at a testimonial of God. (Man didn't make them, yet they are made. Somebody had to make them. If man didn't, then God had to have done it.)

   c. The Scriptures make no bones about crediting the creation to God.

      (1) **Genesis 1-3** details the account of creation by God.

      (2) **John 1:1-5** says all things were made by Him.

3. The earth's symmetry testifies of God's existence.

   a. Observation will reveal the earth to be a very complex and efficient operation which continues day after day.

      (1) Consider the balance of nature, the ability of nature to heal its wounds, changing seasons, rain cycles and multitudes of other natural phenomena.

      (2) The laws of nature are precise: physics, gravitation, centrifugal force, tides, light and sound waves, etc.

   b. Some say these things operate merely by chance without any guidance.

   c. The fact that natural laws operate in harmony with themselves is testimony that God attends its operation.

      (1) The universe has operated for centuries in perpetual motion. Man has neither the ability to generate a system like the universe nor the ability to maintain it.

       (2) **Colossians 1:16-17** says God keeps it operating.

       (3) **Acts 17:24-28** gives further credit to God.

B. The appearances of God testify to His existence.

    1. He *"created"* the universe an undetermined number of years ago, **Genesis 1:1**.

    2. He talked to Adam and Eve in roughly 4000 B.C., **Genesis 3:9**.

    3. He made promises to Abraham in about 2000 B.C., **Genesis 12:1**.

    4. He appeared to Moses in a burning bush around 1500 B.C., **Exodus 3:4**.

    5. He spoke to Elijah in about 900 B.C., **1 Kings 18:1**.

    6. He told Malachi what to say in about 400 B.C., **Malachi 1:1**.

    7. He appeared in the flesh for 33 years from about 4 B.C. to after 29 A.D. See **Matthew, Mark, Luke, John, Matthew 3:15-17**.

    8. He appeared to Paul in about 35 A.D., **Acts 9:3-6**.

    9. He revealed Himself to John in about 96 A.D., **Revelation 1:1-2**.

    10. John looked into the future to at least 1971 plus into the 1000 year millennium, **Revelation 20:3**, and God was there, **Revelation 20:11**.

    11. It would be hard to discount that only God could appear that many times to that many people over that many years. Only God could survive that long.

C. The Bible testifies of God's existence. (See previous chapters)

SECTION TWO

OUR ONE GOD IS A TRIUNE GOD

A. There are not three Gods, there is one God.

  1. *"The LORD our God is one LORD,"* **Deuteronomy 6:4 and Mark 12:29.**

  2. *"It is one God, which shall justify,"* **Romans 3:30.**

  3. *"God is one,"* **Galatians 3:20.**

  4. *"One Lord, one faith, one baptism, One God and Father of all,"* **Ephesians 4:5-6.**

  5. **1 Corinthians 8:6** also verifies this truth.

B. Yet, the one God has three distinct personalities.

  1. **Matthew 28:19** mentions all 3 personalities ... *"Father"*; *"Son"*; *"Spirit."*

  2. **Matthew 3:16-17** shows all three at the same time.

  3. **Ephesians 4:30** mentions Father and Spirit.

  4. **1 Timothy 3:16** mentions Father and Son.

  5. **2 Corinthians 13:14** names all three.

C. The three personalities of God are always in absolute harmony, unity, agreement.

  1. **Genesis 1:1** says, *"In the beginning God* (plural noun) *created"* (singular verb). This shows the harmony of God.

  2. Jesus said, *"I and my Father are one,"* **John 10:30.**

There is no perfect parallel to illustrate the Trinity; however, a chair offers some insight. A chair is one chair, yet it has three dimensions: height, width and length. Each dimension is completely separate and identifiable on its own; however all are necessary to constitute the chair. Without either there is no chair. Even so, there is one God in three persons: Father, Son and Holy Spirit. Each is seen separately throughout the Scriptures, yet all three constitute one God, not three.

Chapter 7

The Father, the Son, and the Holy Spirit

Matthew 28:19

This text specifically mentions the three personalities of the God in whom in our last chapter we professed to believe. The purpose of this chapter is to bring to greater light points we believe about each of these distinct personalities.

SECTION ONE

FIRST, LET US CONSIDER SOME OF THE DISTINCTIONS OF GOD, THE FATHER

A. He is almighty.

1. **Isaiah 40:12-31** shows the awesome might and power of God that no other has.
2. **Chapters 38-39 of Job** show that neither man nor nature is anything before Him.
3. *"There is no power but of God,"* **Romans 13:1**.
4. *"That men may know that thou, whose name alone is JEHOVAH, art the most high over all the earth,"* **Psalm 83:18**.

The Father, the Son, and the Holy Spirit

B. He is also omniscient: (Knows and sees all)

1. **Psalm 139:1-13** is one of the best passages on the subject.

2. God said *"For mine eyes are upon all their ways: they are not hid from my face, neither is their iniquity hid from mine eyes,"* **Jeremiah 16:17.**

3. Paul said *"Neither is there any creature that is not manifest in his sight: but all things are naked and opened unto the eyes of him with whom we have to do,"* **Hebrews 4:13.**

C. He is always just and consistent.

1. You can count on what God says. His nature never varies. There is no reason to think He'll ever deceive you with an inconsistent move.

2. *"Every good gift and every perfect gift is from above, and cometh down from the Father of lights, with whom is no variableness, neither shadow of turning,"* **James 1:17.**

3. Listen to **Numbers 23:19.**

4. He said in **Malachi 3:6**, *"For I am the LORD, I change not."*

5. *"Of old hast thou laid the foundation of the earth: and the heavens are the work of thy hands. They shall perish, but thou shalt endure: yea, all of them shall wax old like a garment; as a vesture shalt thou change them, and they shall be changed: But thou art the same, and thy years shall have no end,"* **Psalm 102:25-27.**

D. Thus, it is easy to see then that He is eternal:

1. There are a host of Scriptures that speak of Him as the everlasting God. **Isaiah 9:6, Genesis 21:33, Romans 16:26,** etc.

2. *"I am Alpha and Omega, the beginning and the ending, saith the Lord, which is, and which was, and which is to come, the Almighty,"* **Revelation 1:8.**

3. **Hebrews 7:3** says he is *"without father, without mother, without descent, having neither beginning of days, nor end of life."*

      4. It is hard to grasp infinity, but He is infinite.

E. Also note that He has both love and wrath.

    1. As a whole, today's world denies His wrath and sees Him as all benevolent.

    2. There's no question that He is a benevolent, loving God.

        a. **John 3:16** shows that He loves the world.

        b. **1 John 3:16** shows the extent of His love.

    3. But, don't ever forget that He is also a God of wrath.

        a. Sinners shall pay, **Ezekiel 18:20** and **Romans 6:23**.

        b. Consider Sodom and Gomorrah, **Genesis 19:23-25**.

        c. **John 3:18** and **36** speak of His wrath and condemnation.

        d. **2 Thessalonians 1:7-9** shows the awfulness of His wrath.

        e. **Proverbs 1:24-32** shows His mercy will not always be available.

SECTION TWO

CONSIDER NOW A FEW POINTS CONCERNING CHRIST, THE SON

A. He is the only begotten Son of God.

    1. This is simply to say He is the sole natural Son of God.

        a. He was by nature a son of God; others by nature are children of sin, **Ephesians 2:1-3**.

        b. Jesus did not become a son by a new birth or adoption as we do. He has always been a son.

2. Listen to the Scriptures.

   a. **John 1:14, 18** and **3:16, 18** all speak of Him as the *"only begotten"* Son.

   b. *"In this was manifested the love of God toward us, because that God sent his only begotten Son into the world, that we might live through him,"* **1 John 4:9**.

B. Jesus was born of a virgin.

   1. It has never happened in history before or since, but Jesus was born of a woman who had never had sexual relations with a man. Thus, He had no earthly, biological father.

   2. It is amazing that Isaiah the prophet could have predicted this event over 740 years earlier, **Isaiah 7:14**.

   3. The Scriptures speak of the event by saying:

      a. Jesus was born *"To a virgin espoused to a man whose name was Joseph, of the house of David; and the virgin's name was Mary,"* **Luke 1:27, Matthew 1:23**.

      b. **Matthew 1:25** says of Joseph that he *"knew her not till she had brought forth her firstborn son: and he called his name JESUS."*

C. Thus, it becomes evident that Jesus was God in the flesh.

   1. The Scriptures show Jesus was conceived of the Holy Ghost thus making Him the God-man, **Matthew 1:20, 18, Luke 1:35**.

   2. **Galatians 4:4** testifies that Jesus was God in the flesh.

   3. The eternality of Jesus is identical to that of the Father. He too is *"the same yesterday, and to day, and for ever,"* **Hebrews 13:8**.

   4. It is most important to know that Jesus, upon whom our hopes rest, is more than a mere man.

SECTION THREE

DISTINCTIONS REGARDING THE HOLY GHOST

A. He is responsible for revealing the Bible.

    1. As we have already observed, **John 16:13, 1 Corinthians 2, 2 Peter 1:21** and other passages show that He inspired the Bible.

    2. It is through the revealed Word that He convicts of *"sin," "righteousness"* and *"judgment,"* **John 16:9-11**.

    3. Whenever anyone rejects God's teachings on any subject, he is thus guilty of resisting the Holy Spirit of God, **Acts 7:51**.

B. The Holy Ghost resides exclusively in saved people.

    1. **1 Corinthians 3:16** says believers constitute the temple of the Spirit.

    2. **Romans 8:9** shows that if the Spirit does not live in a man, he is lost.

    3. **John 14:17** plainly says the Spirit does not live in unconverted men.

C. When the Spirit is given control of a believer's life, a real spiritual revolution for the better will occur.

    1. The Spirit will produce definite qualities or fruit in the life of a believer, **Galatians 5:22-23**.

    2. Thus, **Romans 8:1-14** teaches us to let the Spirit control our lives.

Chapter 8

How the Holy Spirit Convicts the Lost

John 16:8-11

We believe the Holy Spirit of God convicts the lost of sin, righteousness, and judgment, but we do not believe He does it in some mysterious, unexplainable way. We do not believe that the Holy Spirit, on some sort of random basis flies around looking for someone to "woo" to salvation. We believe the Holy Spirit convicts lost men according to a very definite plan which is set forth in the Bible. In short, we believe the Holy Spirit convicts the lost through the Word of God.

SECTION ONE

WE REJECT THE IDEA THAT THE HOLY SPIRIT ENTERS INTO THE HEART OF A SINNER AHEAD OF, APART FROM OR IN ADDITION TO GOD'S WORD AND BEGINS TO "TUG" AT THE HEART AND APPEALS TO THAT PERSON TO BE SAVED

A. We believe that the Holy Spirit only indwells born again persons.

1. To the believers at Corinth Paul wrote, *"Know ye not that ye are the temple of God, and that the Spirit of God dwelleth in you?"* **1 Corinthians 3:16**.

2. Again the truth that the Holy Spirit enters and lives in the saved is set forth in **1 Corinthians 6:19**, *"What? know ye not that your body is the temple of the Holy Ghost which is in you, which ye have of God... ?"*

3. Listen to **2 Corinthians 6:16** on the subject, *"...ye are the temple of the living God; as God hath said, I will dwell in them, and walk in them..."*

4. The promise of the indwelling Spirit was not made to any other than the saved, **John 14:16**; and only these, but all of these, can speak of *"the Holy Ghost which dwelleth in us,"* **2 Timothy 1:14**.

B. The Bible shows that the Holy Spirit does not indwell lost men, all of whom are guilty of rejecting the Son of God and His blood that He shed for the lost.

1. Jesus Christ stated this truth in plain terms, *"Even the Spirit of truth; whom the world cannot receive, because it seeth him not, neither knoweth him: but ye know him; for he dwelleth with you, and shall be in you,"* **John 14:17**.

2. **Romans 8:4, 14** further shows the Spirit's personal dealings and leadership to be with the saved and not the lost.

SECTION TWO

WE BELIEVE THE HOLY SPIRIT REACHES THE LOST THROUGH HIS WORD

A. The Holy Spirit is the producer of the Word of God.

1. Speaking primarily of the Old Testament, Peter said, *"For the prophecy came not in old time by the will of man: but holy men of God spake as they were moved by the Holy Ghost,"* **2 Peter 1:21**.

2. Jesus then showed that the New Testament writers would write under the divine inspiration of the Holy Spirit, **John 16:13**.

Listen to how Jesus put it in **John 16:15**, while speaking of the Holy Spirit, *"...he shall take of mine, and shall shew it unto you."*

3. Thus, Paul the Apostle spent much time showing the Scriptures to be the work of the Holy Spirit. Especially consider **1 Corinthians 2:9-13, 16**.

4. Consider the chapters in the first of this book on divine inspiration.

5. It is in view of the fact that the Bible is the work of the Holy Spirit of God that it is called *"the sword of the Spirit, which is the word of God,"* **Ephesians 6:17**.

B. All of the mighty doctrines of this great work of the Holy Spirit are summarized in three great themes.

1. The three themes as set forth by Jesus in **John 16** are SIN (**verse 9**), RIGHTEOUSNESS (**verse 10**), and JUDGMENT (**verse 11**).

2. The Spirit's book (the Bible) speaks on these subjects warning the sinner, explaining his condition, pleading with him to turn to the righteousness of Jesus; and the truth is that the Spirit's work tells the sinner all he needs to know.

3. The lost person will learn about sin, righteousness and judgement only from the Holy Spirit's Word.

    a. The pagan religions and heathens of this world have amply demonstrated that the truth on these subjects cannot be arrived at by logic, natural reasoning, following the conscience or by yielding to inner feelings.

    b. The Bible says the truth on these subjects can only be arrived at through the revelation of the Holy Spirit, **1 Corinthians 2:14**, which is exactly what we have in the Bible - God's Holy Word.

C. Thus, any time a sinner hears the Word of God, he is being reproved or convicted of sin, righteousness or judgment by the Holy Spirit.

1. Holy Spirit conviction is not a strange mysterious "wooing" in the heart apart from the Word of God.

2. When a person who is lost will open his ears (not just natural ears, but ears of his heart), and hear the truth of the Holy Spirit as set forth in the Word, he will experience Holy Spirit conviction. The Word will make it clear that he is a damnable sinner before Almighty God, that he is without righteousness or hope of saving himself and that he is on his way to the torments of eternal hell. What these truths do to the heart is Holy Spirit conviction: Period.

    a. Some upon hearing these truths become angry, **Acts 7:54**, some are cut to the heart, **Acts 5:33**, some tremble, **Acts 24:25**. There are numerous ways a man may react to these truths and numerous feelings of a mixed variety may well up within his heart. But it all comes under the heading of the convicting power of the Holy Spirit of God through the Word of God.

    b. It should be also noted that reaction to the Spirit's conviction through His Word may not be immediate upon hearing.

        (1) Since the Word is like a natural seed, **Matthew 13:19**, it may lie dormant in a man's heart for a long time before it germinates.

        (2) Even so, all the time it is there, it has a weight of conviction upon the person. Many times some later working of providence or a later exposure to more of the Word of God will cause that long dormant seed to spring up with momentous impact upon a man's heart.

    c. The truth is that there is no power more convicting than the voice of the Holy Spirit of God speaking through His Word. **Hebrews 4:12** says of it, *"For the word of God is quick, and powerful, and sharper than any twoedged sword, piercing even to the dividing asunder of soul and spirit, and of the joints and marrow, and is a discerner of the thoughts and intents of the heart."*

SECTION THREE

WE BELIEVE THIS IS AND ALWAYS HAS BEEN GOD'S METHOD OF CONVICTING THE LOST

A. If **John 16:8-11** was the only light God's Word gave on the subject, then there might be some questions over just *how* the Holy Spirit would go about reproving the world of sin, righteousness, and judgment.

B. If the foregoing information is not sufficient to prove how the Holy Spirit goes about His work of convicting the lost, in **Acts 7** the Word of God adds a very clear-cut proof of how He does it.

   1. In this passage, Stephen under the inspiration of the Holy Spirit of God, **Acts 6:8-15**, preached a tremendous sermon, **Acts 7:2-53**.

   2. When his hearer rejected the words of the Spirit, which he and other inspired men had preached unto them, he accused them of resisting the Holy Ghost, *"Ye stiffnecked and uncircumcised in heart and ears, ye do always resist the Holy Ghost,"* **Acts 7:51**. It wasn't that the Holy Ghost had entered into each of these hearers independently and separately of the Word of God. He did not enter their hearts and start whispering something into the inner ears of the soul. No, the fact was that they had heard God's Holy Spirit speak through this man, and that constituted Holy Spirit conviction. When they resisted it, they were said to be resisting the Holy Ghost.

   3. To make doubly clear that nobody gets a wrong impression of how the Holy Spirit convicts the lost, God through Stephen adds the last phrase of **Acts 7:51**, *"as your fathers did, so do ye."*

      a. Just how did the ancient forefathers of these Jews resist the Spirit?

      b. He (the Holy Spirit) appeared and spoke to the people through their prophets and holy leaders, **2 Peter 1:21**.

         (1) The Lord spoke to Moses, **Numbers 3:1, 9:1**, and in turn Moses told the people so that **Numbers 5:4** says, *"...as the LORD spake unto Moses, so did the children of Israel."*

- (2) Over and over the Old Testament records how the Spirit of God spoke to certain men, and they in turn spoke to the people, **Isaiah 8:5, Jeremiah 30:4, Ezekiel 5:13**, etc.
- c. Very often the people refused to hear and heed, **Ezekiel 33:32**, even imprisoning and killing the prophets, **Matthew 23:37**.
- d. But, the prophets knew that when the people resisted the words which they spoke, they were not merely resisting the prophets; instead they were resisting the Holy Spirit of God Himself, **Judges 3:4**.
- e. Note well that the Spirit did not appear to the people of old, except through the Word. This was His means of convicting them. Stephen says, that's still how it's done.

C. In Old Testament days, the Spirit convicted through His Word. He did the same in early Bible days and we believe that He still does it today. Whereas it was then spoken, now the Bible is written and complete; yet in either form, it is still His Word and He still uses it to convict men. This is Holy Spirit conviction.

Chapter 9

The Nature of Man and the Devil

It will be impossible to understand man's activities or God's dealings with man's activities, unless one understands man's nature and the devil's relationship toward man's nature. We believe man is by nature a sinful creature, void of righteousness by his own efforts; and that Satan works diligently to prey upon the weaknesses of man.

SECTION ONE

THE NATURE OF MAN

A. Man was originally created in holiness and innocence before God, but he voluntarily transgressed God's law and so fell into condemnation.

    1. Look at the Scriptures which show that man was created upright before God.

        a. He was created in the image of God Himself, **Genesis 1:26-27**.

        b. Until man sinned and fell into condemnation, he was seen in a perfect garden without the stigmas which plague men today, **Genesis 3:6**.

      c. Solomon said, *"Lo, this only have I found, that God hath made man upright; but they have sought out many inventions,"* **Ecclesiastes 7:29**.

  2. It is important to note how man sinned and fell from his original state.

      a. Notice that **Ecclesiastes 7:29** says, *"but they have sought out many inventions."*

      b. **Genesis 3:6-24** records the actual sin and fall of man.

      c. *"Wherefore, as by one man sin entered into the world, and death by sin; and so death passed upon all men, for that all have sinned,"* **Romans 5:12**. Sin was man's choice, not God's.

B. From that day forward man became by nature a sinful creature.

  1. Many today argue that man is basically good; and if given the opportunity, he will choose good over evil.

  2. That is not true! To the contrary, man is basically evil and his trend is to choose evil over good.

  3. Listen to the truth of God's Word.

      a. *"For all have sinned, and come short of the glory of God,"* **Romans 3:23**.

      b. **Psalm 14:1-3** shows that all men have *"gone aside"* and turned away from God.

      c. **Genesis 6:5** describes the fallen estate and practice of man.

      d. **Romans 1:21-32** describes the natural tendency of man toward wickedness.

      e. The sinful nature of man is vividly described in **Romans 3:13-18**.

      f. Jeremiah got right to the core of things when he said, *"The heart is deceitful above all things, and desperately wicked: who can know it?"* **Jeremiah 17:9**.

The Nature of Man and the Devil

    g. Ephesians 2:1-3 says plainly that man is by nature a sinful creature.

  4. Men sin and fail over and over again because they have a sinful nature. **2 Peter 2:22** says they repeatedly return to sin even as a dog returns to his own vomit. It's their nature to do it.

C. God describes man in his natural condition and says he is destitute, and absolutely void of righteousness.

  1. Solomon said it this way, *"For there is not a just man upon earth, that doeth good, and sinneth not,"* **Ecclesiastes 7:20.**

  2. *"As it is written, There is none righteous, no, not one: There is none that understandeth, there is none that seeketh after God. They are all gone out of the way, they are together become unprofitable; there is none that doeth good, no, not one,"* **Romans 3:10-12.**

  3. A man's best deeds are unrighteous. *"But we are all as an unclean thing, and all our righteousnesses are as filthy rags; and we do fade as a leaf; and our iniquities, like the wind, have taken us away,"* **Isaiah 64:6.**

  4. As good as the Apostle Paul was, he admitted that his own righteousness was reprehensible, and that his only hope before God was the imputed righteousness that only God can give, **Philippians 3:8-9.**

D. In view of the universal sinfulness of mankind, there is no universal spiritual brotherhood of man in which all are sons of God.

  1. Men are only a part of the universal brotherhood and guilt of sin.

  2. The only way to escape that damnable brotherhood is by faith in Jesus Christ.

    a. When a sinful, condemned man comes in faith to Jesus, the righteousness of Jesus becomes that man's righteousness, **Romans 3:22.** Jesus' righteousness is imputed or given to that man, **Romans 4:5-6.**

b. Thus **Galatians 3:26** says, *"For ye are all the children of God by faith in Christ Jesus."* Notice that it is *"by faith."* No person is automatically a member of the spiritual family of God.

   3. All who are yet in their unconverted natural condition are the children of the Devil, not God, **John 8:44**.

E. Yet in our current humanistic society, we are continually fed a steady diet of soul food that says all of us are a part of a universal brotherhood of men which at heart is fundamentally good, not evil.

   1. That simply is not true according to the Bible and what you can observe in society.

   2. Man is at heart a wicked creature. He may do a few fine deeds for a while; but when he's pushed, he'll turn on you like a mad dog, because that's his nature.

SECTION TWO

THE DEVIL

A. These days, belief in the existence of the Devil and sin is not in style.

   1. The *enlightened* generally regarded the Devil as a mythological character.

   2. Furthermore they do not think *sin* exists. Absolutes are rejected in favor of relativity. Things are not thought to be moral or immoral; good or bad. We are told to think in terms of *what's best for you under the circumstances*. This very anti-biblical concept is called *situation ethics*.

B. On the other hand, the Bible teaches that Satan is a very real person.

   1. **Isaiah 14:12-17** records his expulsion from heaven.

   2. Such passages as **John 8:44, Genesis 3:1-6, 1 Peter 5:8, Ephesians 2:2** speak of him as being very real and alive.

C. Satan's number one job on earth is to cause evil, especially among men.

   1. When he was first seen, he was up to evil, **Genesis 3:1-6**.

   2. He blinds men's eyes, **2 Corinthians 4:4**.

   3. He seeks to destroy, **1 Peter 5:8**.

   4. He accuses men before God, **Job 1:6-12, 2:1-7** and **Revelation 12:10**.

   5. I warn you that the Devil is a trouble-maker who will do his best to stir up the already wicked nature within you.

An understanding of these thoughts will help you see why men often act as they do.

Chapter 10

Blood Redemption, God's Method of Remitting Sins

Hebrews 9:22

We believe that it is impossible for a sinner to have his sins remitted except by the blood of Jesus Christ. This chapter is dedicated to showing you what the scriptures say on the subject.

SECTION ONE

IT IS ABSOLUTELY IMPOSSIBLE FOR A SINNER TO REMIT HIS OWN SINS

A. As previously shown, every man is a sinner in need of having his sins remitted (forgiven or pardoned).

1. Jesus said in **John 3:3, 5** that you cannot go to heaven except by a pardon.

2. Jesus also said, *"Except ye repent, ye shall all likewise perish,"* **Luke 13:3**.

3. **James 2:10** shows that sinners are guilty before God. See also **John 3:18, Romans 3:19**.

B. No man can clear his own guilt.

1. *"O LORD, I know that the way of man is not in himself: it is not in man that walketh to direct his steps,"* **Jeremiah 10:23**.

2. **Galatians 2:16** makes clear that no man can justify his own self.

3. **Titus 3:5** plainly points out that our works do not remove our guilt.

4. Our guilt can only be effectively addressed by Jesus Christ, **2 Timothy 1:9**.

C. A man can try all the methods he desires, but through his own efforts he will never remit even one of his sins; much less all of them.

1. Jesus said He is the way, and no man's sins are remitted except by Him, **John 14:6**.

2. You may try baptism, morality, good works, church affiliation, dedication, faithfulness, sincerity, etc., but they will not remit sins.

3. Jesus said, *"If ye believe not that I am he, ye shall die in your sins,"* **John 8:24**. See also **Hebrews 9:22**.

SECTION TWO

THE ONLY HOPE FOR SINNERS IS THE BLOOD REDEMPTION OF JESUS CHRIST

A. The Bible clearly sets forth blood redemption as God's way of clearing the guilty.

1. Blood redemption is seen as far back as Adam and Eve, **Genesis 3:21**.

2. The necessity of blood redemption is seen in Abel's sacrifice, **Genesis 4:2-7**.

3. Redemption by blood is seen in Israel's deliverance, **Exodus 12:1-13**.

4. Redemption by blood is the heart of the Levitical sacrifices, **Leviticus 16:5, 7-10, 15, 18, 19**.

5. Our text says, *"Without shedding of blood is no remission,"* **Hebrews 9:22**; but God also says, *"When I see the blood, I will pass over you,"* **Exodus 12:13**.

B. Jesus Christ died on Calvary to become our blood sacrifice for sins.

   1. He was God's perfect lamb, **Luke 23:4, 1 Peter 1:19, Mark 1:11**.

   2. His blood was shed.

      a. **John 19:34** records how they pierced Him and His blood came out.

      b. **Hebrews 9:12** says He offered His own blood to God for us.

C. It is through that blood, and it alone, that we are made *"one"* with God. (Sins remitted, pardoned).

   1. **Romans 5:8-11** says by His blood that we receive the forgiveness of sins.

   2. Look at how redemption is in his blood, *"To the praise of the glory of his grace, wherein he hath made us accepted in the beloved. In whom we have redemption through his blood, the forgiveness of sins, according to the riches of his grace,"* **Ephesians 1:6-7**.

   3. *"Whom God hath set forth to be a propitiation through faith in his blood, to declare his righteousness for the remission of sins that are past, through the forbearance of God,"* **Romans 3:25**. Righteousness is by His blood.

   4. Jesus said personally that His blood is for the remission of sins, **Matthew 26:28**.

   5. Listen to **Revelation 1:5** and **Revelation 5:9** on blood redemption.

"And from Jesus Christ, who is the faithful witness, and the first begotten of the dead, and the prince of the kings of the earth. Unto him that loved us, and washed us from our sins in his own blood," **Revelation 1:5**

Blood Redemption, God's Method of Remitting Sins

"And they sung a new song, saying, Thou art worthy to take the book, and to open the seals thereof: for thou wast slain, and hast redeemed us to God by thy blood out of every kindred, and tongue, and people, and nation," **Revelation 5:9**

    6. **1 Peter 1:18-19** shows our redemption is not by vain things, but by blood.

D. When viewed in light of the Scriptures, blood redemption alone is valid for the forgiveness of sins.

    1. It is not only His death that justifies, but also the shedding of His blood.

    2. A person is only saved by the application of the blood of Christ to his life by faith in Christ.

    3. As the text makes very clear that if there is no redemption by blood, then there is no redemption at all. *"And almost all things are by the law purged with blood; and without shedding of blood is no remission,"* **Hebrews 9:22.**

Chapter 11

Faith, God's Method for Appropriating Eternal Salvation

Romans 4:4-5

That salvation is exclusively by faith is one of the clearest teaching in all The Bible, yet it is probably one of the most misunderstood Bible teachings of all. To misunderstand this teaching is to miss heaven. My goal is to present this fundamental truth clearly in this chapter.

SECTION ONE

SALVATION IN NO WAY COMES ABOUT AS A RESULT OF ANY HUMAN WORK OR EFFORT

A. Most religious denominations say it does.

    1. The idea of many is that salvation comes by being *good*, living an upright life.

    2. With others it comes by self-abasement, penance.

    3. With some salvation is by baptism, church membership, communion, prayer, tongues or some similar experience.

    4. Anything that involves an effort on your part is a work of one sort or another.

      a. Praying, being baptized, joining a church are all efforts on your part.

      b. Faith is not an effort; it takes no action, it is strictly a state of the mind (heart).

      c. The Bible speaks of faith as opposed to works. All human efforts are viewed as works. (The Bible doesn't name each individual work, but simply all that is not of faith is work.)

B. If your hope for heaven is based upon your efforts or your plans to continually live right in the future, or if you think there is anything you could ever do or fail to do in the future that would exclude you from heaven, then you have a works for salvation mentality. You are lost and you will never be saved until you change your thinking. That change of thinking is what repentance toward God is. You must get self out of the picture and come by faith, wholly relying upon the work of Christ for your redemption.

C. Listen to how the Scriptures exclude works for salvation.

    1. **Romans 4:1-5** makes it very clear that salvation is not of works.

    2. *"Not by works of righteousness which we have done, but according to his mercy he saved us, by the washing of regeneration, and renewing of the Holy Ghost,"* **Titus 3:5**.

    3. *"Therefore by the deeds of the law there shall no flesh be justified in his sight,"* **Romans 3:20**.

    4. One ought to work, but not in order to obtain salvation, **Ephesians 2:8-10**.

D. Some point to **John 6:29** as proof that faith is a work. *"Jesus answered and said unto them, This is the work of God, that ye believe on him whom he hath sent,"* **John 6:29**.

    1. If faith was a work, then the Bible would be in contradiction of itself on how to be saved from sin's penalty. This passage is not teaching that faith is a work for salvation while the foregoing Scriptures (and others) teach salvation to be by faith apart from works.

2. The work to which Jesus referred was the feeding of the five thousand, **John 6:5-15**. Jesus did this work through the power of God. No man did it.

3. The purpose of this work was to cause men to believe. Faith is not a work.

SECTION TWO

SALVATION IS NOT APPROPRIATED BY A COMBINATION OF FAITH AND WORKS

A. The idea that salvation requires both faith and works is very common.

1. Nearly all religious people will tell you that you must believe in God to be saved.

2. They then start tacking on all these extras.

3. They see salvation as appropriated by some sort of blend of faith and works.

B. Salvation is not a blend of any combination of faith and works.

1. *"And if by grace, then is it no more of works: otherwise grace is no more grace. But if it be of works, then it is no more grace: otherwise work is no more work,"* **Romans 11:6** Salvation is either by faith or it is by works; it is not a combination of the two. The Bible blows to bits the idea of a blend.

2. *"Therefore we conclude that a man is justified by faith without the deeds of the law,"* **Romans 3:28**.

3. Whenever the Word of God tells how to be saved, it always says salvation is by faith. Plus nothing, minus nothing!

C. So far the negative side of the story has been presented; however, there is a positive side which I shall now examine.

SECTION THREE

SALVATION IS APPROPRIATED EXCLUSIVELY BY FAITH IN JESUS CHRIST

A. In appropriating salvation, faith is the one spiritual command you must obey.

1. **Acts 16:31** tells lost people to, *"Believe on the Lord Jesus Christ, and thou shalt be saved."*

2. **John 3:16** says, *"Whosoever believeth in him should not perish, but have everlasting life"* and **verse 18** continues, *"He that believeth on him is not condemned: but he that believeth not is condemned already, because he hath not believed in the name of the only begotten Son of God."*

3. **John 3:36** shows both the positive and negative sides of belief.

4. Jesus says that all believers are saved, **John 5:24**.

5. Consider what Jesus told Martha, **John 11:25-26**.

6. Salvation exclusively by faith was a foregone conclusion to Paul. He said, *"Therefore being justified by faith, we have peace with God,"* **Romans 5:1**.

7. Yet, today there are those (even preachers) who have the audacity to dispute God and say faith is not enough. They say that it takes more, even works.

B. **Romans 4** labors the point that salvation is exclusively by grace through faith in Jesus Christ. This passage destroys the concept of works for salvation.

1. Abraham simply believed God and God gave him righteousness, **verse 3**.

2. Note well these verses as to how salvation is by faith without works, **verses 4-5**.

3. The Lord imputes righteousness without works, **verse 6**.

4. Thus, salvation is of grace, **verse 16**.

5. Salvation was not for Abraham only, but to all who believe, **verses 24-25**.

C. Salvation is there for all who will believe.

    1. It is like a TV beam. It is there and only needs to be received. It is *"unto all,"* but only *"upon all them that believe,"* **Romans 3:22**.

    2. Only by faith in the heart can it be received, **Romans 10:8-9**.

D. Belief in Christ is simple trust or reliance on Him.

    1. **Ephesians 1:13** calls it *"trust."*

    2. It is relying on Christ even *"as a little child,"* **Mark 10:15**.

    3. Belief in this sense is not the mere acceptance of a fact; it is trust, **James 2:19**.

    4. Belief is a matter of trusting Him as your Savior.

E. Eternal salvation for you is solely dependent upon whether or not you come by faith alone to Jesus Christ as your personal Savior.

    1. *"Whosoever believeth that Jesus is the Christ is born of God,"* **1 John 5:1**.

    2. *"If ye believe not that I am he, ye shall die in your sins,"* **John 8:24**.

Chapter 12

The Unpardonable Sin

Matthew 12:31-32

We believe the sin which shall not be forgiven, which Jesus called *"blasphemy against the Holy Ghost,"* **Matthew 12:31**, consists of crediting to Satan the miraculous deeds done by the Holy Spirit through Jesus (and later the Apostles). We do not believe that prolonged rejection of salvation, turning excessively vile in one's thinking, suicide, or committing terrible sins is to commit the unpardonable sin of which Jesus spoke.

In fact, we believe since the cessation of the miraculous works of the Holy Spirit which were performed through Jesus and in the Apostolic Age, it has been impossible for anyone to commit the unpardonable sin. Thus, we do not believe anyone today can commit the unpardonable sin. To the contrary, we believe anyone in sane mind can be saved, which would be equivalent to ALL his sins being forgiven. The capacity is there.

SECTION ONE

THE UNPARDONABLE SIN NOT ONLY INVOLVED THE *"WORDS"* OF TRUTH, BUT ALSO A MIRACULOUS DEMONSTRATION OR *"WORK"* BY THE HOLY SPIRIT TO CONFIRM THAT THE WORDS WERE TRUTH

A. These *"words"* and *"works"* are rightfully considered two witnesses of the truth.

   1. In **John 3:11**, Jesus spoke of His words (own testimony) as being a witness to His hearers. (Repeatedly He bore verbal witness that He was the Christ. **John 8:55-58, John 10:24-25**).

   2. Jesus also said the works that He did were another witness of the truth.

      a. He said, *"The works that I do in my Father's name, they bear witness of me,"* **John 10:25**.

      b. He also said, *"But I have greater witness than that of John:* (John could only witness that Jesus was the Christ with words) *for the works which the Father hath given me to finish, the same works that I do, bear witness of me, that the Father hath sent me,"* **John 5:36**.

B. Jesus personally claimed the strength of a two-fold witness.

   1. His words in **John 8:18** are, *"I am one that bear witness of myself, and the Father that sent me beareth witness of me:"*

      a. Notice first that He bore record of Himself through His words.

      b. But, also notice that the Father bore record of Him through His works.

   2. Jesus thus said, *"I am the Son of God* (His own witness through words)? *If I do not the works of my Father* (the second witness being that of the Father through work) *believe me not,"* **John 10:36-37**.

C. The occasion upon which Jesus introduced the doctrine of the unpardonable sin was a case where a mighty work had been performed through Him in order to cause those who heard Him and saw the miracle to believe in Him.

   1. In the context, you will see that Jesus had performed a mighty miracle (work) of healing on *"one possessed with a devil, blind, and dumb: and he healed him, insomuch that the blind and dumb both spake and saw,"* **Matthew 12:22**.

2. Remember that Jesus said the purpose of such mighty works was to prove who He was and that He spoke the truth, thus causing men to believe in Him, **John 5:36**.

3. After Jesus cast out this devil, He spent considerable time showing that the miracle was proof that He was of God and not of Satan, **Matthew 12:25-30**.

4. On this occasion, the two-fold witness was in clear view: Jesus' words, **Matthew 12:25-30**, and a mighty work of the Holy Ghost through Him, **Matthew 12:22**.

5. The reaction to this two-fold witness was that some believed and some didn't.

   a. Some *"were amazed, and said, Is not this the son of David?"* **Matthew 12:23**.

   b. *"But when the Pharisees heard it, they said, This fellow doth not cast out devils, but by Beelzebub the prince of the devils,"* **Matthew 12:24**.

6. It was this latter group that was guilty of the unpardonable sin. They were exposed to a two-fold witness; but in spite of such positive proof, they rejected the truth of who Jesus was and credited the mighty work and witness of the Holy Spirit to Satan himself, **Matthew 12:31-32**.

SECTION TWO

HAD THERE NOT BEEN A TWO-FOLD WITNESS, SPECIFICALLY A MIRACULOUS WORK BY THE HOLY GHOST TO CONFIRM THE WORDS OF JESUS, THEN THERE WOULD HAVE BEEN NO BLASPHEMY AGAINST THE HOLY GHOST OR UNPARDONABLE SIN

A. Jesus made that truth extraordinarily clear when He said, *"If I had not done among them the works which none other man did, they had not had sin: but now have they both seen and hated both me and my Father,"* **John 15:24**.

1. The sin Jesus spoke of here must be the unpardonable sin. All men commit a wide variety of common sins, **Romans 3:23, Ecclesiastes 7:20.** This is a specific reference by Jesus to a situation where those present both heard Jesus' claim and saw the miracle.

2. In this case Jesus referred to a specific sin which could not be committed separately from the witness of a mighty work of the Holy Spirit. The unpardonable sin is the only sin mentioned in the Bible which required (1) the witness of Jesus or one of His apostles (2) in the presence of a miracle by the power of the Holy Spirit.

3. Notice well that Jesus said that if the mighty work had not been done, then they would have had no sin.

B. This truth is typified and symbolically illustrated in the Old Testament.

1. Under the law, two witnesses were required to put anyone to death. *"He that despised Moses' law died without mercy under two or three witnesses,"* **Hebrews 10:28.**

2. Never could anyone be executed upon the strength of only one witness: *"one witness shall not testify against any person to cause him to die,"* **Numbers 35:30.**

3. God's directive was, *"At the mouth of two witnesses, or three witnesses, shall he that is worthy of death be put to death; but at the mouth of one witness he shall not be put to death,"* **Deuteronomy 17:6.**

4. Even as two physical witnesses were required to put a man to death physically, even so two heavenly witnesses are required to put a man into the category of those who've committed the unpardonable sin and thus seal his fate to eternal death.

SECTION THREE

WE BELIEVE THAT WHEN THE MIRACULOUS WORKS OF THE SPIRIT CEASED, THE ERA OF THE TWO-FOLD WITNESS ENDED. AFTER THAT TIME, IT BECAME IMPOSSIBLE FOR ANYONE TO COMMIT THE UNPARDONABLE SIN.

A. In the age of Jesus and in the Apostolic Age which followed, the Word was accompanied by miraculous works of the Holy Spirit. Thus, a two-fold witness was established and the unpardonable sin could be committed.

  1. It was of this that Jesus spoke when He said, *"it shall not be forgiven him, neither in this world, neither in the world to come,"* **Matthew 12:32.**

  2. The word *"world"* is from the Greek word <u>aion</u> and is used in the sense of "an age"; not in reference to some planet or new creation.

  3. Thus, when Jesus spoke of *"this world"* or His own age, we know from the foregoing points that it was an age of words and mighty works of the Spirit. In that period of time, it was thus possible for men to commit the unpardonable sin.

  4. In *"the world to come"* or the age which followed, which was the age of the Apostles, words and mighty works were also the order of the day. Thus, men were still able to commit the unpardonable sin.

   a. Of God's men in that age, **Hebrews 2:4** says, *"God also bearing them witness, both with signs and wonders, and with divers miracles, and gifts of the Holy Ghost..."*

   b. Paul, an Apostle, said, *"And I, brethren, when I came to you, came not with excellency of speech or of wisdom ... but in demonstration of the Spirit and of power,"* **1 Corinthians 2:1-4.**

  5. There were men in those ages that heard the words of truth and saw the mighty works of the Spirit in confirmation of the words. In spite of such overwhelming divine evidence, some of them didn't believe. Instead they credited the works of the Spirit to Satan. Of those the Scriptures say:

       a. *"Ye cannot hear my word."* **John 8:43.**

       b. *"They could not believe,"* **John 12:39** and they *"cannot cease from sin,"* **2 Peter 2:14.**

       c. *"The last state"* was said to be *"worse than the first,"* **Matthew 12:45.**

B. As the Scriptures were finished at the end of the Apostolic age, the miraculous signs or works of the Spirit ceased, **1 Corinthians 13:8-10.**

   1. See the chapter in this book on *The Completion of the Apostolic Ministry.*

   2. No longer do we see the miraculous works which accompanied Jesus Christ and the Apostles. The two-fold testimony has *ceased.*

   3. Today we have one testimony, that of the Word of God.

       a. In this age, *"faith cometh by hearing, and hearing by the word of God,"* **Romans 10:17.**

       b. Today there are no current mighty signs or works of the Spirit. Men must believe the single witness which is the Word of God. Long ago while God's Word was being given, it was proven to be true by miraculous signs. God's Word is now completed and there are no on-going signs.

       c. Men today must believe upon the strength of a single witness, God's Word. Jesus said of people who believe the Word of God as once given, *"blessed are they that have not seen, and yet have believed,"* **John 20:29.**

C. The unpardonable sin involved the two-fold witness of words and works. Some heard the words as to who Jesus was and saw a confirming miracle. They rejected the truth that Jesus was the Savior and accredited the confirming miracle to Satan. Both the "words" and the "works" were necessary for the unpardonable sin to be committed. Today, men have only the single witness of the Word. There are no current miraculous works to accredit to either the Holy Ghost or Satan. We thus conclude that it is impossible for men to currently commit the unpardonable sin.

The Unpardonable Sin

1. If the circumstances under which the sin could be committed still existed, then the unpardonable sin could be committed, but they don't.

2. Since miraculous works of the Spirit are not performed now, no man today is offered the opportunity to credit them to Satan and in so doing commit the unpardonable sin.

3. The unpardonable sin was a specific sin limited to the ages specified by Jesus Christ. The current age is not included in those ages in which men could commit that sin.

Chapter 13

In Christ We Have Eternal Security

John 6:39

The Bible teaches that once a man comes by faith unto Christ, he is saved forever. He is not saved only as long as he maintains a good testimony and refrains from being too bad. He stays saved *in spite of,* not *because of* his conduct. He can never in any way lose his salvation. In this chapter we shall consider a small portion of the mass of Bible proof there is on this subject.

SECTION ONE

MAN'S SALVATION REMAINS HIS ETERNAL POSSESSION REGARDLESS OF HOW HE LIVES AFTER HIS CONVERSION

A. God does not save men because of their good conduct.

    1. Men are saved strictly by faith in Him, not because of goodness.

        a. Romans 3:22 says God's righteousness is upon all them that believe.

        b. *"By grace are ye saved through faith,"* **Ephesians 2:8**.

       c. John 3:16, Acts 16:31 and many kindred passages show that salvation comes by believing.

  2. Salvation comes to people solely as a gift of God, not as a payment of debt.

       a. Romans 6:23 says that the *"gift of God is eternal life through Jesus Christ our Lord."*

       b. Ephesians 2:8 also calls it the *"gift of God."*

  3. Our goodness was strictly excluded from our being saved.

       a. Ephesians 2:9 says it is *"Not of works, lest any man should boast."*

       b. Titus 3:5 plainly says it is *"not by works of righteousness which we have done."*

B. God didn't save us because of our goodness; neither does He keep us because of our goodness.

  1. Our puny morality becomes no more pleasant to Him after we're saved than it was before, **Isaiah 64:6**.

  2. He saved us because we came to Him in faith or trust, and He keeps us because we trusted Him.

       a. *"Being confident of this very thing, that he which hath begun a good work in you will perform it until the day of Jesus Christ,"* **Philippians 1:6**.

       b. It is in view of the sustaining power of God that Paul rejoiced, **Philippians 3:8-9**.

C. The belief that a man's own goodness keeps him saved is self-incriminating.

  1. All men including saved men sin, **Romans 3:23**. Those who say they don't are liars, **1 John 1:8**.

  2. It is God's view that if a man commits one sin, he is guilty of all, **James 2:10**.

3. Sin brings the condemnation of death, **Romans 6:23, Ezekiel 18:20.**

   4. No man can keep himself on a sinless path. If it were up to any man to keep himself saved, he'd soon be right back in the condemned state where he started.

D. It is God and God alone who keeps us saved.

   1. **1 Peter 1:5** clearly says we *"are kept by the power of God."*

   2. Furthermore, the Scriptures show how Father, Son and Spirit are dedicated to our security.

      a. **Colossians 3:3** says, *"For ye are dead, and your life is hid with Christ in God."*

      b. **Ephesians 1:13** states that we are *"sealed with that holy Spirit of promise."*

      c. Our destruction would require the destruction of God: Father, Son and Holy Spirit.

   3. God did not want, need or allow our help when it came to saving us. Furthermore, He does not allow our help in keeping us saved, **Titus 3:5.**

SECTION TWO

A MAN WILL REMAIN SAVED EVEN THOUGH HE MIGHT RENOUNCE CHRIST

A. It has already been shown that a person is kept by God, **1 Peter 1:5.** God keeps him saved totally apart from any works on his part, **Titus 3:5.** If a person's salvation is up to God, then that person has nothing to do with it. If there was a decision about whether to keep you or let you go back into condemnation, that decision would rest with God, not you.

B. Christ has already decided to never let you go.

1. He specifically said so three times, **John 6:37, 39** and **44**. That claim is either true or God is a liar. He is not a liar; it is true.

2. Furthermore, He will not let you go, and He will not allow anyone (not even you) to separate you from Him, **Romans 8:35-39**.

C. By faith we are placed into the irrevocable relationship of sons of God.

1. By faith we are born again, **John 3:3**, and thus become the sons of God, **1 John 3:1-2**.

2. It is just as impossible for a spiritual son to reverse the spiritual process which made him a son and thus go back to preexistence as it is for a physical son to reverse the natural processes which made him a natural son and go back into preexistence. Either thought is quite preposterous. Thinking people know that both are impossible.

D. It is in view of this that the Bible calls the life we have in Christ *"everlasting,"* and not *"temporary,"* **John 3:16, 36, 4:14; 5:24**.

Chapter 14

The Fatherhood of God and the Brotherhood of Man

John 8:38-44

There is a very common social and religious idea that God is the Father of all men and that all men are brothers in one great family and form some sort of spiritual brotherhood. Since Darwinian Evolution theorizes that man evolved from the *lower animals,* it is commonly believed that the cousins of the man family are the primates, vertebrates, mammals, etc. This position, which has dire ramifications, is embraced and zealously propagated in most intellectual, social and religious circles today. Those who reject it are generally thought to be narrow-minded, illiterate and bigoted. The idea is commonly known as "The Universal Fatherhood of God" and "The Universal Brotherhood of Man."

We reject the contentions of this doctrine, believing them to be absolutely without biblical foundation and in direct opposition to the teachings of God's Holy Word.

We believe God is the Father of only those who are saved from sin's penalty and that the saved form a spiritual brotherhood which is not related to unsaved man.

SECTION ONE

THE UNIVERSALIST IDEA IS APPEALING, YET SINISTER

A. It is based upon a false assumption.

  1. It is assumed that since all men must have come from a first man and God made that first man, then God must be the father of all men.

  2. It is true that all men descended from one man: Adam.

      a. **Genesis 1:26-28** and **2:15-24** record the fact that God made the man and the woman from which all other humans have descended.

      b. Adam is the federal head of the human race and introduced sin to it, **Romans 5:12.**

      c. Since there is a common bond between all men in that they all come from Adam, **1 Corinthians 15:39** says, *"there is one kind of flesh of men..."*

  3. God made Adam and all men came from him, but it does not automatically follow that all those men form one brotherhood and constitute God's spiritual children.

      a. Descending from Adam is not equivalent to membership in God's spiritual family.

      b. The assumption of Universalism is a fleshly assumption which does not reveal the truth. The things of God are *"spiritually discerned,"* **1 Corinthians 2:14.**

  4. The Holy Spirit has discerned and has revealed in the Bible that not all men are members of the same family, nor are they all God's children.

      a. **1 John 3:10** speaks of both *"the children of God ... and the children of the devil."*

      b. Read **Romans 9:6-8**. From God's viewpoint being *"children of the flesh"* does not automatically make people *"children of God."* Note well **verse 8**.

B. In spite of God's Word on the subject, it is assumed that all men are God's dear children and brothers in one big family.

    1. The Jews doubtless had only their race in mind; nevertheless, their words express the Universalist's sentiments to a "tee," *"we have one Father, even God,"* **John 8:41**.

    2. This unscriptural Universalist idea is propagated every day.

        a. Particularly by churches and in religious advertising.

        b. By those endeavoring to advance social reform.

        c. And by thousands of well-meaning, but uninformed people.

C. The Universalist idea has devastating consequences.

    1. It appeals to a man's sense of unity and fairness.

    2. It seems to indicate God would be unfair and inequitable if He makes some His children while others aren't.

    3. There is the thought that even though some are a little more unruly than others, we are all God's children. There is also the *good ole God* idea; He's somehow going to see that everything turns out alright in the end for us all. That kind of thinking gives a sense of security that all is okay.

    4. Thus, man is deceived into thinking all is well with his soul when it really isn't.

        a. His knowledge of guilt and condemnation is deadened and he is deceived, **2 Corinthians 4:4**.

        b. As a result, he plunges on toward hell without even realizing that he is going there.

SECTION TWO

THE TRUTH IS THAT ALL UNBELIEVERS ARE SPIRITUAL CHILDREN OF SATAN AND THEY ARE SPIRITUAL BROTHERS ONLY TO THE UNSAVED

A. Jesus Christ made this very point quite emphatically, **John 8:38-44**.

   1. He spoke of *"your father"* as opposed to *"my Father,"* **verse 38**.

   2. Jesus Christ was the *"only begotten Son"* of *"God,"* **John 3:16**; *"the only begotten of the Father,"* **John 1:14**. There is no question as to whom He was referring when He spoke of *"my Father."* He was speaking of God.

   3. But, He said these unbelieving men did not have the same Father He had, **John 8:45**. He said if God was their Father, they *"would love me,"* **John 8:42,** but they neither loved Jesus nor believed Him. Instead, they *"seek to kill me, because my word hath no place in you,"* **John 8:37**.

   4. Of these unbelieving men, all of whom were natural descendants of Adam, He said, *"Ye are of your father the devil,"* **John 8:44**.

B. Sinners are sons of Satan.

   1. God's will and command is that *"all men every where ... repent,"* **Acts 17:30**. He does not want them to remain in unbelief and perish, **2 Peter 3:9**.

   2. Satan's will is diametrically opposed to God's will, **2 Thessalonians 2:4**. He deceives men and keeps them in unbelief that they might perish, **2 Thessalonians 2:10**.

   3. God's Word says that if you obey Satan's will, you are his servant and every unbeliever is obeying Satan. You belong to him and eternal death is the consequence. *"Know ye not, that to whom ye yield yourselves servants to obey, his servants ye are to whom ye obey; whether of sin unto death, or of obedience unto righteousness?"* **Romans 6:16**.

   4. Every sinner who obeys the will of Satan is not God's spiritual child. To the contrary, he is disobeying the will of God for him and thus falls into the family of Satan.

5. The only way he can become a member of God's family is to obey God's will for him: *"obeyed from the heart that form of doctrine,"* **Romans 6:17**. That *"form of doctrine"* which is God's will is, *"That whosoever believeth in him should not perish, but have eternal life,"* **John 3:15**.

C. The contention that all men are God's children, despite their disobedience of God's will, simply will not stand before the searchlight of the Scriptures: They are Satan's children.

1. *"Children of disobedience,"* **Ephesians 2:2, Ephesians 5:6, Colossians 3:6**.

2. *"Children of wrath,"* **Ephesians 2:3**.

3. *"Children of the devil,"* **1 John 3:10**.

SECTION THREE

ONLY BY FAITH DOES ANY MAN BECOME GOD'S CHILD

A. The Scriptures declare it.

1. *"For ye are all the children of God by faith in Christ Jesus,"* **Galatians 3:26**. Only by faith.

2. Notice in **John 1:12** that membership in the spiritual family of God is only for them that believe.

3. **Deuteronomy 32:6** asks, *"...is not he thy father that hath bought thee?"* and every believer has been bought by God, **1 Corinthians 6:19-20**, with the precious *"blood of Christ,"* **1 Peter 1:18-19**.

4. It is not a common place thing to be one of God's sons. It is a miraculous thing through faith. *"Behold, what manner of love the Father hath bestowed upon us, that we should be called the sons of God,"* **1 John 3:1**.

B. By faith, a spiritual birth occurs and God becomes the spiritual Father of the believer.

1. **1 John 5:1** states it well. *"Whosoever believeth that Jesus is the Christ is born of God."*

2. Of these, **2 Corinthians 6:17-18** says *"I will receive you. And will be a Father unto you, and ye shall be my sons and daughters, saith the Lord Almighty."*

3. These can say, *"to us there is but one God, the Father,"* **1 Corinthians 8:6**.

4. These can address God as their Father: **Romans 8:14-17, Galatians 4:5-7, Matthew 6:9**.

C. Believers become sons of God, and as such they are true brethren.

1. It matters not whether we be Jew or Gentile, bond or free, black or white. All believers are *"children of the living God"* and brethren with all other believers, **Romans 9:23-26**.

2. Through faith there is *"one God and Father of all,"* **Ephesians 4:6**, and all the saved make one great family with God as Father, **John 11:52**. On the other hand, not one unsaved person is a true spiritual brother to believers. Neither can he call God his Father.

Chapter 15

God's Threefold Salvation

2 Corinthians 1:10

This chapter is designed to present a simple truth which every Christian should know well. Though it is central in the Scriptures, many Christians have never seen it. The understanding of this truth will shed light on a great many other Bible truths and make many difficult passages easy to understand. In fact, a good understanding of this will do as much, if not more, to enhance a person's overall understanding of the Scriptures than any other single truth.

The infinitive verb "to save" and its various derivatives (saved, salvation, etc.) come from the Greek word sos which, according to Strong's Greek Dictionary, means "to save, to deliver or, to protect." When we read the word in the Bible or hear it in a sermon, we normally think of the word as a religious word; however, it is not correct to limit the word to a religious sense. Though this word is used to express a mighty Bible truth, it is at the same time appropriately used in everyday situations. Any time anyone is delivered from any given peril, one can rightfully say he was saved. A child can be saved from an onrushing car, a man can be saved from a lynch mob, or a soul can be saved from eternal damnation.

There are three major senses in which the word is used in the Scriptures. Most people think that when the word is in a Bible context, it always refers to deliverance from the eternal damnation of hell, (to miss hell and gain heaven). That is not true. Sometimes the word refers to the deliverance we have from daily temptations and perils, which ruin our testimonies and spiritual lives. The word also refers to deliverance from sin's presence, which shall one day take place. In any given Bible text where salvation is under consideration, it is vital to understand the sense in which it is used. For example, people who have trusted Christ as personal Savior are already saved from sin's penalty which is eternal separation from God in the lake of fire. Not all texts which speak of salvation are about sin's penalty; many texts are all about the help of God which saves or delivers us from the daily efforts of Satan to wreck our day-to-day lives. This is salvation from sin's power. It is not difficult to see how misleading and confusing it is to use a Scripture like this to lead a lost sinner to Christ. Sadly, many well-meaning soul winners do it every day. The most common Scripture which is misused in this way is Romans 10:13. It is vital to use Scriptures in context. It is a grave offence before God to use them in a different sense than He intended.

We cannot overstress the importance of determining the sense in which a word is used in any given Scripture. Whatever the word, especially *salvation*, it should always be used in the proper biblical sense.

You can see that all three senses of the word *saved* are mentioned in our text, **2 Corinthians 1:10**. We will now analyze the infinitive verb *to save* in each of its three primary biblical senses.

SECTION ONE

SALVATION FROM THE PENALTY OF SIN

A. The penalty of sin is eternal death or separation from God, **Romans 5:12**, and those who have experienced salvation in this first sense have been delivered from this death, which is sin's penalty.

   1. It is thus that believers are said to have *"passed from death unto life,"* **John 5:24**.

   2. **1 John 3:14** says of us who have believed, *"We know that we have passed from death unto life."*

3. Jesus referred to this type of salvation or deliverance by saying, *"I am the resurrection, and the life: he that believeth in me, though he were dead, yet shall he live,"* **John 11:25**.

B. Notice that this salvation is always past tense for those who have experienced it.

1. **John 5:24** says the believer *"is passed from death unto life"*. That would be a completed, finished work of the past.

2. Jesus spoke to a woman who had just believed on Him and said, *"Thy faith hath* (past tense) *saved thee,"* **Luke 7:50**.

3. Paul said that the saints at Ephesus *"are ... saved through faith,"* **Ephesians 2:8**.

4. **2 Timothy 1:9** speaks of Jesus Christ, *"Who hath saved us."*

5. It is thus that **1 Corinthians 1:18** can speak of us *"which are saved."* That is a completed work which *has been,* not *is being* accomplished.

6. Salvation from sin's penalty is not a progressive delivering, taking a lifetime to perform. It is a deliverance which occurs completely and finally at belief. The deliverance is finished then, and continuously thereafter, we are saved. We can forever thereafter look back to that event when we were delivered wholly and instantly from all of sin's penalty.

C. As the previous Scriptures show, we experience this salvation at belief.

1. This is what Paul told the Philippian jailor, *"Believe on the Lord Jesus Christ, and thou shalt be saved,"* **Acts 16:31**.

2. **John 3:36** says, *"He that believeth on the Son hath everlasting life."*

3. Re-examine **John 5:24** and **John 11:25**.

D. Salvation in this sense is accomplished by Christ's dying.

1. **1 Thessalonians 5:9-10** says, *"For God hath not appointed us to wrath, but to obtain salvation by our Lord Jesus Christ, Who died for*

us, that, whether we wake or sleep, we should live together with him." Note: Salvation was made possible by His dying.

   2. He delivered us from death by taking our death on Himself, **Romans 5:8**, as our substitute; and by this death, reconciled us to God, **Colossians 1:21-22**.

E. It was in His office of good shepherd that Christ performed this salvation (deliverance), for it is the good shepherd that *"giveth his life for the sheep,"* **John 10:11**.

F. Deliverance or salvation in this sense is the saving grace of God, **Ephesians 2:8**.

G. Now notice some of the facts of this salvation.

   1. It is past tense.

   2. It is a finished deliverance; not progressive.

   3. It is from sin's penalty.

   4. It is experienced at the point of belief.

   5. It is accomplished by Christ's death.

   6. Christ performs this salvation as a good shepherd.

   7. This is God's work of saving grace.

SECTION TWO

SALVATION FROM THE DOMINION OF SIN

A. Satan would cause us to backslide, ruin our testimony and rob us of joy, fruitfulness and happiness. But, God would deliver or save us from this peril or danger.

   1. When Paul surveyed these dangers, knowing he could be robbed of fellowship with God and all the benefits that result from it, **Romans 7:15-23**, he stated there is deliverance or salvation in Christ, **Romans 7:24-25**.

2. Paul referred to salvation in this sense when he said, *"For the law of the Spirit of life in Christ Jesus hath made me free from the law of sin and death,"* **Romans 8:2**.

3. Again he referred to it by saying, *"For sin shall not have dominion over you,"* **Romans 6:14**.

B. Salvation in this sense is present tense and progressive.

1. We need this kind of deliverance day by day, even moment by moment.

2. Paul needed this daily, ever-present, deliverance. Thus he asked the Philippian Christians to pray for him. *"For I know that this shall turn to my salvation through your prayer."* He said this salvation was equivalent to the fact *"that in nothing I shall be ashamed, but that with all boldness, as always, so now also Christ shall be magnified in my body...,"* **Philippians 1:19-20**.

3. It is in view of God's saving us in this sense that David said, *"God is our refuge and strength, a very present help in trouble,"* **Psalm 46:1**.

C. Salvation in this sense is the sustaining grace of God.

1. It is of salvation in this sense that God speaks in **2 Corinthians 12:9**, *"My grace is sufficient for thee."*

2. We are promised deliverance from the daily perils of life. *"There hath no temptation taken you but such as is common to man: but God is faithful, who will not suffer you to be tempted above that ye are able; but will with the temptation also make a way to escape, that ye may be able to bear it,"* **1 Corinthians 10:13**.

D. Only the believer who is walking in truth, whose life is submitted to the will of God can expect to experience this salvation.

1. If a man will yield himself to God and walk according to truth, God will deliver or save him in this sense.

   a. God's word says, *"But whoso looketh into the perfect law of liberty, and continueth therein, he being not a forgetful hearer, but a doer of the work, this man shall be blessed in his deed,"* **James 1:25**.

      b. It is in this sense that Paul speaks of salvation in **Philippians 2:12-13**, *"Wherefore, my beloved, as ye have always obeyed, not as in my presence only, but now much more in my absence, work out your own salvation with fear and trembling. For it is God which worketh in you both to will and to do of his good pleasure."* Note that there is no work involved in salvation from sin's penalty, but salvation from sin's dominion or power requires much work.

      c. This truth is further seen in **2 Timothy 2:21**, *"If a man therefore purge himself from these, he shall be a vessel unto honour, sanctified, and meet for the master's use, and prepared unto every good work."*

      d. It is in this sense that **1 Peter 3:21** says, *"baptism doth also now save us..."*

  2. On the other hand, the believer, who stiffens himself against God's will and does not walk in truth will that find he is not delivered or saved from the things which would ruin his life.

      a. The Lord is only *"nigh unto all them that call upon him, to all that call upon him in truth,"* **Psalm 145:18**.

      b. Listen to how Isaiah put it in **Isaiah 59:1-2**, *"Behold, the LORD's hand is not shortened, that it cannot save; neither his ear heavy, that it cannot hear: But your iniquities have separated between you and your God, and your sins have hid his face from you, that he will not hear."*

E. Believers who lose their salvation in this sense, **Galatians 5:4**, regain it through prayer.

  1. We have this promise in **1 John 1:9**, *"If we confess our sins, he is faithful and just to forgive us our sins, and to cleanse us from all unrighteousness."*

  2. This is what **Romans 10:13** is talking about, *"For whosoever shall call upon the name of the Lord shall be saved."*

  3. Ananias told Paul to wash away his sins by *"calling on the name of the Lord,"* **Acts 22:16**.

4. And, Peter told Simon, whose heart was not right, **Acts 8:23**, to *"Repent therefore of this thy wickedness, and pray God...,"* **Acts 8:22**.

F. Salvation in this sense is accomplished by Christ's living.

    1. It is thus that **Hebrews 7:25** says, *"Wherefore he is able also to save them to the uttermost that come unto God by him, seeing he ever liveth to make intercession for them."*

    2. As one who lives and is passed into the heavens, **Hebrews 4:14**, He acts there as our Living High Priest, **Hebrews 4:15**, inviting us to come to Him for all the daily salvation or deliverance we need, **Hebrews 4:16**.

G. It is in His office of great shepherd that Christ performs this deliverance (salvation), for it is the great shepherd who lives and regularly tends the sheep. **Hebrews 13:20-21** thus says, *"Now the God of peace, that brought again from the dead our Lord Jesus, that great shepherd of the sheep, through the blood of the everlasting covenant, Make you perfect in every good work to do his will, working in you that which is wellpleasing in his sight, through Jesus Christ; to whom be glory for ever and ever. Amen."*

H. Notice particularly these facts of this salvation.

    1. It is present tense.

    2. It is continuous; progressive.

    3. It is from sin's dominion.

    4. It can be lost.

    5. It is regained by prayer from a repentant heart.

    6. It is accomplished by Christ's life.

    7. Christ performs this salvation as great shepherd.

    8. This is God's work of sustaining grace.

SECTION THREE

SALVATION FROM THE PRESENCE OF SIN

A. One day the believer shall be taken to be with the Lord where there'll be no more sin; and in this place, he shall miss or be delivered from all of God's wrath which shall ultimately be poured out on sin and unconverted sinners.

1. **Romans 5:9** speaks of this deliverance by saying, *"we shall be saved from wrath through him."*

2. **Romans 13:11** speaks of this coming deliverance and says, *"And that, knowing the time, that now it is high time to awake out of sleep: for now is our salvation nearer than when we believed."*

3. Peter says that believers are *"kept by the power of God through faith unto salvation ready to be revealed in the last time,"* **1 Peter 1:5**.

B. You will notice that this salvation is future tense.

1. We *"shall be saved"* which speaks of something yet future, **Romans 5:9**.

2. It is not yet a reality, but as the foregoing verses show it will come.

C. Salvation in this sense will be accomplished by Christ's returning.

1. It is then that the old bodies will be made new, **1 Corinthians 15:51-55**.

2. We shall then all be changed and be ever with the Lord where sin cannot enter and we'll be safe from all wrath, **1 Thessalonians 4:13-17**.

D. We can only wait for this salvation to materialize. **Titus 2:13**, teaches us to look, *"for that blessed hope, and the glorious appearing of the great God and our Saviour Jesus Christ."*

E. Salvation in this sense is the glorifying grace of God.

1. Paul spoke of this grace by saying, *"I have fought a good fight, I have finished my course, I have kept the faith: Henceforth there is laid up for me a crown of righteousness, which the Lord, the righteous judge, shall give me at that day: and not to me only, but unto all them also that love his appearing,"* **2 Timothy 4:7-8.**

2. Peter said there's a tremendous inheritance *"reserved in heaven"* for the saints of God, **1 Peter 1:4-5.**

3. The Lord will glorify his children, **Romans 8:17, 30.** It is called final grace, **1 Peter 1:13.**

F. It will be in His office of chief shepherd that Christ will perform this salvation (deliverance). Peter said, *"And when the chief Shepherd shall appear, ye shall receive a crown of glory that fadeth not away,"* **1 Peter 5:4.**

G. Notice some of the outstanding facts of this salvation.

1. It is future tense.

2. It is from sin's presence.

3. It will be experienced when the Lord returns.

4. It will be accomplished by Christ's returning.

5. Christ will perform this salvation as chief shepherd.

6. This is God's work of glorifying grace.

Chapter 16

The Difference Between Son-ship and Fellowship

Hebrews 12:5-7

I use this section of Scripture as a text because it has the idea of being more than just a son of God. This passage not only deals with God's children, but it also deals with God's special dealings with his children.

The purpose of this chapter is to show you that it is one thing to be a son of God, but it is quite another to be in fellowship with God. Many believers have never grasped this simple truth; and though they are children of God, they are not children in fellowship with Him. They stopped at son-ship thinking all the things that are to be done in order to have fellowship with God are not important now that they have become a son of His.

Only believers have either son-ship or fellowship, while unbelievers have neither. It may also be said that all believers have son-ship, **John 3:36**, while only a few believers have fellowship.

SECTION ONE

HERE ARE SEVERAL IMPORTANT FACTS RELATED TO SON-SHIP

A. Son-ship deals with our standing, relationship, or position before God.

    1. The Bible calls the saved the *"sons"* or *"children of God."*

        a. This text speaks of saved people as both *"children"* and *"sons,"* **Hebrews 12:5-7**.

        b. **1 John 3:1-2** calls the saved *"sons."*

        c. **Galatians 3:26** says, *"for ye are all the children of God by faith in Christ Jesus."*

        d. **Galatians 4:6** says, *"ye are sons..."*

    2. All of the saved have entered into this direct and close relationship before God.

B. This relationship is reached exclusively by faith in Him as personal Savior.

    1. Notice that **Galatians 3:26** says we become children of God *"by faith in Christ Jesus."*

    2. **1 John 5:1** says *"Whosoever believeth that Jesus is the Christ is born of God."*

    3. **Romans 4** is devoted to showing how our relationship with God is obtained by faith alone.

C. Whether or not we have good fellowship with a relative has no bearing upon whether that relative is ours. Relationship is predicated upon birth.

    1. It is a physical birth that makes us natural sons.

    2. It is a spiritual birth that makes us God's sons.

        a. It is in view of this that Jesus told Nicodemus he had to be born again in **John 3:1-7**.

The Difference Between Son-ship and Fellowship

      b. Therefore, **1 Peter 1:23** says believers are *"born again"* and **1 John 5:1** says they are *"born of God."*

  3. A son is not a son because he's good or bad; he's a son because he was born that way.

D. The result of son-ship is life.

  1. The only way a child may have life is from his parents.

  2. When we are born again as sons of God, He gives us life.

      a. Jesus said, *"I am come that they might have life,"* **John 10:10**.

      b. He said He's heaven's bread that gives life to the world, **John 6:33**.

      c. He made known *"the ways of life,"* **Acts 2:28**.

      d. **John 20:31** says that in *"believing ye might have life through his name."*

      e. Jesus said men might have life through Him, **John 8:12**.

E. The duration of the life we receive from Him through son-ship is eternal.

  1. In other words, son-ship is not ours merely as long as nothing goes wrong.

  2. It is an eternal standing or relationship.

      a. Many scriptures call it *"eternal,"* **John 3:15, 6:54, Romans 6:23**.

      b. Others call it everlasting. **John 3:16, 36** and **5:24**.

F. The relationship of son-ship is maintained by the power of God, apart from our efforts.

  1. In other words the relationship is not dependent upon us.

  2. **1 Peter 1:5** clearly says we are *"kept by the power of God."*

G. The relationship is unaffected by our conduct or sins.

1. It grows no stronger or weaker regardless of how we act.
2. **Romans 8:35-39** says nothing shall sever the relationship.
3. It would be preposterous to think the sins of a child could ever sever his relationship to his parents.

H. Thus, son-ship is a relationship which never has to be regained.
   1. Since we can't lose it, we will never need to get it back.
   2. **Hebrews 9:12** says, *"by his own blood he entered in once into the holy place, having obtained eternal redemption for us."*

SECTION TWO

A COMPARISON OF RELATIONSHIP AND FELLOWSHIP REVEAL THAT THEY ARE ALTOGETHER DIFFERENT

A. Fellowship deals with communion, concord, or agreement with God.
   1. Son-ship deals with relationship, standing, position.
   2. Numerous Scriptures speak of fellowship, **1 John 1:3, 6, 7**.

B. Fellowship is reached by the believer wholly dedicating himself unto the Lord.
   1. Son-ship comes by faith, but fellowship is by submission and dedication to Him.
   2. Jesus said in **Luke 9:23**, *"If any man will come after me, let him deny himself, and take up his cross daily, and follow me."*
   3. That, in a nutshell, is the sum total of our responsibility before God as sons, **Matthew 22:37**.

C. Our fellowship with God is predicated upon our conduct.
   1. Conduct will not affect your relationship to another, but it will grossly affect your fellowship or communion with that person.

The Difference Between Son-ship and Fellowship

    2. **1 John 1** deals entirely with having fellowship and that our conduct or walk before God affects it.

    3. **2 Corinthians 6:14-17** shows how poor conduct seriously hinders fellowship.

    4. The whole scope of our conduct including baptism, church affiliation, prayer, worship, service, etc. is directly related to the degree of fellowship we will have with God.

        a. If our conduct is good, fellowship will be good.

        b. If our conduct is bad, fellowship will be bad.

D. Sin will break and destroy fellowship.

    1. Remember that sin has no bearing at all on son-ship.

    2. But, sin will break one's fellowship with God.

        a. This is specifically stated in **Isaiah 59:2**.

        b. **2 Corinthians 6:14-17** emphasizes this truth.

        c. **1 John 1:6** makes it quite clear.

E. Thus, it becomes evident that once a person has achieved fellowship with God, the walk should continue upright in order that fellowship might be maintained.

    1. Son-ship depends upon the power of God, while fellowship is maintained by a right walk before Him.

    2. Listen to the Scriptures.

        a. **Romans 12:1** says yielded bodies are acceptable to God.

        b. God is pleased as we walk in truth, **2 John 4**.

    3. If a man is purged and clean, he can be useful to God, **2 Timothy 2:21**.

    4. Note well that unlike son-ship which is eternal, fellowship is temporary and maintained only as long as one is walking in truth. See **Galatians 5:1, 4**.

F. Once fellowship is lost it can only be regained through confession.

    1. Because son-ship cannot be lost, it does not need to be regained.

    2. But, fellowship, which can be lost, can only be regained through confession. See **1 John 1:9**.

        a. Notice **Acts 22:16**, *"…wash away thy sins, calling on the name of the Lord."*

        b. Also see **Psalm 32:1-5** and **Psalm 51**.

G. The result of fellowship is joy and abundant life.

    1. Son-ship brings life.

    2. Fellowship brings abundant life.

        a. Happiness comes in doing God's will, **John 13:17**.

        b. A man is blessed by implementing the principles set forth in the Word of God, **James 1:25**.

        c. Jesus said, *"I am come that they might have life, and that they might have it more abundantly,"* **John 10:10**.

    3. No man knows what it means to really enjoy living until he lives in fellowship with God.

        a. Here he can pray, **James 5:16**; be useful to God, **Romans 6:13**; have victory over sin, **Romans 6:14**; and the list goes on for a long time.

        b. Without fellowship, chastening must and will come into the life of a child of God, **Hebrews 12:5-7**.

Chapter 17

The Truth About Romans 10:13

"For whosoever shall call upon the name of the Lord shall be saved," **Romans 10:13**.

This is a most misused text. **2 Timothy** commands us to *"rightly divide"* the Scriptures. It seldom happens in the case of **Romans 10:13**.

A comprehension of some of the Bible's most basic concepts is necessary for a proper understanding of this text. In this chapter, we shall endeavor to show you the proper perspective and consequent truth of this passage.

SECTION ONE

HERE IS A BRIEF LOOK AT HOW THIS SCRIPTURE IS SO COMMONLY MISUSED

A. There are many who use this verse of Scripture in an effort to show a lost man how he may have eternal life. They tell the lost sinner to pray a prayer to be saved. They understand calling upon the Lord to mean a prayer.

    1. It is from this concept that the idea of prayer salvation has arisen.

    2. Also the idea of "praying through."

B. The very next verse soundly disproves this interpretation of the verse.

    1. The very next words are *"How then shall they call on him in whom they have not believed?"* **Romans 10:14.** You would do well to try and answer that question.

    2. The point Paul made is that they cannot call upon Him in whom they have never believed.

C. Nowhere in the Scriptures is a lost sinner ever asked to pray that he might have eternal life.

    1. In fact, it is well-established in the Bible that a lost sinner cannot pray or call upon the Lord at all.

        a. *"Now we know that God heareth not sinners...,"* **John 9:31.**

        b. In **Ezekiel 20:31**, God tells wicked Israel, *"As I live, saith the Lord GOD, I will not be enquired of by you."*

        c. **Proverbs 15:29** says, *"The LORD is far from the wicked."*

        d. Job said that God will not hear the cry of wicked hypocrites, **Job 27:8-9.**

        e. Of God-rejecters, David said in **Psalm 18:41**, *"They cried, but there was none to save them: even unto the LORD, but he answered them not."*

        f. Solomon made it clear that God will not honor the prayer of unconverted men when he said, *"The sacrifice of the wicked is an abomination to the LORD,"* **Proverbs 15:8.**

D. The one thing that God tells lost sinners to do is believe on the Lord Jesus Christ.

    1. *"Verily, verily, I say unto you, He that heareth my word, and believeth on him that sent me, hath everlasting life,"* **John 5:24.**

    2. Paul said, *"Believe on the Lord Jesus Christ, and thou shalt be saved,"* **Acts 16:31.**

    3. **Romans 1:17** says, *"The just shall live by faith."*

4. I defy anyone to show that God ever propagated any method for justifying the lost other than faith.

E. Except a sinner believe, there is absolutely no hope for him.

   1. Listen to the Scriptures.

      a. Jesus said, *"...he that believeth not the Son shall not see life; but the wrath of God abideth on him,"* **John 3:36**.

      b. *"...he that believeth not is condemned already, because he hath not believed in the name of the only begotten Son of God,"* **John 3:18**.

      c. Jesus also said, *"...if ye believe not that I am he, ye shall die in your sins,"* **John 8:24**.

   2. God himself shall appear *"In flaming fire taking vengeance on them that know not God, and that obey not the gospel of our Lord Jesus Christ,"* **2 Thessalonians 1:8**.

   3. Regardless of whatever else you do, including praying, you shall die a hell bound sinner if you do not believe in Jesus Christ, **Acts 4:12** and **John 14:6**.

F. One thing is certain, this Scripture is not telling a lost sinner what he must do to have eternal life.

SECTION TWO

TO UNDERSTAND THIS SCRIPTURE PROPERLY, IT IS NECESSARY TO REALIZE THAT THE BIBLE SPEAKS OF BEING SAVED IN THREE DISTINCTLY DIFFERENT SENSES

A. The Bible speaks of being saved from the penalty of sin, which was accomplished through Christ dying for us as our good shepherd.

   1. This is missing Hell and gaining Heaven.

   2. Such verses as **John 5:24, John 3:36, John 3:16** refer to it.

B. The Bible also speaks of being saved from the dominion of sin, which is accomplished through Christ living for us as our great shepherd.

  1. This is having the strength to live an honest and upright life in this world despite the temptations of Satan.

  2. Such verses as **Philippians 2:12, James 1:25** and **Romans 6:13** refer to it.

C. Finally the Bible speaks of being saved from the presence of sin, which shall be accomplished through Christ returning for us as our Chief Shepherd.

  1. When He returns we shall be caught up to Heaven beyond the reach of Satan's temptations.

  2. Such verses as **Romans 5:9, Philippians 3:21** and **Revelation 21:4** refer to it.

D. Whenever you hear the Bible referring to being saved, you must understand the sense in which the word *saved* is being used. Otherwise, you are not likely to understand the truth of the verse.

  1. Understanding the proper sense and usage of a word or phrase is to *rightly divide* the Word of Truth.

  2. If you fail to do this, you are likely to misuse the Scripture. For example, many Scriptures speaking of salvation are instructing saved believers about how to have deliverance or victory over Satan's daily efforts to defeat them. To use one of those passages to tell a lost sinner how to be saved from sin's penalty is deceptive and highly misleading. No doubt many die lost as a direct result of this misuse of the Scriptures.

    a. You can't bring a lost person to salvation by instructing him to do what only believers have a right to do.

    b. God's plan for Christian victory is quite different from His plan for saving lost sinners.

SECTION THREE

ROMANS 10:13 IS NOT A SCRIPTURE SHOWING A LOST SINNER HOW TO BE SAVED FROM THE PENALTY OF SIN; IT IS A SCRIPTURE SHOWING THE BELIEVER HOW TO BE SAVED FROM THE ATTACKS OF SATAN UPON HIS CHRISTIAN LIFE

A. That view is in harmony with the teachings of the Scriptures as a whole.

1. God tells His children who are out of fellowship with Him to call upon Him.

    a. **1 John 1:8-9** tells backsliders to *"confess"* their sins for forgiveness.

    b. Ananias said, *"arise, and be baptized, and wash away thy sins, calling on the name of the Lord,"* **Acts 22:16**.

    c. David did just this to get right with God, **Psalm 51:4**.

    d. Peter told Simon to pray that God would forgive him, **Acts 8:22**.

2. The right of prayer is the blessed and exclusive right of believers.

    a. The Bible says, *"If any man be a worshipper of God, and doeth his will, him he heareth,"* **John 9:31**.

    b. **Proverbs 15:8** says, *"the prayer of the upright is his delight."*

    c. To believers He says, *"Ask, and it shall be given you,"* **Matthew 7:7-8**.

    d. **Psalm 145:18** says, *"The LORD is nigh unto all them that call upon him, to all that call upon him in truth."*

B. What a blessed privilege for a son of God prayer is!

1. Believers can call on Him and find His grace is sufficient for every Christian, **2 Corinthians 12:9**.

2. David exemplifies the truth so well in **Psalm 22:12-21**.

3. The attacks of Satan sometime seem too great to bear, but then God's child can run to Him in prayer.

   a. *"God is our refuge and strength, a very present help in trouble,"* **Psalm 46:1**.

   b. In **Romans 10:13**, Paul was pointing out this great truth.

Chapter 18

Prayer Is Exclusively for the Children of God

Proverbs 15:29

We believe that prayer is exclusively for the children of God. We reject the contention that any unbeliever can pray a prayer which God would hear. (Note that in this study we use the word hear in the sense of honor or respect. We recognize full well that God hears the prayers of all men in the sense of awareness; even the prayers of unbelievers are fully known to Him. Consider **Psalm 139:1-12** and **Hebrews 4:13**. In this sense, God hears [knows] all prayers; but He only honors or respects the prayers of believers, who are His children.) We believe the idea that an unbeliever, even a sinner desiring to be saved from the penalty of sin, can pray and God will hear him is without scriptural foundation. Thus, we do not believe in the so called "sinner's prayer," which some claim is an exception to God's teaching that He does not hear sinners.

SECTION ONE

THE BIBLE CLEARLY DECLARES THAT GOD DOES NOT HEAR SINNERS' PRAYERS

A. Several Scriptures are unmistakable on this point.

1. Every unbeliever has turned away from or been disobedient to the truth, **2 Thessalonians 1:8**, and **Proverbs 28:9** says, *"He that turneth away his ear from hearing the law, even his prayer shall be abomination."* Does not every unbeliever fall into this category?

2. The text declares, *"The LORD is far from the wicked."* It is evident that this is particularly true with regard to prayer, for the remainder of the verse says, *"...but he heareth the prayer of the righteous,"* **Proverbs 15:29**.

3. Job spoke of lost, unconverted people, **Job 27:7**. He asked, *"For what is the hope of the hypocrite, though he hath gained, when God taketh away his soul? Will God hear his cry when trouble cometh upon him?"* **Job 27:8-9**. David indicated that God will not hear the cry of wicked, unconverted people. He said, *"When he shall be judged, let him be condemned: and let his prayer become sin,"* **Psalm 109:7**.

4. Of a group of unconverted men, the Scriptures testify, *"They cried, but there was none to save them: even unto the LORD, but he answered them not,"* **Psalm 18:41**.

5. In Jesus' day, most Jews did not recognize who He was, **John 9:25**. They rejected Him as the Messiah or Christ, **John 9:29**. Even these unbelieving people realized the truth that God does not honor sinners' prayers. One man among them pointed out that God does not hear the prayers of unconverted sinners. They all recognized his statement as a valid scriptural argument. *"Now we know that God heareth not sinners: but if any man be a worshipper of God, and doeth his will, him he heareth,"* **John 9:31**.

B. The Bible declares that God hears the prayers of righteous men.

1. Remember that the latter half of **Proverbs 15:29** says, *"He heareth the prayer of the righteous."*

2. The only way any man becomes righteous is by believing on Christ, for it is stated in **Romans 10:10**, *"with the heart man believeth unto righteousness."* When one believes, God's righteousness is given or imputed to that man, **Romans 4:5-6**.

3. No unbeliever is righteous; and if God hears only the prayers of the righteous, then He does not hear the prayers of unbelievers.

4. It is in view of this truth that **James 5:16** states, *"The effectual fervent prayer of a righteous man availeth much."*

SECTION TWO

PRAYER IS THE MEANS BY WHICH GOD'S CHILDREN TALK TO HIM, AND NONE EXCEPT BELIEVERS ARE GOD'S CHILDREN

A. Jesus taught that in prayer we are to address God as *"Our Father."*

1. In teaching us how to pray, Jesus said, *"After this manner therefore pray ye: Our Father ...,"* **Matthew 6:9.**

2. Jesus was speaking to believers about their prayers when He said, *"... your Father knoweth that ye have need of these things,"* **Luke 12:30.** He did not include those of whom He is not the Father.

B. It is easily established from the Scriptures that only believers are God's children.

1. Jesus said unbelievers are children of the devil, **John 8:44.**

2. Only those who are born spiritually into God's family are His children, **John 3:3-7**, and this new birth occurs only at belief, **1 John 5:1.**

3. Thus, the statement is made, *"For ye are all children of God by faith in Christ Jesus,"* **Galatians 3:26.**

C. It is not difficult to see how a person who rejects all that God has done for him and who by his disbelief stands in continuous rebellion and disobedience to the truth has no right to approach the throne of grace and ask God for anything.

SECTION THREE

THE ONE THING GOD CALLS ON UNBELIEVERS TO DO IS BELIEVE ON CHRIST

A. Everywhere in God's Word where a sinner is being told what to do that he might have life, the one thing required of him is that he believe.

    1. *"Believe on the Lord Jesus Christ, and thou shalt be saved...,"* **Acts 16:31.**

    2. Belief is a matter of turning by faith unto the Lord, **Isaiah 55:7.**

B. Nowhere is a lost sinner told to do anything else in order to be saved from sin's penalty.

    1. Some have attempted to use Scriptures directed to the children of God as if they were directed to lost sinners.

        a. Such passages as **Romans 10:13** and **Acts 22:16** discussed elsewhere in this book are examples.

        b. The dangers of misapplying Scriptures directed to the saved to those who are yet in unbelief and unsaved are readily apparent.

        c. **Luke 18:9-14** is a passage which is often misused to support the contention that lost sinners must pray in order to be saved.

            (1) Notice here that two circumcised Jews went up to the house of God. Had they not been circumcised, thus Jews, they could not have entered the temple, **Ezekiel 44:7.**

            (2) They went to pray, (**verse 10**) which is to worship; and the publican prayed, *"God be merciful to me a sinner,"* (**verse 13**).

            (3) Why should anyone suppose this man was lost? Saved men need mercy from God just as lost men do; and one thing the child of God gets in prayer is "*mercy,*" **Hebrews 4:16**. Who among the saved of God has not sinned, thus making him a sinner even as this publican was? **1 John 1:8, 10**. The publican was a saved sinner, but a sinner nonetheless.

(4) Furthermore, why should anyone suppose this publican was asking God to save him from the penalty of sin? He never once asked for salvation, rather he asked for mercy?

(5) Yet, there are those who assume the publican was a lost sinner praying the sinner's prayer.

(6) This publican requested that God look toward him in the same way He looks toward the atoning blood of the Mercy Seat. In order to legitimately make such a request, he had to have been previously identified with the blood sacrifice of Jesus Christ.

2. Why should a sinner be told to do a second thing until he has done the first thing God told him to do?

   a. Why should he be told to pray until he first believes?

   b. Does true salvation from sin's penalty come by belief plus prayer? If so, why doesn't the Bible say so, somewhere, at least one time?

   c. Furthermore, if prayer is essential to salvation from the penalty of sin, then why did Paul mislead that Philippian jailor, **Acts 16:30-31**? Why did Christ mislead all of us by failing to tell us to believe and pray, **John 3:15-16**?

   d. If the sinner's prayer has saving merits, then why is it that so many who have prayed it dozens of times and testified later that they were still lost? Every person who has believed, though he never uttered a prayer, has been saved, **John 3:36**.

3. Telling a lost sinner to pray for salvation is a dangerous practice.

   a. If he depends on that prayer to save him, thus not wholly believing on Christ, then the person remains lost.

    b. Telling a person to pray makes it appear there's more to being saved than believing.

    c. Many a worker and preacher have delivered a wonderful presentation of the Gospel to an individual or a congregation in which the truth of salvation by grace through faith was clearly set forth. Then in an invitation or further explanation, he undercut what he just said by telling his lost listeners to pray a prayer to be saved. He just finished explaining that salvation is simply and only by faith. How confusing!

    d. Is it any wonder that so many earnest sinners go away lost and that there are so many unconverted church members?

4. The truth is that a man may say what he wants to say, but if he does not believe, he will remain lost. He may say nothing; but if he believes, he will be saved. Thus it becomes clear that God saves a man because he believes, not because of what he says or doesn't say. Man receives salvation by believing in the heart. With his mouth he simply confesses (acknowledges) before men the salvation he received in his heart by faith. Consider **Romans 10:9-10**.

5. We contend that a man is saved from sin's penalty by grace, through faith, apart from any work he might perform, **Ephesians 2:8-9**, be it baptism, prayer, pilgrimages, reformation, tithing, or whatever he chooses.

C. Prayer is for a child of God.

  1. It is the means by which he takes care of sin's defilement in order that he might have fellowship with his heavenly Father, **1 John 1:9**.

  2. It is also his means of receiving help or salvation from sin's dominion, **Romans 10:13, Acts 22:16**.

Chapter 19

Under Discipline

Deuteronomy 8:5

The title of this chapter is *Under Discipline*. The text is **Deuteronomy 8:5**, *"Thou shalt also consider in thine heart, that, as a man chasteneth his son, so the LORD thy God chasteneth thee."* When many people get out of line with God, they wonder whether or not He will really take disciplinary action toward them. The answer is a clear *"Yes."*

SECTION ONE
GOD DOES DISCIPLINE HIS OWN CHILDREN

A. The Scriptures often speak of the disciplinary nature of God our Father.

    1. The key verse for this chapter says the Lord chastens us just as a loving father would chasten his son, **Deuteronomy 8:5**.

        a. It should be noted that the Lord chastens *His* sons. Though God may allow lost people to continue in their sins, He will correct sins in His own children.

        b. If you have never been born again, you can go on sinning and appear to escape punishment. Punishment for you is reserved in hell fire. Such is not the case for God's children. If you are God's dear child, God will discipline you when you sin.

      c. Furthermore, if you sin and go on without discipline from God, you are not a child of God. *"But if ye be without chastisement, whereof all are partakers, then are ye bastards, and not sons,"* **Hebrews 12:8.**

  2. God says, *"As many as I love, I rebuke and chasten,"* **Revelation 3:19.**

  3. **Hebrews 12:6-7** declares, *"For whom the Lord loveth he chasteneth, and scourgeth every son whom he receiveth. If ye endure chastening, God dealeth with you as with sons; for what son is he whom the father chasteneth not?"*

B. According to *Strong's Greek Dictionary of the New Testament*, chastening means *to discipline, teach, train, or nurture.*

  1. The discipline or chastening of the Lord is not retaliatory. It doesn't come because God *is mad at us.* God's discipline is corrective.

  2. His discipline is designed to drive away the evil from us and to encourage and strengthen the good.

  3. Paul wrote, *"But when we are judged, we are chastened of the Lord, that we should not be condemned with the world,"* **1 Corinthians 11:32.**

  4. Do not feel ill will toward God when His disciplinary hand falls upon you. In reality, *"Blessed is the man whom thou chastenest, O LORD,"* **Psalm 94:12.**

  5. We should heed such passages as **Job 5:17** and **Hebrews 5:12**. Listen to **Proverbs 3:11-12**, *"My son, despise not the chastening of the LORD; neither be weary of his correction: For whom the LORD loveth he correcteth; even as a father the son in whom he delighteth."*

SECTION TWO

THE QUESTION ARISES, "WHY DOES GOD BRING DISCIPLINARY ACTION UPON ONE OF HIS CHILDREN?"

Under Discipline

As just explained, discipline is designed of God to correct something that is wrong in the life of His child. It is an evil or combination of evils in that child's life that initiates the disciplinary action.

A. God literally hates sin, **Psalm 119:104**. When you, as one of God's children, allow sin to creep into your life, do not imagine that God is going to let it stay there unaddressed.

B. Sin tolerated and embraced in the life of a child of God is rebellion against God. It is in direct opposition to the will and program of God.

   1. Suppose you told your son one thing, but he did the exact opposite. Doubtless you'd recognize his action as rebellion.

   2. The Bible says God views rebellion *"as the sin of witchcraft, and stubbornness is as iniquity and idolatry,"* **1 Samuel 15:23**.

C. It is not surprising that **Isaiah 59:2** says, *"...your iniquities have separated between you and your God, and your sins have hid his face from you..."*

D. Because of David's sin he said, *"The LORD hath chastened me sore,"* **Psalm 118:18**.

E. Let's be more specific.

   1. Many Christians recognize that obvious sins will bring the discipline of God upon His children: lying, murder, drunkenness, adultery, fornication, stealing, etc. Many great men of the Bible found themselves under the disciplinary hand of God as a direct result of glaring sins: Noah, **Genesis 9:20-25**, Abraham, **Genesis 12:10-20**, and David, **2 Samuel 11** and others.

   2. It is easy to ignore the fact that some of the more subtle, innocent-looking sins can also ruin your fellowship with God and bring His discipline upon you. Sins like hatred, strife, envying, lust, a proud look, a talebearer, and sowing discard are abominations unto God, **Proverbs 6:16-19**. The Bible confirms that when a Christian begins to neglect church, prayer and Bible study he begins to backslide. Often he grows self-righteous and legalistic. When the world

comes to mean more and the things of God mean less, that person is asking for the discipline of God upon his life.

SECTION THREE

AS LONG AS SIN PREVAILS OR GOES UNCONFESSED, THE DISOBEDIENT CHILD OF GOD LIVES UNDER DISCIPLINE WHICH IS A CONTINUOUS STATE OF CHASTENING

A. Sins (even those of Christians) must be paid for, and Christians pay most for theirs while they live on this earth.

1. The Bible says, *"Be not deceived; God is not mocked: for whatsoever a man soweth, that shall he also reap. For he that soweth to his flesh shall of the flesh reap corruption...,"* **Galatians 6:7-8**.

2. It is true that some will not be properly settled until the judgment seat of Christ, **2 Corinthians 5:10**, where many *"shall suffer loss,"* **1 Corinthians 3:15**, but much is paid for here on earth.

    a. A man can commit sins in his youth which can bring shame, suffering and reproach for the rest of his life, **Job 20:11**. Even beyond discipline, the scars and long-term consequences of sin often remain.

    b. A child of God can especially realize how true this is as he suffers with a disability, financial bondage or an addiction.

B. Note well that this chastening is not always a short act which occurs and is quickly over. The chastening or discipline continues as long as the rebellious condition continues.

1. The Bible says, *"If we say that we have fellowship with him, and walk in darkness, we lie, and do not the truth,"* **1 John 1:6**.

2. As long as the iniquity continues, you will remain out of fellowship, **Psalm 66:18**.

Under Discipline

C. It is only when a child of God repents of his sins and confesses them to God that the discipline of God is lifted.

  1. **1 John 1:9** says, *"If we confess our sins, he is faithful and just to forgive us our sins, and to cleanse us from all unrighteousness."* John the Baptist warned against false, empty confession without true repentance, **Matthew 3:8**.

  2. **Proverbs 28:13** thus reads, *"He that covereth his sins shall not prosper: but whoso confesseth and forsaketh them shall have mercy."*

SECTION FOUR

HERE IS A BRIEF LOOK AT WHAT HAPPENS TO A MAN UNDER THE DISCIPLINE OF GOD

A. The first thing that happens is that a man's spiritual state begins a steady decline.

  1. True, abiding joy and happiness seem to vanish away.

    a. Joy and happiness in life come in knowing and doing what you know is right before God, **John 13:17**.

    b. On the other hand, the man who knows right and doesn't do it is condemned by his own guilty conscience, **James 4:17**. David illustrates this reality, **Psalm 51:3**.

  2. A man or woman under discipline generally grows uneasy and uncomfortable around the church or other Christians who are serving God.

  3. Most of the time people under discipline begin to gravitate to and associate with other disgruntled backsliders. They usually become picky and critical of anybody who is faithfully serving God. (Most of them take a certain comfort in lowering others to their level; it seems to soothe their conscience.) Because of their evil, they begin to love darkness and resent light, **John 3:19**.

  4. Almost always personal misery, disgust, frustration, restlessness, and bitterness take root and grow in people under discipline.

5. It may well be that some who read this book realize that they are under the disciplinary hand of God.

B. Not only does the spirit of one under discipline grow tormented, but sometimes God deals with a man's body and life.

1. Christian, *"It is a fearful thing to fall into the hands of the living God,"* **Hebrews 10:31**.

2. Remember that while David was under discipline he said, *"The LORD hath chastened me sore...,"* **Psalm 118:18**. When a Christian lives in such a way as to bring God's hand upon him, he is asking for untold trouble.

3. When God decides to fight, the Bible asks, *"...who shall be able to stand?"* **Revelation 6:17**. God doesn't fight with conventional means and there is no defense against Him.

4. God sometimes uses sickness and death, **1 Corinthians 11:24-30**, loss of money, loss of children, great calamities, loss of job and other such disciplinary actions.

5. With Jonah it was a storm and three days in a fish's belly, **Jonah 1-2**,

6. David's daughter was raped by his own son, **2 Samuel 13:14**. Another of his sons publically raped his stepmother, David's wife, **2 Samuel 16:22**. One of his sons died before him in a macabre way, **2 Samuel 18:33**.

7. I have prayed that God will never have to touch my loved ones in order to get my attention and correct me. I know that to correct us He can use our children, a dreaded disease or take away something very precious including all of your material goods. All of us have a weak spot and God knows exactly where it is.

8. Before following through with evil and finding ourselves under the discipline of God, it is wise to think twice and turn from the evils in our lives. Let every one of us think long and hard about what it means to be *Under Discipline*.

Chapter 20

Sanctification

1 Thessalonians 4:3-4

We believe that every believer should walk respectably before God. He has been justified and now he should be set apart. "To sanctify" means to consecrate, to dedicate, to keep holy, to set apart. The word sanctify is seen in the Scriptures in two major ways.

SECTION ONE

SANCTIFICATION IS SOMETIMES USED TO DESCRIBE THE ETERNAL POSITION ALL BELIEVERS HAVE IN CHRIST

A. Several Scriptures employ the word in this way.

   1. For example, Paul said to the Corinthian believers, *"And such were some of you: but ye are washed, but ye are sanctified, but ye are justified in the name of the Lord Jesus, and by the Spirit of our God,"* **1 Corinthians 6:11.**

   2. By Jesus' blood He has sanctified us, **Hebrews 13:9-12.**

   3. **1 Corinthians 1:2** and **Jude 1** both address those that are sanctified.

B. As believers in Christ, we forever have a position that is set apart from all other positions.

    1. We are sons of God, **1 John 3:1.**

    2. We are the *"elect"* of God, **1 Peter 1:2. Romans 8:33** asks, *"Who shall lay any thing to the charge of God's elect?"*

    3. In view of this, we who are sanctified are also perfected forever, **Hebrews 10:10, 14.**

C. A beautiful Old Testament type illustrates this truth.

    1. Before an Old Testament priest could serve in the Lord's house, he had to be washed completely. See **Exodus 40:12-15, Leviticus 8:12** and **Exodus 28:41.**

    2. Once the priest was set apart (sanctified) in this manner, he never again required a complete rewashing or sanctification.

    3. Jesus applied this truth to believers when He told Peter that only his feet needed washing, **John 13:5-10.** In other words, once one is set apart as a son, he needs never to again be set apart as a son. He will be a son forever.

SECTION TWO

SANCTIFICATION IS MOST OFTEN USED TO SHOW HOW THE BELIEVER'S LIFE SHOULD BE SET APART TO THE GLORY OF GOD

A. This truth is also seen in the Old Testament type.

    1. In order to qualify as acceptable in the Tabernacle and in the Temple, Old Testament priests had often to wash the dirt and filth of the world from their hands and feet, **Exodus 30:17-21.**

    2. Jesus drew the parallel when He told Peter that in order to be useful to the Lord, believers in Christ also need continual cleansing, **John 13:5-10.**

B. The Word of God often uses the word sanctify to show how believers should separate themselves unto holy use in God's service.

  1. Paul spoke of this when called on believers to be *"wholly"* separated unto the Lord, **1 Thessalonians 5:23**.

  2. Look at **2 Timothy 2:15-26** where Paul discussed this matter at length.

     a. Notice that *"sanctification"* here refers to growing in grace. It is a progressive work by which the believer becomes more and more consecrated to the will of God.

     b. Sanctification in this sense is not a state of sinless perfection attained through some *second blessing* or *baptism of the Holy Ghost*.

  3. Oh how Christians need to be set apart, holy, consecrated, dedicated vessels of the Lord; not filthy, polluted and marked with the stains of this world, **1 Thessalonians 4:3-4**! How we should be people who are willing to be different from the world!

     a. We are to be people who are set aside and peculiar, **Titus 2:14**.

     b. We long for people who will grow in grace, **2 Peter 3:18**.

     c. It is sad to observe that in this current age there are not many really sanctified people.

C. The Word of God shows us how to be sanctified unto the Lord.

  1. First we must yield ourselves unto the leadership of the Holy Spirit.

     a. 2 Thessalonians 2:13 and **1 Peter 1:2** both speak of sanctification by the Holy Spirit.

     b. Romans 15:16 also shows this truth.

  2. We must also consider the Word of God.

    a. **John 17:17** says we're sanctified by His truth. See also **1 Peter 1:22**.

    b. As we look into the truth of God's Word, we are changed for the better, **2 Corinthians 3:18, Romans 12:1-2**.

3. Prayer is also essential to sanctification in this sense, **1 Timothy 4:5**.

4. The key to sanctification is denial of self and total commitment to God, **Luke 9:23**.

Chapter 21

Doubtful Things

1 Corinthians 10:22-23

The purpose of this chapter is to shed Bible light on borderline activities. Quite often people who are saved engage in activities which are questionable, then defend themselves by arguing that the activity or questionable practice is not specifically forbidden in God's Word.

SECTION ONE

PERHAPS IT CAN BE PROVEN THAT A PARTICULAR PRACTICE IS NOT SPECIFICALLY FORBIDDEN IN GOD'S WORD, BUT THAT DOES NOT PROVE THE PRACTICE IS GOOD, NOR DOES IT GIVE ANYONE AN OPEN LICENSE TO PRACTICE IT

A. A false assumption that it does has led many Christian people into sinning against God by practicing questionable activities such as:

1. Social drinking.

2. Frequenting night clubs.

3. Dancing which is not akin to the dancing mentioned in the Scriptures.

4. The use of profanity and vulgar language.

5. Male and female swimming events where the modesty taught in the Bible is clearly violated.

6. Activities which blur or erase the distinction of the sexes. Examples include such issues as hair length, immodest dress and cross dressing.

7. Compromising activities by married people with others than their own marriage partner.

8. Many other activities could be named. They may seem lawful and innocent enough, yet they should never be practiced by a child of God. The *"appearance of evil"* is to be avoided by God's people, **1 Thessalonians 5:22**.

B. There is a Bible principle which forbids certain practices, even though they may be borderline, questionable and not specifically forbidden in God's Word.

1. The Bible teaches that if a thing would hinder or cast reflection and doubt upon the cause of Christ, then the thing shouldn't be done. All Christians do should strengthen and build up the work of God, **1 Corinthians 10:31**.

2. If one persists on doing the thing, in spite of its reflection on the cause of Christ, the thing becomes sin to him. That is true even though the practice was lawful and not specifically forbidden. Christianity is not all about the letter of the law; it is also about the spirits and attitudes of God's people.

    a. If a practice or activity brings reproach upon the cause of Christ, then it is not good. James said, *"...to him that knoweth to do good, and doeth it not, to him it is sin,"* **James 4:17**.

    b. **1 Corinthians 8:12** specifically speaks about things which are Biblically lawful for a Christian, yet which hurt a weaker brother and so brings reproach on the cause of Christ. *"But when ye sin so against the brethren, and wound their weak conscience, ye sin against Christ."*

3. A practice or activity is not automatically approved by God simply because He did not specifically forbid it in His Word.

SECTION TWO

THE BIBLE SPELLS OUT THIS PRINCIPLE ON DOUBTFUL THINGS

A. The principle as biblically stated.

1. *"All things are lawful for me, but I will not be brought under the power of any,"* **1 Corinthians 6:12.**

2. The principle is stated again in **1 Corinthians 10:23**, *"All things are lawful for me, but all things are not expedient: all things are lawful for me, but all things edify not."*

3. Simply because a thing is legal for us does not mean we should go right out and practice it.

B. There are two Bible reasons for this principle.

1. Some things have the characteristic of bringing people under their power. A Christian should abstain from things which would bring him under their power. This is the argument of **1 Corinthians 6:12**, *"All things are lawful unto me, but all things are not expedient: all things are lawful for me, but I will not be brought under the power of any."*

   a. Such things as liquor, tobacco and drugs have an addictive power within them.

   b. Put yourself in certain association with members of the opposite sex, and your sex passion can overpower you.

   c. What this principle says is that you shouldn't subject yourself to these practices which tend to bring you under their power. They may be lawful, but they are not wise.

2. The second reason is that some things which are lawful for you will offend and cause a weak brother to stumble. They may even keep someone from being saved.

- **a. 1 Corinthians 10:23** argues that some legal things *"edify not:"*

  - **(1)** Christians should always give consideration to the implications of their speech and behavior. They should engage in such a way as to help and never hurt another person, especially a brother. *"Let no man seek his own, but every man another's wealth,"* **1 Corinthians 10:24.**

  - **(2) Philippians 2:4** says, *"Look not every man on his own things, but every man also on the things of others."*

  - **(3)** The principle says a Christian shouldn't hurt and cause his brother in Christ to stumble. Parents consider your children.

- **b.** Neither should a Christian do anything to keep a lost man from being saved.

  - **(1)** Imagine saying, "Well, I don't think there's anything wrong with it" and by your action turning a man to hell.

  - **(2)** Paul argued against doing things to keep sinners from being saved. *"Even as I please all men in all things, not seeking mine own profit, but the profit of many, that they may be saved,"* **1 Corinthians 10:33.**

- **c.** In general the principle says, *"Give none offense, neither to the Jews, nor to the Gentiles, nor to the church of God,"* **1 Corinthians 10:32.**

C. The results of violating this principle.

1. Seeing how much we can get away with tries the patience of God. *"Do we provoke the Lord to jealousy? are we stronger than he?"* **1 Corinthians 10:22.** What a foolish and shameful way for a son to act!

2. Violation of this principle is sin. It becomes a stumbling block to the weak. **1 Corinthians 8:9** says, *"But take heed lest by any means this liberty of yours become a stumblingblock to them that*

are weak." And **verse 12** says, *"...when ye sin so against the brethren, and wound their weak conscience, ye sin against Christ."*

SECTION THREE

THE GUIDING PRINCIPLE FOR THE EARNEST CHILD OF GOD IS SPELLED OUT IN 1 CORINTHIANS 10:31, *"WHETHER THEREFORE YE EAT, OR DRINK, OR WHATSOEVER YE DO, DO ALL TO THE GLORY OF GOD:"*

A. For a child of God, the guiding idea should be that "if a practice is injurious to the cause of Christ, and brings no glory to God; then I want no part of it."

B. The child of God should have the attitude.

    1. "My life belongs to God." **1 Corinthians 6:19-20** says, *"... ye are not your own? For ye are bought with a price: therefore glorify God in your body, and in your spirit, which are God's."*

    2. "Therefore, I will yield it to Him and ever seek to up-build and strengthen His work; I will never yield to Satan to discredit and cast reflection on Christ's work."

C. A child of God should say:

    1. "I'll not be the kind of son who sees just how far I can go without getting into too much trouble with my heavenly Father."

    2. "I will be the best son I can, living as near to what I ought to be as I possibly know how, doing all I do to the glory and not the dishonor of my God."

Chapter 22

Water Baptism: Every Believer Should Be Baptized

Acts 2:41

We believe it is the will of God that every born again believer should be baptized. No unbeliever is eligible for baptism. The first thing one who is save should do is be scripturally baptized.

SECTION ONE

THE FIRST ACT OF OBEDIENCE FOR A BELIEVER SHOULD BE SCRIPTURAL BAPTISM

A. Consider the Scriptures on this matter.

    1. Look to **Matthew 28:19**. Water baptism is the first thing to be done after salvation.

    2. Peter told these unconverted Jews *"Repent, and be baptized every one of you...,"* **Acts 2:38**. They repented and the first thing they did was be baptized. *"Then they that gladly received his word were baptized,"* **Acts 2:41**.

    3. The first thing the Philippian jailor did after he was saved was be baptized, **Acts 16:31-33**.

4. The first thing the Ethiopian man wanted and got after being saved was water baptism, **Acts 8:36-38**.

  5. Peter commanded new converts to be baptized, **Acts 10:47-48**.

  6. Ananias told newly converted Paul to be baptized, **Acts 22:12-16**.

B. It is evident from the commands of our Lord as well as from scriptural precedents that the very first thing a new convert should do is follow the Lord in scriptural baptism.

SECTION TWO

A PERSON WHO IS UNSAVED IS NOT A CANDIDATE FOR BAPTISM

A. The Scriptures make this truth unquestionably clear.

  1. **Matthew 28:19** shows the order to be salvation first and baptism second.

  2. **Acts 8:36-37** is perhaps the clearest Scripture on the subject.

     a. When the eunuch desired baptism, Philip told him, *"If thou believest with all thine heart, thou mayest,"* **Acts 8:37**.

     b. Before he was baptized, the eunuch confessed he did believe on Christ, **Acts 8:37-38**.

     c. If the eunuch had not believed, Philip would not have baptized him.

  3. The Scriptures in Section One show that salvation always preceded baptism.

B. Salvation comes through faith, not through ordinances such as baptism.

  1. Sacrifices and religious ceremonies do not forgive sinners, **Hebrews 9:12-14**.

  2. Salvation by grace through faith is the only method of salvation the Bible ever gives.

- a. Salvation is by grace through faith, not by works, **Ephesians 2:8-9**.

- b. *"Believe on the Lord Jesus Christ, and thou shalt be saved,"* **Acts 16:31**.

- c. **John 3:16, 36** and **John 5:24** all show salvation to be by faith.

- d. **John 14:6** shows there is no other way. See also **Acts 4:12**.

C. The inherent picture in water baptism shows clearly that salvation must precede baptism.

1. The mechanics of baptism portray a death, burial, resurrection, **Romans 6:4-6**.

2. When we believe in Christ as personal Savior, God reckons the death, burial, and resurrection of Christ to our account, **1 Corinthians 15:1-4**.

3. It is in view of this that Paul can say, *"For ye are dead, and your life is hid with Christ in God,"* **Colossians 3:3**.

4. In baptism, one publicly testifies to the world that through Christ he has died, been buried and is raised a new creature in Christ.

   - a. How can an unsaved man say that?
   - b. The baptism of a lost man is a lie.
   - c. Until a person is in Christ by faith, he cannot truthfully testify in baptism of the death, burial, and resurrection.

D. The conclusion is that it is useless to baptize a lost person.

1. There is no power in the water to wash away sins; the power to wash away sins lies exclusively in the blood of Christ.

2. Thus it is vain to baptize babies or anyone else who has not willfully, consciously made a commitment by faith in Christ.

3. It should also be noted that all persons who were not believers prior to their baptism have really never been baptized at all.

Chapter 23

Water Baptism: Immersed by a New Testament Church

Acts 2:41

We believe baptism must be conducted in a right manner by a right administrator in order to be scriptural and recognized by God.

SECTION ONE

THE METHOD OF BAPTISM MUST BE IMMERSION

A. Through their examples, Bible men taught us immersion.

  1. In **Matthew 3:6**, John baptized saved people in the Jordan River. Why would he go to the mighty Jordan River just to get enough water to sprinkle or dampen a candidate?

  2. **Matthew 3:16** says, *"And Jesus, when he was baptized, went up straightway out of the water."*

     a. In order to go *"out of"* water, He had to be down in the water.

     b. Such a statement is only possible if immersion is in mind.

c. The idea of Jesus standing in the water with John sprinkling Him or pouring water over Him does not harmonize with this text.

   3. **Acts 2:41, Acts 8:12, John 4:1-2** and many other scriptures use the word *"baptize"* or *"baptized"* to describe what happened to believers. As the following point shows, the word means immersion. The examples we have show believers were immersed.

B. The word *"baptize"* means immerse.

   1. It comes from the Greek word <u>baptizo</u> which means to fully cover with a liquid. By implication it means submersion, ducking or immersion.

   2. A different Greek word must be used to speak of sprinkling, pouring or wetting with a cloth.

C. The picture inherent in baptism can only be portrayed by immersion.

   1. **Romans 6:4-6** explains that baptism is a picture of the death, burial and resurrection of Christ.

   2. In a literal burial, a person is covered fully; the dead person is put into the ground and fully covered under the surface. The person is literally immersed.

   3. How could sprinkling, wetting, pouring or similar means of baptism show this picture?

D. The truth is that if a person was not immersed in baptism, he was never truly baptized.

SECTION TWO

THE ADMINISTRATOR OF BAPTISM MUST BE A NEW TESTAMENT CHURCH

A. God gave the authority to baptize only to His church.

1. God gave the commission to baptize to those men who became the first members of the church in Jerusalem, **Matthew 28:19**.

2. In all places in the Bible where you find baptism being practiced, it is done under the authority of some New Testament church.

    a. The Jerusalem Church conducted baptisms, **Acts 2:41**.

    b. Both Peter and Philip baptized under authority from the Jerusalem Church, **Acts 10:48, Acts 8:38**.

    c. Paul baptized under the authority of the Antioch church, **Acts 15:35-41**.

3. No individual or other institution ever received authority or the right to baptize.

B. A group of baptized believers in covenant relationship who are teaching the fundamental truths of the Bible is a scriptural New Testament Church.

1. It is quite possible for a group to call itself a church, yet not be one which God recognizes, **Revelation 2:5**.

2. We believe that only a group that teaches the truth about the plan of salvation constitutes a church of Jesus Christ.

    a. God's Word exhorts us to preach the Gospel.

    (1) To every creature, **Mark 16:15**.

    (2) Preaching is our number one task, **1 Corinthians 1:17, 15:1**.

    (3) Preaching the gospel is God's method of saving the lost, **Romans 1:16, 1 Corinthians 1:21**.

    b. Damnation rests upon all who do not hear and obey the gospel of Christ, **2 Thessalonians 1:8, 1 Peter 4:17**.

    c. Both **Galatians 1:6-7** and **2 Corinthians 11:12-15** warn against those who would pervert the Gospel or preach another gospel.

d. We are warned against hearing another gospel, and *"woe"* is pronounced upon those who preach anything other than the gospel of Christ for salvation.

  (1) Let him be accursed who preaches *"another gospel,"* **Galatians 1:8-9**.

  (2) Paul said, *"Woe is unto me, if I preach not the gospel,"* **1 Corinthians 9:16**.

e. It is our conclusion that groups that believe a false gospel are accursed and not true churches of Jesus Christ.

  (1) This includes most professing Christianity.

  (2) We cannot accept baptism from any church that is not straight on the plan of salvation. Such groups are not truly churches.

3. There is a definite stigma on all of the *daughter churches* which stemmed from the Roman Catholic Church. A look at both the doctrine and history of that Church will quickly reveal that it is far from the Bible and that its descendants cannot be true New Testament churches. Since only a true church has the authority to baptize, we believe all those who have not been baptized by a true New Testament church have not been truly baptized.

Chapter 24

The Bible Does Not Teach Baptismal Regeneration

1 Peter 3:21

We categorically reject the common belief that water baptism is essential to salvation from the penalty of sin. As set forth in chapter eleven of this book, we believe faith alone to be God's method for appropriating eternal salvation. We believe those who teach baptism to be essential to salvation from sin's penalty have perverted the Scriptures, attempting to make them say what they never did say nor were intended to say.

SECTION ONE

IF THE BIBLE TEACHES SALVATION FROM SIN'S PENALTY BY BAPTISM (WHICH IT DOESN'T), THEN IT CONTRADICTS ITSELF

A. In dozens of places, by type and symbol, by implication, and by direct statement, the Bible teaches man is justified before God by faith alone.

   1. *"But to him that worketh not, but believeth on him that justifieth the ungodly, his faith is counted for righteousness,"* **Romans 4:5.**

2. *"Therefore being justified by faith, we have peace with God through our Lord Jesus Christ,"* **Romans 5:1.**

3. *"For by grace are ye saved through faith; and that not of yourselves: it is the gift of God: Not of works, lest any man should boast,"* **Ephesians 2:8-9.**

4. *"Believe on the Lord Jesus Christ, and thou shalt be saved,"* **Acts 16:31.**

5. The Apostle Paul advocated that his justification before God was wholly apart from anything he had ever done, **Philippians 3:4-9.**

6. Consider **John 3:15-16, John 3:36, Titus 3:5** and **1 Corinthians 1:21.**

B. The Bible clearly teaches that there is only one way to be saved from the penalty of sin.

1. Jesus said, *"I am the way, the truth, and the life: no man cometh unto the Father, but by me,"* **John 14:6.**

2. *"Neither is there salvation in any other: for there is none other name under heaven given among men, whereby we must be saved,"* **Acts 4:12.**

3. **1 Timothy 2:5** declares, *"For there is one God, and one mediator between God and men, the man Christ Jesus."*

4. **Romans 11:6** makes clear that salvation is by only one mean, but not by two or three different means.

C. If the Bible also teaches that water baptism is essential to eternal life, as some believe, then there are two plans of salvation. Thus the Bible is in error when it teaches that there is only one plan.

1. One Bible plan is that salvation is clearly by faith. Salvation by baptism is clearly another plan. Plan one plus plan two equals two plans. 1+1 still equals two.

2. Such illogical and unbiblical reasoning would place Jesus in error. He claimed there is one and only one way to heaven and that way is exclusively by faith in Him, **John 14:6.** If God's Word is in error, then we are all deceived.

3. Furthermore, if one argues that regeneration comes only by water baptism, then that argument invalidates and contradicts all the Scriptures that plainly state salvation to be by faith.

4. Following their argument to its logical conclusion, those who teach baptism to be essential to salvation back themselves into an inescapable corner. They pit Scripture against Scripture and make the Bible contradict itself.

D. We believe that Jesus told the truth and that there is no contradiction in God's Holy Word. When it declares you are *"saved through faith,"* **Ephesians 2:8**, that is exactly how it is.

SECTION TWO

THOSE WHO ADVOCATE BAPTISMAL REGENERATION ARE HARD PRESSED TO EXPLAIN THE SALVATION OF THOSE WHO HAVE BEEN JUSTIFIED BEFORE GOD WITHOUT EVER BEING BAPTIZED

A. There are a number of Bible cases of people who were saved from the penalty of sin apart from water baptism.

1. Abraham is a clear case.

    a. The Bible specifically says Abraham was justified by faith *"before God,"* **Romans 4:2-3**. **James 2** speaks of his justification before man. **Romans 4:3** reads, *"Abraham believed God, and it was counted unto him for righteousness."*

    b. Abraham lived and died centuries before water baptism was ever initiated and practiced.

2. John the Baptist was apparently the first to baptize, **Matthew 3**. He began to baptize around 25 A.D. That being true, then all who were saved prior to that time were saved without being baptized. That includes a great host of people.

    a. David was one, **Romans 4:6**.

    b. **Hebrews 11:1-40** is a whole chapter naming many, and referring to a great company of others who were saved.

      c. There were apparently 7,000 in Israel in Elisha's day alone who were saved without being baptized, **1 Kings 19:18**.

      d. The fact that many *"saints"* rose from the dead on the day Christ was crucified, testifies to the fact that men were saved before baptism was ever practiced, **Matthew 27:50-53**.

  3. The thief who believed in Christ and then died before being baptized is undeniable proof that a man can go to heaven without being baptized. He was not baptized, but Jesus said to him, *"Verily I say unto thee, To day shalt thou be with me in paradise,"* **Luke 23:43**.

B. The water baptismalists really have no valid answers for these cases.

  1. Some of them argue that before Christ's death, people lived in a different dispensation and were saved in a different way than those since.

      a. According to this argument, there have been two plans of salvation: one before Christ's death, and another after. That argument makes a liar out of Jesus Christ, **John 14:6**.

      b. If there already was one plan of salvation apart from the sacrificial work of Christ on the cross, the work of Christ on the cross was a useless thing!

      c. The truth is that the Mosaic Law by which the water baptismalists say Old Testament people were saved never justified a single person. The Apostle Paul spoke of that law and said, *"Knowing that a man is not justified by the works of the law, but by the faith of Jesus Christ, even we have believed in Jesus Christ, that we might be justified by the faith of Christ, and not by the works of the law: for by the works of the law shall no flesh be justified,"* **Galatians 2:16**.

      d. **Romans 4** makes unquestionably clear that all men from Adam to the last one who shall ever be justified are justified in the exact same way; by faith. Especially note **verses 16-17, 23-24**.

2. This argument is indicative of the weakness of the whole position of water baptism regeneration.

   a. Someone once pointed out that if water is your savior, then when the plug in the baptistery is pulled, your savior goes down the drain.

   b. Someone also pointed out the weakness of this argument. He said that if your sins are washed into the water, then after the water is released and reaches a stream or reservoir. If a cow happens to drink some of the water with your sins or those of another in it and recycle that water into milk, then by drinking that milk you get back your sins or the sins of some other sinner. What ridiculous reasoning!

SECTION THREE

THOSE WHO TEACH WATER BAPTISM SALVATION PERVERT A SERIES OF SCRIPTURES AND BUILD THEIR FALSE DOCTRINE UPON THESE PERVERSIONS

A. The perversion of **Acts 2:38**.

"Then Peter said unto them, Repent, and be baptized every one of you in the name of Jesus Christ for the remission of sins, and ye shall receive the gift of the Holy Ghost," **Acts 2:38**.

1. This is probably the most common *proof text* of those who teach salvation from sin's penalty by water baptism.

2. Many who read this verse assume that both *"repent"* and *"be baptized"* are equally essential to the remission of sins.

   a. Other Scriptures speaking on this subject make clear that such an assumption is absolutely false.

      (1) The Bible states *"repentance"* is *"unto life,"* **Acts 11:18**, and *"baptism"* is unto *"death,"* **Romans 6:4**. In other words, repentance is what produces life while baptism testifies of our personal participation by faith in Christ's death.

(2) John the Baptist refused to baptize anyone who did not offer substantial evidence that they had already repented, **Matthew 3:7-11**. He said that *"baptism"* is *"unto"* (because of) *"repentance,"* **verse 11**.

b. The grammatical fact is that in **Acts 2:38**, *"repent"* is the primary action and *"be baptized"* is the secondary action.

(1) Every man should repent. That will result in the remission of sins. He should then be baptized without delay as a result of sins remitted.

(2) That is in perfect harmony with Bible teaching elsewhere.

(a) As a preceding chapter shows, following belief in Christ as personal Savior, the next thing a person should do is be baptized.

(b) Note well what John preached. Baptism is the secondary action. Repentance is the primary action, **Matthew 3**.

c. *"Repent"* and *"be baptized"* are not equally joined in **Acts 2:38** or elsewhere. The *"repentance"* should stimulate the *"baptism."*

3. Furthermore, many who read **Acts 2:38** assume the preposition *"for"* means "in order to obtain."

a. According to *Strong's Hebrew and Greek Dictionaries,* the word *"for"* in **Acts 2:38** is translated from the Greek word eis which can translate numerous ways including "for", "unto", "indeed" and "what."

b. The scholars in no way ever indicate that it could translate "in order to obtain."

c. The word eis is translated at least 1,700 times in the King James Bible, many times in the sense of *because of.* It is never once translated "in order to obtain."

d. The people who believe water baptism salvation think **Acts 2:38** is saying, "repent and be baptized every one of you in the name of Jesus Christ, in order to obtain the remission of sins." Notice how ridiculous several other passages of the same mood and case would appear if "in order to obtain" were used in the place of "for" or "unto:"

(1) *"Take therefore no thought (for)* in order to obtain *the morrow,"* **Matthew 6:34**.

(2) *"I will say to my soul, Soul, thou hast much goods laid up (for)* in order to obtain *many years,"* **Luke 12:19**. [Note: just remove the italics on the added words and added it to the "for"]

e. In **Acts 2:38**, the Apostle Peter used the preposition *"for"* as it is nearly always used in the Bible, to mean *because of*.

(1) He told men to repent. That will remit their sins. He then told them to be baptized because of their repentance. You will notice that the phrase about baptism is set in commas. That shows it to be an action resulting from the main or primary action.

(2) When we say a man went to prison "for" stealing, nobody interprets that the man went to prison in order to steal, but rather because of his stealing. Somehow when Peter said be baptized for the remission of sins, many have assumed he meant a person is to be baptized *in order to* have his sins remitted.

B. The perversion of **Mark 16:16**.

"He that believeth and is baptized shall be saved; but he that believeth not shall be damned," **Mark 16:16**.

1. Many pervert this Scripture to mean, "He that believeth and is baptized shall be saved from past sins by his death."

a. If that is what this Scripture means (and it does not), then in order to be consistent a kindred verse, **Romans 5:9**, would have to read, *"Being now justified by his blood, we shall* *be saved from* past sins by his death." Otherwise the Bible would be in contradiction of itself.

    b. The fact is **Romans 5:9** says nothing about past sins or Christ's death. It says, *"Being now justified by his blood* (not baptism), *we shall be saved from wrath* (not past sins) *through him."* This future tense salvation is by his life, not his death, **Romans 5:10**.

    c. Neither **Romans 5:9** nor **Mark 16:16** say anything about "past sins" or "His death."

2. The fact is that the future tense is used in **Mark 16:16** with relation to *"saved."* This refutes the idea that the salvation referred to is past tense salvation from past sins only.

3. **Mark 16:16** is a passage that teaches the threefold aspects of salvation.

    a. *"He that believeth"* speaks of deliverance from the penalty of sin.

    b. *"And is baptized"* puts the believer into the house or church of God where access to the High Priest enables him to be delivered from the power of sin in his life as he lives from day-to-day.

    c. *"Shall be saved"* speaks of the future when Christ returns to receive His children.

C. The perversion of **Galatians 3:27**.

"For as many of you as have been baptized into Christ have put on Christ," **Galatians 3:27**.

1. Those who teach salvation from sin's penalty by water baptism say this Scripture teaches water baptism is literally the way a man gets into Christ; and thus without water baptism, he can't be in Christ.

2. To maintain this position, this interpretation poses a set of problems which the water baptism salvation crowd is neither prepared to answer nor ready to accept.

      a. **John 15:4** teaches that the saved are *"in Him"* and He is *"in"* them. See also **Colossians 3:3** and **1 Corinthians 6:19**.

      b. If baptism in water literally puts a man into Christ, then eating of the Lord's Supper must literally put Christ into the man. **Matthew 26:26-28** says, *"this is my body ... this is my blood."*

      c. It would be inconsistent to hold to one of the positions and yet reject the other; however, most of those who teach that water literally puts a person into Christ also teach that as the Lord's Supper elements are eaten, they only symbolically, not literally, represent Christ's blood and body.

  3. We believe that the Lord's Supper symbolizes our participation in Christ's body and blood. Likewise, we believe that baptism symbolizes the believer is submerged in Christ by faith.

  4. We believe according to the Scriptures that at faith a man is placed in Christ, **Romans 5:1-2**, and Christ in the person of the Holy Spirit takes up abode in the man, **Romans 8:9, 1 Corinthians 3:16**.

D. The perversion of **Acts 22:16**.

"And now why tarriest thou? arise, and be baptized, and wash away thy sins, calling on the name of the Lord," **Acts 22:16**.

1. As you must suppose, scores of people assume from this verse that a man can literally wash away his sins by water baptism.

2. Such a view is not logical, let alone scriptural.

      a. Ananias told Paul (Saul) to *"wash"* away his sins.

      b. If baptism will do it thoroughly, as the water baptism crowd contends, then why did Ananias tell Paul to *"wash"*?

      c. After all, had Paul obeyed the first part and been *"baptized,"* his sins would have already been gone and there would have been no need for him to *"wash."* Washing after he was already cleansed of sin would have been like electrocuting a dead man.

3. The truth is that **Acts 22:16** refers to deliverance from the daily dominion (not penalty) of sin which Paul (and we) needed.

   a. On the road to Damascus and before he arrived in Jerusalem and spoke to Ananias, Paul had already been saved from sins penalty, **Acts 22:6-10**.

   b. When he arrived in Jerusalem and God's man began to instruct him about what he should do as a new believer, Ananias told him exactly what Jesus had said ought to be told new believers. He told him to *"be baptized,"* **Matthew 28:19**. That is the first act of obedience, and *"the answer of a good conscience toward God,"* **1 Peter 3:21**.

   c. Following his baptism as an obedient son, he would be in a position to pray, **Psalm 66:18**. By *"calling on the name of the Lord,"* Paul could have cleansing from daily sins, **1 John 1:8**. That daily cleansing would be vital to his remaining in fellowship with God, **1 John 1:9**. The first two aspects of threefold salvation are in view: Paul (1) believed in Christ and was baptized. This put him into a position from which he could (2) pray or call upon the Lord. This is salvation from sin's power which is the second aspect of salvation. This is the aspect of salvation under consideration in **Romans 10:13**. Of course, salvation from sin's presence is the third aspect of salvation. That aspect is not in view in **Mark 16:20**.

   d. By calling on the name of the Lord, not by baptism, a man can wash away the sins which would otherwise rob him of spiritual strength and deliverance.

E. The perversion of **1 Peter 3:21**.

"The like figure whereunto even baptism doth also now save us (not the putting away of the filth of the flesh, but the answer of a good conscience toward God,) by the resurrection of Jesus Christ," **1 Peter 3:21**.

1. The water baptismal crowd naturally jumps to the conclusion that the word *"save"* in this text refers to salvation from the penalty of sin.

2. Most seem unaware that the Bible refers to three major aspects of God's salvation. (See the chapter on *God's Threefold Salvation*.)

3. **1 Peter 3:21** unquestionably refers to the second aspect of salvation.

    a. Baptism does not save us from sin's penalty by the *"putting away of the filth of the flesh."*

    b. To the contrary, baptism makes us obedient sons. The Lord commanded us to be baptized, **Acts 2:41, Matthew 28:19**. Baptism thus gives us *"a good conscience toward God."*

F. When you consider that our Lord views *"rebellion"* as *"the sin of witchcraft,"* **1 Samuel 15:23**, it is obvious that baptism does save us from a great amount of chastening, **Hebrews 12:5-8**. As other chapters in this book show, obedience to our Lord delivers us from many a devastating defeat at the hands of our great adversary, Satan.

Chapter 25

Baptized into the Body

1 Corinthians 12:13

We believe that when a person is saved, he becomes a member of the family of God. We do not believe that automatically makes him a member of the Lord's church, which we believe is His body. To become a member of the church, he must follow the Lord in scriptural water baptism. In so doing, he becomes a member of the church.

This chapter is designed to show why we believe this and at the same time to show the truth of **1 Corinthians 12:13**. There are many assumptions about this verse.

SECTION ONE

THE BODY UNDER CONSIDERATION IN THIS TEXT IS A LOCAL CHURCH

A. The context of **1 Corinthians 12** shows the subject under discussion to be the body of Christ, which in this case was the church at Corinth.

   1. **1 Corinthians 12:12** says the natural body is made up of many members, but is one body. In the same way, the body of Christ has many members, but is one body.

2. It was to those many members in Corinth that Paul addressed this book. He called them *"the church of God which is at Corinth,"* **1 Corinthians 1:2**. He said to this identical group, *"Now ye are the body of Christ, and members in particular,"* **1 Corinthians 12:27**.

   3. Notice that these Corinthians were not called a part of the body, but they were the body just as each human constitutes a whole body. Likewise, each church constitutes the body of Christ.

B. The body, which is the Lord's church, has always existed and is a visible local body of born again, scripturally baptized believers, called out to assemble in a specific place at a specific time to carry out definite work.

   1. Only a local church could assemble and observe the ordinances which are prescribed in **1 Corinthians 11:2, 17-34**.

   2. Scripturally the officers of a church were only to serve one particular congregation. They were to never serve in a general sense over two or more congregations.

   3. God gave instructions only to churches or bodies to administer discipline, bind and loose with heaven's authority, **Matthew 18:17-18**.

C. The Bible specifically declares the body to be the church.

   1. **Colossians 1:18** plainly says, *"He is the head of the body, the church..."*

   2. This truth is again clearly set forth in **Ephesians 1:22-23**, *"And hath put all things under his feet, and gave him to be the head over all things to the church, Which is his body..."*

   3. Since there is *"one body,"* **Ephesians 4:4**, and the local church is definitely a body, **1 Corinthians 12:27**, then the only kind of church that exists is a local visible church.

   4. Since other chapters of this book are devoted to showing that the body and the church are one and the same as well as the fact that both speak only of a local assembly, we shall not labor the point here.

5. We simply want to make clear that the body, into which the baptism of **1 Corinthians 12:13** puts one, is a local church.

SECTION TWO

THE BAPTISM WHICH PUTS ONE INTO THE CHURCH (BODY) IS WATER BAPTISM

A. We emphatically reject the contention that the baptism referred to here is some mystical *Holy Spirit baptism*.

   1. **Ephesians 4:5** says there is *"One Lord, one faith, one baptism."*

   2. If believers automatically receive a Holy Spirit baptism at the time of the New Birth, then water baptism must be a second baptism. Such a contention as that would render untrue Paul's Holy Spirit inspired statement that there is *"one baptism."*

   3. We know that at faith one is *"born"* of the Spirit, **John 3:5** and **1 Peter 1:23**, but a birth in no way is a baptism.

   4. Unbelievers shall experience a baptism of fire (**Matthew 3:11**, compare **2 Thessalonians 1:8**) and the Apostles were baptized in (not by) the Holy Ghost at Pentecost, **Acts 1:5**. The only baptism for each individual believer is water baptism.

B. That people are added to the church by water baptism is seen elsewhere in God's Word.

   1. In **Acts 2:41** the Bible says, *"Then they that gladly receive his word were baptized: and the same day there were added unto them about three thousand souls."*

   2. Notice that only saved and baptized people were added to the Church by the Lord. Compare verses **41** and **47**.

   3. It is easy to see that there is a vast difference in being *"added to the Lord"* as we shall discuss in the next section and in being added unto *"them,"* **Acts 2:41**. *"Them"* refers to the church at Jerusalem, **Acts 2:47**. Since the church is *"not one member, but many,"* **1 Corinthians 12:14**, it is easy to see that the expression *"them"* refers to the *"many"* who constituted the church or body that was at Jerusalem.

4. **Acts 18:8** shows exactly how the Corinthians had been formed into a church. It says, *"many of the Corinthians hearing believed, and were baptized."*

5. We conclude that the Corinthians became members of the Corinthian church by water baptism, just as the Jerusalem believers became members of the Jerusalem church by water baptism.

C. Thus, we believe Paul's teachings in **1 Corinthians 12:13** to be in perfect harmony with God's single means of adding to His church. When a believer is scripturally baptized in water, he is added to the local church.

SECTION THREE

A MAN MUST BE IN THE SPIRIT BEFORE HE CAN BE SCRIPTURALLY BAPTIZED INTO THE BODY

A. We believe the correct translation of the word *"by"* in **1 Corinthians 12:13** is "in".

"For by one Spirit are we all baptized into one body, whether we be Jews or Gentiles, whether we be bond or free; and have been all made to drink into one Spirit," **1 Corinthians 12:13**.

1. According to *Strong's Greek Dictionary of the New Testament*, page 28, number 1722, the word from which *"by"* is translated is a preposition which can mean "by, in, on", and others.

2. To render the word *"in"* is in harmony with other Scriptures which address the relationship a person must have with Christ in order to be a candidate for baptism.

    a. At the moment of the New Birth, believers are *"added to the Lord,"* **Acts 5:14**, (not church, but Lord).

    b. The result is that believers *"live in the Spirit,"* **Galatians 5:25**, for all believers we are completely *"sealed"* with the Spirit, **Ephesians 1:13**.

    c. **Romans 8:9-10** also shows that believers are *"in the Spirit."*

3. Thus, in keeping with the teaching of God's Word as to the position that believers are in (in Christ), we believe the clearest translation of **1 Corinthians 12:13** into English is, *"For in one Spirit are we all baptized into one body."* That is how the American Standard Version translates this preposition.

B. In order to be baptized, a person must be in the Holy Spirit.

1. Note **verse 13** as well as the context of this passage. The word *"Spirit"* is capitalized, thus denoting the Holy Spirit. There is no doubt that the Holy Spirit is the Spirit under consideration (**verse 11**). To make this verse suddenly deny that the Holy Spirit is under consideration would be to wrest the continuity of Scripture and pervert the meaning.

2. We thus reject the belief that this Scripture teaches that a believer must be in a certain attitude or "spirit" (non-capital "s") in order to be scripturally baptized.

C. Only believers, all of whom are in the Holy Spirit, are eligible for water baptism and resulting church membership.

1. Only if a man believes may he be baptized, **Acts 8:37**, and honestly show forth his personal participation in Christ's death, burial, and resurrection, **Romans 6:4-5**.

2. It is useless to baptize a non-believer because he is not in the Spirit, **John 14:17**. Only by being saved, which comes exclusively by faith in Christ, can a person be in the Spirit and thus a legitimate candidate for water baptism.

3. Consider the first chapter on *Water Baptism* in this book.

Chapter 26

Church Membership

Ephesians 5:25

We believe the church today is God's most important earthly institution. In this chapter we will see that it is the will of God that every saved person becomes an active member of a church.

SECTION ONE

FIRST CONSIDER THE TRUTH THAT THE CHURCH IS GOD'S MOST IMPORTANT AND PRIZED EARTHLY INSTITUTION

A. God has a tremendous love for His church.

1. Our text, **Ephesians 5:25**, makes that clear. It says, *"Christ also loved the church, and gave himself for it."*

2. **Ephesians 5:2** exhorts us to *"walk in love, as Christ also hath loved us, and hath given himself for us an offering and a sacrifice to God for a sweetsmelling savour."*

3. *"Take heed therefore unto yourselves, and to all the flock, over the which the Holy Ghost hath made you overseers, to feed the church of God, which he hath purchased with his own blood,"* **Acts 20:28**.

4. There can be no questions as to the sincerity and dedication of that kind of love.

   a. For one to die and shed his blood is the supreme sacrifice.

   b. Jesus said, *"Greater love hath no man than this, that a man lay down his life for his friends,"* **John 15:13**.

   c. Jesus has done this for His church ... He paid the supreme sacrifice.

B. To this institution that He loves so much, He has given the responsibility of conducting His spiritual work on earth today.

   1. That really is quite an honor to the church.

   a. He could have raised up stones, appointed individuals, selected mission boards, associations, conventions, fellowships, but He didn't. He gave the precious task to His church.

   b. It is not surprising that Peter said Christ *"hath called us to glory and virtue,"* **2 Peter 1:3**.

   2. In **Matthew 28:19-20**, God set forth a three step plan of spiritual endeavor.

   a. The steps are: make believers, baptize them and then teach them.

   b. Note well that this commission was to the Apostles, who were the first ones Christ set in the church, **1 Corinthians 12:28**. He built that church, **Matthew 16:18**, which was meeting in Jerusalem on the day of Pentecost, **Acts 2:1**.

   3. After Christ's resurrection, every time the responsibility of spiritual labor is under consideration, that responsibility rests upon the church. It does not rest upon individuals or institutions outside the church.

   4. **Ephesians 3:21** makes clear where the work is to be done when it says, *"Unto him be glory in the church by Christ Jesus throughout all ages, world without end. Amen."*

C. Many people may consider the church to be a small and unimportant institution, but it is certainly not that way with God.

SECTION TWO

HIS CHURCH IS THE MAIN OBJECT OF HIS CONCERN

A. He desires glory from it.

1. We have seen in **Ephesians 3:21** that He specifically wants glory in the church *"throughout all ages."*

2. In general, He wants His people to be active in His church.

   a. He states that He wants it attended, **Hebrews 10:25**.

   b. He expects His people to support it financially, **Malachi 3:10, 1 Corinthians 16:2**.

   c. The Scriptures speak of the church worshipping, **Acts 20:7**, sending out missionaries, **Acts 13:3** and serving Him in many ways.

3. Individuals are told *"Whatsoever ye do, do all to the glory of God,"* **1 Corinthians 10:31**, and when you look at **Ephesians 3:21**, you see the glory is to be *"in the church."*

   a. Any souls won, any prayers answered, any missionaries sent, the glory should be to God through the Lord's church, not otherwise.

   b. The soil from which every Christian plant grows should be the church, which is *"the pillar and ground of the truth,"* **1 Timothy 3:15**.

B. God promises to particularly protect and bless those in His church.

1. **Ephesians 5:23** says, *"Christ is the head of the church: and he is the saviour of the body."*

2. **Hebrews 10:21** says He does His High Priest work over the church, *"...an high priest over the house of God."*

3. He can cause all things to work for the church, **Ephesians 1:19-23**.

4. In **Matthew 16:18**, He promised to build up the church and so protect it that *"the gates of hell shall not prevail against it."*

5. It becomes obvious that He has gone to great lengths to watch over and care for His church.

SECTION THREE

ANY PERSON WHO NEGLECTS AND IGNORES GOD'S CHURCH IS STANDING IN OPEN DEFIANCE OF GOD

A. The foregoing points are ample to show God's concern and love for His church.

   1. He loves it and watches over it.

   2. He clearly warns us not to forsake it, **Hebrews 10:25**.

B. If and when we do forsake it, we are standing in open rebellion and disobedience of God, **James 4:17**.

C. When this occurs, our fellowship with God is broken.

   1. **1 John 1:6** says, *"If we say that we have fellowship with him, and walk in darkness, we lie, and do not the truth."*

   2. When this happens, we are chastened, **Hebrews 12:5-8**. If we continue to rebel, death can occur, **1 Corinthians 5:5**.

D. It is evident that church membership and activity is not essential to being saved and a child of God, but it is essential to fellowship.

E. This being true, every believer should become a member of God's church and labor faithfully therein.

Chapter 27

Joining and Attending Church

Hebrews 10:24-25

The previous chapter showed why we believe every believer should also become a member of the Lord's church. Here we plan to give further reasons why believers should join a church. Additionally, we believe those in a church should actively support and attend it.

SECTION ONE

TO BE AN ACTIVE MEMBER OF THE LORD'S CHURCH IS TO ABIDE IN THE SPECIAL FAVOR OF GOD

A. Believers are provided many privileges in and through the church.

1. The church provides fellowship with other Christians, **1 John 1:6-7**.

2. It also provides edification through preaching and teaching, **Acts 4:2, Matthew 28:20**.

3. The church provides you a place to worship God. There you can sing, **Psalm 66:1**; give, **1 Corinthians 16:2**; pray, **Matthew 6:1-10**; take the Lord's Supper, **1 Corinthians 11:23-31** and hear preaching, **1 Corinthians 1:21**.

4. Through the church you are provided the opportunity to participate in God's mission plan, **Romans 10:13-15, Acts 1:8**.

5. The church provides you the opportunity to unite with others as the body of Christ for the purpose of carrying on Christ's work, **1 Corinthians 12** and **Ephesians 4:14-16**. (There is strength in numbers.)

6. The church provides you the opportunity to prove your love for Christ by being obedient to His commands, **Hebrews 10:25**.

B. Christ promises special care over His church.

1. The gates of Hell shall not prevail against it, **Matthew 16:18**.

2. He promises to act as High Priest only over those in His church, **Hebrews 10:21**.

3. He acts as Savior over His church, **Ephesians 5:23**.

4. He is able and prepared to cause all things to work for its well-being, **Ephesians 1:22-23**.

5. Consider the awful plight of anyone cast out of the church, **1 Corinthians 5:5**.

C. Thus, we believe that all saved persons should become a part of one of the Lord's churches. They should join it.

SECTION TWO

THOSE WHO ARE A PART ONE OF THE LORD'S CHURCHES SHOULD ATTEND IT REGULARLY AND FAITHFULLY

A. Attendance of just some of the services is not regular, faithful attendance.

1. God holds His children accountable for being in every service unless providentially hindered, **Matthew 18:18**.

2. In the Day of Judgment, His people will answer to God for neglect of His church, **Romans 14:11-12**.

      a. Excuses succeed only in hurting those who make them, but they do not fool God.

      b. Those who neglect church have an issue with God, not merely the preacher or other church members.

B. Attendance is not everything, but there is not anything without it.

    1. If no one attends, it is impossible to conduct a worship service or have a church.

    2. Though there are numerous other things important to having a good church, attendance is a basic rudimentary essential. Attendance is possibly the most rudimentary need of a church; it is undeniably the first step in the right direction.

    3. The more faithful a believer is in attendance, the greater his potential to grow in grace, experience revival, assume responsibility, support the church financially, pray effectively and reach lost people. This list could be much longer.

C. Those who forsake assembling (do not attend) commit at least a sevenfold sin against the church.

    1. They rebel against God, **Hebrews 10:25a.**

    2. They discourage the hearts of those who are faithful, **Hebrews 10:25b.**

    3. They rob God of His substance, **1 Corinthians 16:2, Malachi 3:8-9.**

    4. They neglect God's Word, **2 Timothy 2:15.**

    5. They implant in their children a disregard for the church, God, God's Word and obedience to God, **Proverbs 22:6.**

    6. They refuse to help the lost find Christ. Men are to be reached through the church, **Ephesians 3:21.**

    7. They fail to give God the praise which is rightfully His, **Hebrews 2:12.**

SECTION THREE

THOSE WHO ARE MEMBERS OF THE LORD'S CHURCH SHOULD BRING OTHER PEOPLE TO IT

A. This will bring about growth of the church.

   1. If only the members of a church attended, the church wouldn't grow.

   2. To have an increase, others must be reached.

   3. To *"Enlarge the place of thy tent,"* **Isaiah 54:2**, should be the aim of every church member.

B. The very purpose of a Christian's pilgrimage on earth boils down to his promoting the cause of Christ on earth.

   1. The saved are to open the eyes of others, **Acts 26:16-18**.

   2. **Matthew 28:19** and **Mark 16:15** teach us to promote Jesus to others.

   3. The Jerusalem church did it, **Acts 5:42**.

   4. **Luke 14:23** teaches us to compel them to come in.

C. One of the very best things you can do is to enthusiastically promote your church by bringing people to it, **Psalm 126:5-6**.

Chapter 28

The Completion of the Apostolic Ministry

We believe the Apostles were *"Baptized with the Holy Ghost,"* **Acts 1:5**, which resulted in the gifts of the Spirit being bestowed upon them, **Hebrews 2:4**. These gifts, which are not the same as the fruits of the spirit, are definable. Every Apostle was endowed with all of the gifts, **2 Corinthians 12:12**, and could bestow the gifts to others by the laying on of hands, **Acts 8:18**. We also believe that only the Apostles had the power to bestow these gifts to others.

We believe these gifts of the Spirit were given to a specific group (the Apostles and those upon whom they laid their hands), during a specific time period (while the New Testament of the Bible was being given), for a specific purpose (to edify and perfect the saints and confirm the words of God's men to be Truth). We refer to that age of time, and to the functions of the Apostles and those upon whom they conferred gifts as the Apostolic Ministry. Theirs was a ministry of delivering the Word of God and of edifying the saints therein.

We believe that when the Bible was completed, there was no longer a need for the special Apostolic Ministry. It had served its purpose. We contend that when the purpose ceased, the Apostolic Ministry was completed and ceased. Thus, we believe that no one since the completion of the Apostolic Ministry has had the gifts of the Spirit. We believe the gifts of the Spirit, which enabled the possessors to perform mighty signs, wonders, and miracles, was limited to the Apostolic Ministry, which ceased with the death of the Apostles and those upon whom they laid their hands.

THE MIGHTY WORKINGS OF THE APOSTOLIC MINISTRY

SECTION ONE

THE GIFTS OF THE SPIRIT BY WHICH THE SUPERNATURAL WORKS OF THE APOSTOLIC MINISTRY WERE PERFORMED ARE CATALOGUED IN 1 CORINTHIANS 12:8-10

A. The word of wisdom that involved a supernatural power to reason.

B. The word of knowledge that provided insight or illumination of things not known through study.

C. Faith by which a man could perform works of such scope as to prove his miraculous power.

D. Gifts of healing by which the possessor of the gift could restore one instantly to health, regardless of the degree of his ailment or lack of faith by the ailing.

E. The power to perform miraculous works which are impossible by natural powers and from a human standpoint.

F. Prophecy. This was the power to tell or declare the mind of God to other people, including things to come prior to its fulfillment. It was done completely separate from any means of knowing apart from the personal revelation of God.

G. Discerning of spirits which was the ability to discern at once whether or not the spirit prompting any speech or authoring any action was of God.

H. Divers kinds of tongues which was the ability to speak in a language unfamiliar to him.

I. The interpretation of tongues which was the ability to interpret to an audience that which one who spoke in a tongue said.

SECTION TWO

THE HOLY SPIRIT WAS THE POWER THAT MADE THESE GIFTS WORK, WHICH ALLOWED THE MANY MIGHTY WORKS OF THE APOSTOLIC MINISTRY TO BE PERFORMED

A. 1 Corinthians 12:4 says, *"Now there are diversities of gifts, but the same Spirit."*

B. After naming those gifts, the Scriptures say, *"But all these worketh that one and the selfsame Spirit...,"* **1 Corinthians 12:11**.

C. Jesus told the Apostles, *"Ye shall receive power, after that the Holy Ghost is come upon you,"* **Acts 1:8**.

D. None of the mighty works of the Apostolic Ministry were performed apart from the power of the Holy Spirit.

E. While some who were not apostles exercised some of these gifts, all of them received this supernatural power only from the apostles who alone could administer the Spirit.

SECTION THREE

THERE ARE NUMEROUS CASES IN THE NEW TESTAMENT WHERE THE MIGHTY WORKINGS OF THE APOSTOLIC MINISTRY ARE SEEN

A. The Apostles went about doing mighty works.

    1. The Apostles are named in **Matthew 10:2-4**.

        a. **Acts 1:25** shows Judas Iscariot fell from Apostleship (not eternal life as he never had that, **John 6:64**). Thereafter he was no longer numbered as an apostle, **Acts 1:20**.

        b. **1 Corinthians 9:1-5** shows that Paul was numbered with the Apostles.

    2. Of those Apostles, **Mark 16:20** says, *"And they went forth, and preached every where, the Lord working with them, and confirming the word with signs following. Amen."*

a. **Mark 16:14** shows that this text applies only to the Apostles.

b. Jesus spoke and then was taken up, **Mark 16:19**. **Acts 1:2** records the same event saying, *"He was taken up, after that he through the Holy Ghost had given commandments unto the apostles whom he had chosen."*

c. The signs that were to follow these apostles are stated in **Mark 16:17-18**.

d. Jesus said, *"These signs shall follow them that believe,"* **Mark 16:17**. *"Afterward he appeared unto the eleven as they sat at meat, and upbraided them with their unbelief and hardness of heart, because they believed not them which had seen him after he was risen,"* **Mark 16:14**.

e. The words *"believed not"* used in **verse 17** refer directly to those apostles who did not believe He had risen. Thomas was one of them, **John 20:25-29**.

f. It does not refer to belief in Christ as personal Savior (as many contend) because those signs (**verses 17-19**) did not follow all believers in Bible days. Today they still do not follow all believers, but the *"signs"* did follow the eleven, **verse 20**.

3. In speaking of these apostles, **Hebrews 2:3-4** reads, *"How shall we escape, if we neglect so great salvation; which at the first began to be spoken by the Lord, and was confirmed unto us by them* (Apostles) *that heard Him. God also bearing them witness, both with signs and wonders, and with divers miracles, and gifts of the Holy Ghost, according to his own will?"* A requirement for Apostleship was that they had seen the Lord," **Acts 1:21-22**. Of the apostles it is said, *"Am I am not an apostle? am I not free? have I not seen Jesus Christ our Lord? are not ye my work in the Lord?"* **1 Corinthians 9:1**.

4. Paul spoke to the Corinthians of the apostolic work which he performed, **Acts 14:3**. Later he wrote, *"Truly the signs of an apostle were wrought among you in all patience, in signs, and wonders, and mighty deeds,"* **2 Corinthians 12:12**.

5. Jesus Christ came doing mighty works, **John 5:36**. He prayed to the Father, *"As thou hast sent me into the world, even so have I also sent them* (particularly the Apostles) *into the world,"* **John 17:18**. The apostles went forth with the same mighty power that Jesus had. Their miracles confirmed their words just as Jesus' miracles confirmed His words.

6. Peter and John, who were apostles, went up to the temple and raised up a lame man, **Acts 3:1-11; 4:14-16, 22**.

7. **Acts 4:33** says, *"And with great power gave the apostles witness of the resurrection of the Lord..."*

8. **Acts 5:12** says, *"And by the hands of the apostles were many signs and wonders wrought among the people."*

9. Paul spoke of himself to the Galatians as one that *"...worketh miracles among you,"* **Galatians 3:5**.

10. Paul wrote to the Romans, *"For I will not dare to speak of any of those things which Christ hath not wrought by me, to make the Gentiles obedient, by word and deed, Through mighty signs and wonders, by the power of the Spirit of God,"* **Romans 15:18-19**.

11. It is in view of such miraculous power in the apostles that Paul spoke for all of them and said, *"And my speech and my preaching was not with enticing words of man's wisdom, but in demonstration of the Spirit and of power,"* **1 Corinthians 2:4, 1 Thessalonians 1:5**.

B. Those upon whom the Apostles laid their hands also performed miraculous works.

1. **Acts 6:5-6** records the laying on of the hands of the apostles on Stephen. The results are quickly seen, *"And Stephen, full of faith and power, did great wonders and miracles among the people,"* **Acts 6:8**.

2. The apostles laid their hands on Philip, **Acts 6:5-6**. Mighty works through him followed, **Acts 8:5-13**.

3. Spiritual gifts were also bestowed on some who were not apostles, **Acts 8:18, Acts 10:44-46**.

C. Miraculous works characterized Apostolic Ministry, but never apart from the direct or indirect ministry of an Apostle.

Chapter 29

The Purpose of the Apostolic Ministry

SECTION ONE

THE APOSTOLIC MINISTRY, WHICH WAS DISTINGUISHED BY SIGNS, WONDERS AND GIFTS OF THE SPIRIT, WAS OPERABLE IN A DAY WHEN THE BIBLE, WHICH IS GOD'S WORD, WAS NOT FULLY REVEALED

A. During the time that this Apostolic Ministry was in operation, you will note that the Word of God was being revealed.

    1. As the *"signs ... wonders ... miracles ... and gifts"* are considered, **Hebrews 2:4**, note that **Hebrews 2:3** is talking about divine revelation.

    2. The Apostles who went forth *"with signs following"* were declaring God's *"Word,"* **Mark 16:20**.

    3. These Apostles had a ministry of penning the Word of Truth as the Spirit revealed it to them, **John 16:13**. Paul, who was one of them, stated how God told him his purpose was to deliver the revelations of God. He said in **Acts 26:16**, *"But rise, and stand upon thy feet: for I have appeared unto thee for this purpose, to make thee a minister and a witness both of these things which thou hast seen, and of those things in the which I will appear unto thee."*

The Purpose of the Apostolic Ministry

4. In the same book where the mighty Apostolic Power is seen, **1 Corinthians 2:4**, and the gifts are discussed at length, **1 Corinthians 12-14**, divine revelation is clearly seen to have been in process. **1 Corinthians 2:10** thus says, *"God hath revealed them unto us by his Spirit."* **Verses 12-13** continue, *"Now we have received, not the spirit of the world, but the spirit which is of God; that we might know the things that are freely given to us of God. Which things also we speak."*

5. Many other passages showing divine revelation to be still in process during the times when the Apostolic Ministry was being exercised could be cited, but these are sufficient to establish the point.

B. These early saints did not have the completed Bible to guide and edify them.

1. It is true that they had Moses and the prophets, **John 1:45**, but they did not have the books on the life of Christ, the teachings of the church, the doctrines of growth, the Second Coming and dozens of other teachings which are contained in the 27 books of the New Testament.

2. It is in view of that reality that we have such descriptions of this era as:

   a. *"For we know in part, and we prophecy in part."* **1 Corinthians 13:9**.

   b. *"For now we see through a glass, darkly..."* **1 Corinthians 13:12**.

C. Without the written Word of God before them, these saints were greatly handicapped in carrying on the work of the Lord.

1. They had no completed Bible by which to *"try the spirits,"* **1 John 4:1**, *"Edify,"* **Romans 14:19**, teach or preach as we do. We quote from book, chapter and verse. They didn't have the *book,* let alone *chapter* and *verse* indexing.

2. Since it is impossible for man to walk properly before God apart from the revealed Word of God (compare **Jeremiah 10:23, Proverbs 11:14** and **Psalm 119:5**), it was essential that these early saints be furnished with some sense of divine direction for the duration of the period in which the Word of God was being revealed and completed.

SECTION TWO

THE APOSTOLIC MINISTRY WAS ESTABLISHED FOR THE PURPOSE OF CONFIRMING THE WORD ALONG WITH EDIFYING AND UNIFYING THE SAINTS

A. The miraculous gifts were means by which these saints could tell the genuine from the counterfeit.

   1. There were many lying, false prophets and teachers claiming to be spokesmen for God, **2 Peter 2:1, Jude 4, 2 Corinthians 11:13**.

   2. Without the completed Revelation, it was difficult for those early Christians tell who was of God and who was not; however, they could see the miraculous confirmations by those who were truly delivering the Word of God, **1 Corinthians 2:16**. They could see the *"signs and wonders, and ... divers miracles, and gifts of the Holy Ghost,"* **Hebrews 2:4**, and thereby know assuredly who was of God and speaking the truth.

B. Thus, it becomes ever clearer that the main purpose of the Apostolic Ministry was to confirm the divine revelation of God. This miraculous ministry was a divine stamp of His approval by words spoken with miraculous confirmation. Over and over the Scriptures show the miraculous workings of the Spirit in and through the message bearers. These mighty works confirmed what they spoke to be true.

   1. Hear it in **Hebrews 2:3-4** where the Word *"at the first began to be spoken by the Lord* (and in Him miraculous works confirmed it to be the truth, **John 5:36**) *and was confirmed unto us by them that heard him; God also* (just as He did with Jesus) *bearing them witness, both with signs and wonders, and with divers miracles, and gifts of the Holy Ghost, according to his own will?"*

   2. Remember also how Paul said that he came *"not with enticing words of man's wisdom, but in demonstration of the Spirit and of power,"* **1 Corinthians 2:4**. The Apostolic Power proved his words to be true.

3. The Apostles *"preached every where, the Lord working with them, and confirming the word with signs following. Amen,"* **Mark 16:20.**

4. *"And with great power gave the apostles witness of the resurrection of the Lord Jesus,"* **Acts 4:33.** Again, signs confirmed truth.

5. Paul believed that the workings of the Apostolic Ministry were sufficient proof that he delivered the revealed truth of God. He said to the Thessalonian Christians, *"For our gospel came not unto you in word only, but also in power, and in the Holy Ghost, and in much assurance,"* **1 Thessalonians 1:5.**

C. The result of the Apostolic workings (by the apostles and those to whom they administered the gifts) was confidence in each other, edification and unity among the saints of God.

1. Their confidence that what they heard was from God is seen in **1 Thessalonians 2:13.** *"For this cause also thank we God without ceasing, because, when ye received the word of God which ye heard of us, ye received it not as the word of men, but as it is in truth, the word of God..."* The thing that caused them to receive it as such was the fact that it came to them in power and in demonstration of the Holy Ghost, **1 Thessalonians 1:5.**

2. Paul knew the gifts would establish, edify and unify the Christians in the churches. He wrote to the Romans, *"For I long to see you, that I may impart unto you some spiritual gift, to the end ye may be established; That is, that I may be comforted together with you by the mutual faith both of you and me,"* **Romans 1:11-12.**

3. The threefold result of the Apostolic working is set forth in **Ephesians 4:11-14:**

    a. For the perfection of the saints or that they might grow.

    b. For the work of the ministry that their service might be both intelligent and acceptable.

    c. For the edifying of the body of Christ which is the establishing or building up of the church.

    d. The outcome of these three for the saints is that they *"be no more children, tossed to and fro, and carried about with every wind of doctrine."*

4. Where the gifts are named and discussed at length, **1 Corinthians 12-14**, their result is that *"there should be no schism in the body; but that the members should have the same care one for another,"* **1 Corinthians 12:25**, and *"that the church may receive edifying,"* **1 Corinthians 14:5**.

SECTION THREE

THE APOSTOLIC MINISTRY WAS A SPECIAL MINISTRY. ITS PURPOSE WAS TO CONFIRM THE WORD, EDIFY THE SAINTS AND UNITE THE CHURCHES DURING THE TIME WHEN GOD'S WORD WAS BEING REVEALED.

A. We ask those who claim to have the gifts today: "What purpose does what you are doing serve?"

B. From this study of the Scriptures, it is clear that in Bible days miraculous gifts were inseparable from divine revelation.

   1. They were in direct confirmation of revealed truths.

   2. Furthermore the gifts worked transitionally in others to produce the edification and unity which the completed revelation of truth (The Bible) would produce in them. It took a few years for the Bible to be finalized.

C. If these supposed charismatic gifts of today do not serve the same purpose they served in Bible days, then they either serve no purpose or serve a purpose one that is unscriptural.

D. If a modern advocate of charismatic power is so bold as to claim that they are still serving in confirmation of divine revelation, let him hear what God says about modern revelations which would add to the Bible, *"For I testify unto every man that heareth the words of the prophecy of this book, If any man shall add unto these things, God shall add unto him the plagues that are written in this book,"* **Revelation 22:18**.

E. The truth is that the Apostolic Ministry is not for today. Its purpose, which was to confirm the Word and edify the churches, has been served. The next chapter in this book will further substantiate this claim.

Chapter 30

The Apostolic Ministry Was Limited to the Apostles and Those to Whom They Administered the Gifts

SECTION ONE

THOUGH MANY EXERCISED THE GIFTS OF THE SPIRIT, NOT ONE PERSON DID SO APART FROM THE DIRECT MINISTRY OF AN APOSTLE. THE APOSTLES ALSO COULD CONFER A GIFT TO ANOTHER PERSON.

A. Many people other than the apostles had one or more of the gifts and worked mighty signs, wonders, and miracles.

    1. *"And Stephen, full of faith and power, did great wonders and miracles among the people,"* **Acts 6:8.**

    2. Philip performed such powers. **Acts 8:5-7** says the people of Samaria, *"hearing and seeing the miracles which he did. For unclean spirits, crying with loud voice, came out of many that were possessed with them: and many taken with palsies, and that were lame, were healed."*

    3. When Peter and John arrived in Samaria, **Acts 8:14,** *"then laid they their hands on them* (the Samaritan believers, **Acts 8:14**), *and they received the Holy Ghost,"* **Acts 8:17.** (The receiving of the Holy Ghost here refers not to the person, but to the *"power"* of the Holy Ghost. They were already believers and all believers are indwelt by the Holy Spirit, **Romans 8:9**. The Samaritan believers already had *the person*; they did not have *the power* to do the miracles they had seen in Philip.

4. At Cornelius' house, *"The Holy Ghost fell on all them which heard the word. And they of the circumcision which believed were astonished, as many as came with Peter, because that on the Gentiles also was poured out the gift of the Holy Ghost. For they heard them speak with tongues, and magnify God,"* **Acts 10:44-46**. Later Peter told the other Apostles of this event saying, *"Forasmuch then as God gave them the like gift as he did unto us...,"* **Acts 11:17**. Peter mentioned this again in **Acts 15:8**.

5. There were men who received the baptism of John the Baptist without conversion (belief in Christ). Paul met some of them in Ephesus. Once they received Christ by faith, they were baptized. *"And they spake with tongues, and prophesied,"* **Acts 19:6**.

6. There can be no doubt from considering **1 Corinthians 12-14** that many, if not all of the Corinthian men, possessed one or more of the gifts of the Spirit.

7. The Galatians exercised gifts, **Galatians 3:5**.

8. To say that only the Apostles exercised spiritual gifts would be foolish and untrue. These examples are sufficient to show that many who were not apostles exercised spiritual gifts.

B. Note well that all of those non-Apostles who exercised spiritual gifts received their power to do so from an Apostle or group of Apostles. No one ever received this special power apart from the personal ministry of an Apostle.

1. The Apostles laid hands on Stephen and Philip. This laying of *"their hands on them,"* refers to the conveying of miraculous gifts, **Acts 6:6**.

2. The Samaritans received divine power when Peter and John (Apostles) *"laid they their hands on them,"* **Acts 8:17**.

3. Peter was the Apostle who gave the gifts of the Spirit to the people at Cornelius' house, **Acts 15:7**.

4. The believers of Acts 19:5 received their power only when Paul (an Apostle) *"had laid his hands upon them,"* **Acts 19:6**.

5. Paul personally ministered in Corinth, **Acts 18:1**, and administered the Spirit to the Galatians, **Galatians 3:5**.

6. You will not find a single case where any person or group of people ever exercised spiritual gifts, wrought signs, wonders or miracles apart from the ministry of an Apostle or group of Apostles!

SECTION TWO

THE MINISTRY OF IMPARTING THE GIFTS OF THE SPIRIT WAS EXCLUSIVELY THAT OF THE APOSTLES

A. Though many exercised spiritual gifts and powers, there is not one case where anyone other than an Apostle ever imparted such gifts or powers to another person.

B. The Scriptures show that the ministry of imparting spiritual gifts was exclusively that of the Apostles, not those to whom they imparted such gifts.

1. Paul spoke of himself to the Galatians as, *"He... that ministereth to you the Spirit...,"* **Galatians 3:5**.

2. Knowing that he had the power to impart the spiritual gifts, Paul wrote to the Romans, *"For I long to see you, that I may impart unto you some spiritual gift...,"* **Romans 1:11**. If these believers could have had the gifts of the Spirit apart from the ministry of an Apostle or by merely believing (which they'd already done, **Romans 1:7**), one cannot help wondering why they didn't already have the gifts, and why Paul needed to *"see"* them in order for them to have the gifts.

3. The Apostles laid their hands on believers and in so doing conveyed the gifts of the Spirit to them, **Acts 6:6, 8:17, 19:6**, but let it be known that none except the Apostles ever laid

hands on anyone else and in so doing imparted to him a spiritual gift.

4. When it came to the imparting of spiritual gifts, Simon the sorcerer was quick to realize, what many gullible people today don't realize, that those gifts were imparted *"Through laying on of the apostles' hands,"* **Acts 8:18.**

C. When someone other than an apostle wanted the exclusive Apostolic Power to impart the gifts, he was quickly told that he had no part in that ministry, **Acts 8:13-21.**

1. Simon the sorcerer wanted that power. **Acts 8:18-19** says of him, *"And when Simon saw that through laying on of the apostles' hands the Holy Ghost was given, he offered them money, Saying, Give me also this power, that on whomsoever I lay hands, he may receive the Holy Ghost."* This context and wording is so clear that no one should fail to see that what Simon wanted was power to impart these gifts just as the Apostles could.

2. Note well that Simon saw that only the Apostles had the power to impart the gifts to others.

a. Philip had been in Samaria for an extended time exercising the gifts of the Spirit, doing miracles before them, **Acts 8:6-7**; however, he had not imparted his power to a single person.

b. It was only when the Apostles came that the power was imparted. Even then only the Apostles did it, **Acts 8:14-18.**

3. To Simon who wanted the power to impart the gifts of the Spirit, the Apostles answered, *"Thou hast neither part nor lot in this matter: for thy heart is not right in the sight of God,"* **Acts 8:21.**

a. *"This matter"* referred to that which only an Apostle could do, the ministry of which only they had a *"part."*

b. **Acts 1:25-26** establishes this point by recording that Matthias was ordained to *"...take part of this ministry and apostleship, from which Judas by transgression fell, that he might go to his own place. And they gave forth their lots; and the lot fell upon Matthias; and he was numbered with the eleven apostles."*

By his ordination, Matthias received exactly what Simon asked for, but could not have. Simon wanted a part in this matter of conferring Apostolic Powers to others. Only the Apostles had a *"part"* in that ministry.

4. Neither Simon or Philip or Stephen nor any other man save only the Apostles had *"part"* in the *"matter"* or business of administering or imparting spiritual gifts.

5. Furthermore, those who claim to have part in such matters today fall into the same condemnation as did Simon. It must be said of them as of him, *"Thy heart is not right in the sight of God,"* **Acts 8:21**.

SECTION THREE

BASED UPON THE FOREGOING BIBLE FINDINGS, CERTAIN CONCLUSIONS ARE INESCAPABLE

A. Since only the Apostles had the power to administer spiritual gifts (and no one ever exercised such gifts apart from the ministry of an Apostle), it is obvious that when the Apostles died, no more gifts were imparted. Furthermore, when all of those who received their powers from the Apostles died, the Apostolic Ministry ceased. No one since has been able to perform Apostolic Powers.

B. This being true, there is no one today able to exercise a gift of the Spirit or Apostolic Power.

C. We conclude that all who claim to have charismatic or Apostolic Powers are frauds, imposters and counterfeits.

Chapter 31

The Apostolic Ministry Ceased When It Served Its Purpose

Remember that at the time of the mighty workings of the Apostolic Ministry, the New Testament was being revealed. The Apostolic Ministry of miracles was given by God to confirm that the apostles and those to whom they conferred the miraculous gifts were indeed truthful messengers from God.

SECTION ONE

THIS MINISTRY HAD AN EDIFYING AND UNIFYING IMPACT ON THE CHURCHES

A. **Hebrews 2:3-4** points out that the *"signs and wonders, and divers miracles, and gifts of the Holy Ghost"* *"bore"* *"witness"* that that those who did them were of God.

B. *"The word"* that the apostolic workers spoke was confirmed *"with signs following,"* **Mark 16:20**.

C. Such miraculous workings had the effect of assuring the hearts of those who saw them (**1 Thessalonians 2:13, 1 Thessalonians 1:5**) and establishing or edifying them, **Romans 1:11-12**.

D. Thus by the working of the Apostolic Ministry, the saints were edified, **1 Corinthians 14:5**, and unified, **1 Corinthians 12:25**.

SECTION TWO

THE HOLY BIBLE TODAY SERVES THE SAME PURPOSE THAT THE MIGHTY WORKINGS OF THE APOSTOLIC MINISTRY SERVED

A. Those who preach, teach or in any way testify to the truth today, do not need to perform a miraculous work to confirm that they are of God and what they speak is the truth.

B. To the contrary, men who would communicate the truth of God today simply need to *"Preach the word,"* **2 Timothy 4:2**. The Word of God has already been revealed and confirmed to be the truth, **Hebrews 2:3-4**. As long as a man limits himself to declaring what is written in the Bible, he speaks the truth. The fact that what he says can be established from the Bible is all the proof or confirmation of truth that is needed.

C. This can be said without contradiction.

  1. God *"cannot lie."* **Titus 1:2**.

  2. Jesus said, *"Heaven and earth shall pass away, but my words shall not pass away,"* **Matthew 24:35**.

  3. As long as one rightly divides the Bible to you, you can be sure that he is telling the truth.

  4. Since no more Scripture is being written, **Revelation 22:18**, it is useless to reconfirm with another miraculous sign what was already confirmed when it was initially given. Does the Holy Ghost of this universe have to continually reconfirm what has already been confirmed? We say "No." One confirmation was sufficient for the Scriptures. Since its completion, the Bible determines the truth or falsehood of any statement.

  5. Furthermore, the body (the church) is unified and edified with the Bible.

  a. Colossians 2:7 teaches us to be *"rooted and built up in him, and stablished in the faith, as ye have been taught."* Early Christians were taught the Word, **2 Timothy 4:2**, and it had the effect of building up (edifying) and establishing (unifying) them.

    b. Rather than wait for some miracle or gift of the Spirit to unify and edify us, we are told to *"study to shew thyself approved unto God, a workman that needeth not to be ashamed, rightly dividing the word of truth,"* **2 Timothy 2:15**.

6. We believe that the completed Bible serves the same purpose that the Apostolic Ministry served in the days before the Bible was completed.

SECTION THREE

IN VIEW OF THIS TRUTH, THOSE OF THE APOSTOLIC ERA LOOKED FORWARD TO THE COMING COMPLETION OF THE SCRIPTURES. THEY UNDERSTOOD THAT THE APOSTOLIC MINISTRY WAS ONLY TO SERVE UNTIL THAT DAY ARRIVED.

A. Paul discussed Spiritual gifts in **1 Corinthians 12** and after a long discussion of them, he said in **verse 31**, *"Yet shew I unto you a more excellent way."* Paul was clearly in the business of revealing the Word of God, **1 Corinthians 2**. Revealing the Word of God allows the Lord's work to be carried on successfully without the gifts of the Spirit.

B. Paul indicated that eventually *"the unity of the faith"* would come, by which the saints could know the knowledge of the Son of God and become *"perfect"* or mature, **Ephesians 4:11-14**.

C. Jude spoke of *"the faith which was once delivered unto the saints,"* **Jude 3**. It is obvious that Jude clearly recognized that the Word would be completely delivered. Divine revelation would not go on indefinitely. Jude foresaw that humanity would have the completed Revelation as we now have in the Bible.

D. The mighty workings of the Apostolic Ministry were designed to cause men to believe that which was spoken to be the truth. John mentioned the Written Word and said that it would be alone sufficient to cause men to believe. *"But these are written, that ye might believe,"* **John 20:31**. When Thomas saw Jesus resurrected,

John 20:26-28, and the many miraculous things which Jesus did, **Acts 1:2-3**, he believed, **John 20:29**. Note well Jesus' striking response. *"Blessed are they that have not seen, and yet have believed,"* **John 20:29**. That which is written is sufficient evidence today to cause anyone to believe. No person needs a miracle to convince him.

E. **2 Timothy 3:16-17** says, *"All scripture* (the completed Word) *is given by inspiration of God, and is profitable for doctrine, for reproof, for correction, for instruction in righteousness: That the man of God may be perfect, throughly furnished unto all good works."* The word *"perfect"* means mature or complete. This is the same word that is used in **Ephesians 4:13** and **1 Corinthians 13:10**. Both these passages refer to the finished or completed Scriptures. If the Bible thoroughly or completely furnishes all good works unto us, what possible thing could signs, wonders, miracles and gifts of the Spirit add to us today?

F. After a detailed discussion of Apostolic gifts, Paul said they shall *"cease,"* **1 Corinthians 13:8**. He used the Greek word pauo which means literally to stop, quit, to come to an end. See *Strong's Greek Dictionary of the New Testament*. In the next verse, Paul spoke of the time in which he lived as an era in which *"we know in part, and we prophesy in part,"* **verse 9**. He mentions knowing *"in part,"* **verse 12**. At that time there was no completed Bible. It was impossible for them to be *"...throughly furnished"* or to be *"perfect"* or mature. Thus, Paul said *"Now we see through a glass, darkly,"* **verse 12**. He then spoke of the day when the Word would be complete. He called it the day *"...when that which is perfect is come."* (This is not a reference to the Second Coming of Christ. Christ is masculine, and He is never referred to as *"that,"* which is neuter. Furthermore, nowhere in this context is the Second Coming of Christ under consideration. To say this is a reference to the Second Coming is to completely disregard the context.) When that which is complete (the finished Bible) is come, Paul said, *"...then that which is in part shall be done away,"* **verse 10**. The Apostolic Ministry was a ministry *"in part."* All of the truths were not yet assembled into one whole. Once they were, the ministry *"in part"* was *"done away."*

G. Again, we conclude that the Apostolic Ministry ceased with the completion of the Bible.

SECTION FOUR

NOTE THESE SIMPLE CONCLUSIONS

A. Once the Bible was completed, the Apostolic Ministry had served its purpose. The Bible today serves the purpose the Apostolic Ministry once served.

B. Thus, the Apostolic Ministry is not needed today. It would serve no purpose.

C. The ministry of gifts was given to the Apostles and no one else. Thus, with the death of the Apostles, which occurred about the time the Bible was completed, there was no further ministering of the gifts. After that time, no one else received the gifts.

D. When all those to whom the Apostles administered the gifts died, no one since has exercised a miraculous gift of the Spirit.

E. Those who claim Apostolic Power and spiritual gifts today are mistaken. No one since the Apostolic Age has miraculous spiritual gifts.

F. We conclude that the charismatic renewal is not at all a bona-fide scriptural movement.

Chapter 32

Unknown Tongues

1 Corinthians 12:10

We believe that the spiritual gift of tongues ceased with the completion of the Apostolic Ministry. Although, in view of the heavy emphasis which is being currently laid on tongues, it is important that we look specifically into this gift of the Spirit called, *"divers kinds of tongues."*

As the previous chapters have shown, we believe the gift of tongues is not in effect today. We also maintain that all who practice "speaking in tongues" today are frauds and not of God. Furthermore, the "tongues speakers" of today bear minutely little, if any, resemblance to the speaking in tongues which was done during the Apostolic Age.

SECTION ONE

IT IS IMPORTANT TO UNDERSTAND THE GIFT OF TONGUES AS TAUGHT IN THE BIBLE AND PRACTICED IN THE APOSTOLIC AGE

A. The gift of tongues was the ability to instantly speak fluently in a language previously unknown to the speaker.

   1. When tongues are referred to in the New Testament, the word *tongues* (sometimes tongue) is translated from the Greek word glossa. The word is defined in *Strong's Greek*

Dictionary and in *An Expository Dictionary of New Testament Words* by W. E. Vine to mean (1) The tongues like as of fire, which appeared at Pentecost, (2) The tongue as an organ of speech, and (3) a language.

2. Always, when speaking of the gift of tongues, the word *tongues* refers to another language, which was not previously learned or known by the speaker.

3. **Acts 2** illustrates this truth.

   a. When the twelve Apostles (compare **Acts 1:26** with **Acts 2:1**) spoke with other tongues, **verse 4**, *"every man heard them speak in his own language,"* **verse 6**.

   b. To show that the *"tongues"* were known languages the hearers asked, *"And how hear we every man in our own tongue, wherein we were born?"* **verse 8**.

   c. This passage is most often cited by the modern tongues movement to prove tongues to be speech in some strange Gibberish or utterance unknown to any people anywhere apart from a heavenly revelation.

   d. Such was obviously not the case. The fact that amazed the multitude here is that every man, (and a wide spectrum of languages was present, **verse 5**), heard; not in unknown utterance; but in his *"own tongue."*

   e. These Apostles were simply speaking languages and each listener was hearing in his own language.

4. Always tongues as a gift refers to another language; never to a mysterious, ecstatic Gibberish. There is not one word, phrase, or context in the entire New Testament that even vaguely suggests such ecstatic utterance was ever done.

5. To a man who spoke only Hebrew, other tongues would be Arabic, Greek, Chinese, Chaldee, etc. For a modern English speaker, other tongues would be Spanish, German, Russian, Japanese, Portuguese, etc.

6. The gift of tongues was to speak perfectly these languages without having ever learned them. This was speaking in tongues or languages.
7. This is not how the modern *tongues speakers* do it.
   a. Their speaking is not in some other language; instead it is a conglomeration of sounds and utterances unknown to be any language on earth.
   b. Consequently, the modern tongues movement does not even vaguely resemble the tongues gift practiced by some of the early Christians.
8. It is noteworthy that there is no indication that the *"tongues"* spoken in Bible days were *"unknown"*.
   a. The word *"unknown"* does not appear in the ancient manuscripts.
   b. When it was used in the King James Bible, it was purposely italicized by the translators to tell the reader that the word did not appear in the original manuscripts. It was added by the translators for clarity.
   c. The translators were attempting to show that the *"tongue"* or *"language"* was unknown to the person speaking it. It was not unknown as an earthly language.

B. Any person endowed with the gift of tongues could speak in many different languages as the Spirit gave him utterance.
   1. You will notice that **1 Corinthians 12:10** mentions *"kinds of tongues"*:
      a. Though the word *"divers"* is italicized in the King James translation, nevertheless the plurality of languages is seen.
      b. Both *"kinds"* and *"tongues"* are plural, showing the speaker could speak in more than one language.
      c. The statement of this verse also shows that the same person could speak in these different kinds of tongues. Notice *"to another* (singular) *kinds of tongues"* (plural). It was

not a matter of having a different person to speak each foreign language.

2. **Acts 2:4-11** illustrates this as the twelve Apostles spoke in a number of languages, *"other tongues,"* **verse 4**. Notice too, that they were only able to do it *"as the Spirit gave them utterance,"* **Acts 2:4**. **1 Corinthians 12:11** indicates the gift was only operative by the Spirit. It was not that a man learned these languages; he had no knowledge of the language except as the Spirit revealed it to him.

3. This is very different from the "tongues movement" of today!

   a. Today's speakers utter an ecstatic Gibberish, not another tongue

   b. Regardless of the speaker, the Gibberish is always almost exactly the same.

C. There are no *"kinds"* (plural) of Gibberish in the modern charismatic movement, let alone *"kinds"* of languages. Instead, with today's Charismatics, the Gibberish is one kind with a distinctive sameness.

SECTION TWO

THE SPIRIT OF GOD DECIDED WHO RECEIVED THE GIFT OF TONGUES

A. Not everyone received the gift of tongues.

1. In describing the gifts in **1 Corinthians 12**, Paul explained that different ones received different gifts (**verses 8-10**), but not everyone (except the Apostles) had all the gifts.

   a. He asked, *"Do all speak with tongues,"* **verse 30**. The context answers "No."

   b. Various members of this church had differing abilities; not every member had the same abilities of every other member, **verses 14-24**.

2. No woman received the gift of tongues (nor any of the gifts).

   a. In the context dealing with tongues, **1 Corinthians 12-14**, Paul said, *"Let your women keep silence in the churches: for it is not permitted unto them to speak,"* **1 Corinthians 14:34**.

   b. He continued in **1 Corinthians 14:35**, *"it is a shame for women to speak in the church."*

3. This is very different from the modern tongues movement.

   a. The modern *tongues speakers* generally claim that everybody can and must speak in unknown tongues to be saved.

   b. Tongues are supposedly evidence of being filled with the Holy Ghost.

   c. In this movement, women and men speak in tongues and, generally, the women are first and foremost in speaking in tongues.

   d. Of course, none of the Bible women and few of the Bible men ever spoke in tongues. If tongues are essential to salvation as the present charismatics contend, then these Corinthian *"saints,"* **1 Corinthians 1:2**, were not saints or saved, **1 Corinthians 15:2**. They were lost, and the Spirit who inspired Paul to say they were saved saints was mistaken.

4. This truth alone is sufficient to expose the fallacy in the charismatic movement.

B. The Spirit of God selected who would receive the gift of tongues.

1. In speaking of the gifts, including tongues, the Scriptures say, *"all these worketh that one and the selfsame Spirit, dividing to every man severally as he will,"* **1 Corinthians 12:11**.

2. The gifts were not self-chosen; the Spirit determined who got which gift.

3. On the Day of Pentecost, the Apostles spoke in other tongues, **Acts 2:4**. It is noteworthy that they were not praying at some altar in order that they might receive the gift and speak in tongues.

a. To the contrary, they were merely waiting for the fulfillment of Jesus' promise of **Luke 24:49** and **Acts 1:5, 8**.

b. As the resurrection of Christ fulfilled the prophecy of the Feast of First-fruits, **1 Corinthians 15:20**, likewise, the miraculous manifestation of the Spirit at Pentecost fulfilled the Old Testament prophecy of the feast of Pentecost. As there could only be one resurrection, there can only be one Pentecost.

c. The definite fact is that there was no self-seeking or self-choosing of what happened at Pentecost; it was in fulfillment of promise.

4. Furthermore, there was no self-choosing of a gift when the gifts of the Spirit were conferred by the laying on of Apostles hands.

    a. This was true of Cornelius' house, **Acts 10:45-46**, and of John's disciples, **Acts 19:6**.

    b. You will also note that in neither case were they at an altar begging for the gifts.

5. The Holy Spirit, not the Apostles or the man receiving, decided who would receive which gift, **1 Corinthians 12:11**.

    a. This is totally different from the modern tongues movement.

    b. In today's Charismatic Movement, everyone is to choose tongues.

    c. Furthermore, the seekers are to get *down at the altar* and pray persistently until they receive the gift.

    d. It is evident that what happened in the Bible was not the same as what is happening today.

SECTION THREE

HOW THE GIFT OF TONGUES WAS TO BE GOVERNED WHENEVER PRACTICED

A. The gift of tongues was only to be exercised when unbelieving Jews were present.

1. The main purpose of tongues was to reach unbelievers. Paul said, *"Wherefore tongues are for a sign, not to them that believe, but to them that believe not,"* **1 Corinthians 14:22.**

2. When an unbeliever came into the services of the church and could not understand the language being spoken, the service meant nothing to him. Those members with the gifts of knowledge, prophecy, etc. could not reach him; however, the man with the gift of tongues could. It is not difficult to imagine the impact tongues had on an unbeliever. His language was unknown to all present; however, one of the members spoke fluently to him in his own language. No human could do it. He knew this was a God-thing.

3. **1 Corinthians 14:21** shows the tongues gift was for unbelieving Jews.

   a. This verse quotes **Isaiah 28:11-12** saying, *"With men of other tongues and other lips will I speak unto this people."*

   b. The gift of tongues fulfilled this prophecy.

   c. *"This people"* speaks directly of Jews, **1 Corinthians 14:21**. **Isaiah 28** shows *"this people"* to be Jews.

4. Tongues were not for everybody; they were *"a sign"* for unbelieving Jews.

B. Furthermore, the gift of tongues was only to be exercised when an interpreter was present.

1. **1 Corinthians 14:28** plainly says, *"if there be no interpreter, let him keep silence in the church."*

2. The interpretation of tongues was another gift of the Spirit, **1 Corinthians 12:10.**

3. The interpretation of tongues is confusing to many.

   a. The question arises, "Why did they need an interpreter if the speaker was speaking in a known language?"

   b. The answer lies in the fact that the known language was the language of the unbelieving Jew. It was not known by the speaker of tongues or by the church.

   c. Without an interpreter to translate the message for the church, the speaking in tongues was meaningless and unedifying to them.

4. Since all things were to edify the church (*"Let all things be done unto edifying,"* **1 Corinthians 14:26**, then tongues were intended to edify.

5. As the man with the gift of tongues spoke in the language of the unbelieving Jew, the interpreter translated it into the language spoken by the church.

6. The interpreter did not interpret to the unbeliever; he didn't need it. He was miraculously hearing in his own language. The interpreter interpreted for the church.

7. Note well that if no interpreter was present, no tongues were to be spoken, **1 Corinthians 14:28**.

8. Here is further proof that these tongues were not to be jargon or unintelligible Gibberish.

   a. **1 Corinthians 14:6-10** says that whatever is spoken must be easy to understand and not in some strange lingo which no one would comprehend.

   b. **1 Corinthians 14:11** shows that if language is not comprehendible, no communication is done.

   c. If there was no interpreter to translate to the church, **1 Corinthians 14:28**, then silence in tongues was to prevail. While still in the context of *"tongues"* Paul said, *"in the church I had rather speak five words with my understanding, that by my voice I might teach others also, than ten thousand words in an unknown tongue,"* **1 Corinthians 14:19**.

C. In no service were more than three men to speak in tongues.

   1. *"If any man speak in an unknown tongue, let it be by two, or at the most by three,"* **1 Corinthians 14:27**.

   2. Notice that that this is a reference to worship services, not to the unique, one-time wait for the promise of the Spirit which occurred in **Acts 2**.

D. No two were to speak in tongues simultaneously.

   1. After **1 Corinthians 14:27** says only two or three per service were to speak, the verse then says, *"and that by course."*

   2. One was to speak, then another, but not all at the same time.

   3. Everything in the church was to be done decently and in order. **1 Corinthians 14:33** declares, *"God is not the author of confusion, but of peace, as in all churches of the saints."*

E. As previously mentioned, women were forbidden to speak in tongues.

   1. *"Let your women keep silence in the churches: for it is not permitted unto them to speak; but they are commanded to be under obedience, as also saith the law. And if they will learn any thing, let them ask their husbands at home: for it is a shame for women to speak in the church,"* **1 Corinthians 14:34-35**.

   2. Nowhere in Scriptures did anyone except a few Spirit-selected men ever receive the gift of tongues.

F. This is all so very different from the modern tongues movement.

   1. They give no consideration to whether or not an unbelieving Jew, who can't speak their language, is present. Their Gibberish is not for unbelievers. By their own admission, it is supposedly "evidence that the speaker is filled with the Holy Ghost."

   2. Since the speaker is speaking a jargon and not another language, there is no way to check whether or not his interpretation is correct. This is a very convenient escape device. There is no objective way to measure the legitimacy

of the activity. It plays upon the superstition of the hearers, and protects the tongue speaker and the interpreter from exposure.

3. Also, the modern tongues people insist that everybody, including women, should speak in tongues in each service. Tongues have become a sort of litmus test of spirituality.

4. Generally modern *tongues speakers* all speak at the same time and create a great state of disorder and confusion.

5. They also insist that the women must speak in tongues.

    a. Some say speaking in *tongues* is essential to salvation.

    b. Others, who will not go so far as to say tongues are essential to salvation, maintain that tongues are good for everybody. They insist that everyone really should speak in them as evidence of a second blessing or deeper spiritual life.

6. The modern tongues phenomena is nowhere similar to the gift of tongues which was practiced during the days before completion of the Bible. The modern movement contradicts the Bible practice of tongues at almost every point.

SECTION FOUR

THE GIFT OF TONGUES WAS NOT GIVEN TO GLORIFY ITS RECIPIENT

A. All the gifts, including tongues, were to strengthen and edify the church.

1. Remember that **1 Corinthians 14:26** says, *"Let all things be done unto edifying,"* and **1 Corinthians 14:7-11** condemns the practice of anything which does not edify.

2. Instead of clamoring for gifts, Paul said, *"seek that ye may excel to the edifying of the church,"* **1 Corinthians 14:12**.

3. Like the human body, the church body needs a variety of members in order to be complete and function well. See **1 Corinthians 12:14-30**. In those days before completion of the Bible, God provided these gifts of the Spirit, *"That there should be no schism in the body; but that the members should have the same care one for another,"* **1 Corinthians 12:25**.

4. As the preceding studies have shown, the gifts served to confirm the Word and edify the church until the Word was completed. Thus, the gifts of the Spirit were for the benefit of the whole church and not for the glory of an individual member.

B. In the listing of the spiritual gifts, tongues and interpretations come last.

1. You will find this to be true in both **1 Corinthians 12:8-10** and **1 Corinthians 12:28-30**.

2. In spite of this, you will see in the context of **1 Corinthians 12-14** that many of the Corinthians had elevated tongues to the rank of premier gift.

3. Though Paul told them it was not wrong to speak in tongues at that time (see preceding chapters), he made clear that tongues were not the foremost gift, **1 Corinthians 14:39**.

4. In view of the Bible principle that men ought to humble and abase self, **Luke 14:11**, none of the gifts were to cause anyone to become proud with a superior air about them.

C. In contrast to the Bible standard, most modern tongue speakers are highly puffed up and think themselves to be superior to everybody else.

1. Tongue speaking is seen as the most important thing anyone is to do.

2. The message comes across that once you've spoken in tongues, you've really *arrived*. You are in a very elite group of God's *in circle*. Those who haven't spoken in a tongue are usually regarded as inferior, if saved at all. They're not yet

deep. To *arrive*, you need to be in a *Full Gospel* church. The obvious implication is that all of the other churches are not *full*.

3. The modern movement does not produce the same effect the Bible gift produced.

SECTION FIVE

THE GIFT OF TONGUES WAS TO CONTINUE ONLY UNTIL THE WORD OF GOD WAS COMPLETED

A. The ministry of gifts was a ministry in part.

1. In that day, Paul said, *"we know in part, and we prophesy in part,"* **1 Corinthians 13:9**.

2. The completion of the Scriptures was then in process. Consequently, they did not have the whole or completed Bible.

3. Therefore, these early saints could not go to the Bible for the guidance and counsel necessary to their edification and the well-being of the church.

4. During this period, they were given these gifts by which the church could carry on without handicap.

B. The ministry of the church was not to remain permanently a ministry in part.

1. In the midst of defining the gifts (ministry in part), Paul said, *"yet shew I unto you a more excellent way,"* **1 Corinthians 12:31**. He indicated that something better than this ministry of gifts was coming.

2. At that very time, the more excellent or complete way was being developed. It would not be a ministry *"in part."*

   a. Jesus said to the Apostles, *"the Comforter, which is the Holy Ghost, whom the Father will send in my name, he shall teach you all things, and bring all things to your remembrance, whatsoever I have said unto you,"* **John 14:26**. He also said, *"I have yet* many things to say unto you, but ye cannot bear them now. Howbeit when he, the Spirit of truth, is come, he will guide you into all truth: for he shall not speak of himself; but whatsoever he shall hear, that shall he speak: and he will shew you things to come,"* **John 16:12-13**. When you put what Jesus had done and taught with what He would teach, you have the whole.

    b. During the time of the gifts, they were putting *the parts together,* **1 Corinthians 2**. Paul, an Apostle *"born out of due time,"* **1 Corinthians 15:8**, said, *"that by me the preaching might be fully known,"* **2 Timothy 4:17**.

    c. Jesus said, *"the things concerning me have an end,"* **Luke 22:37**; therefore, Paul could look forward to the day when the Word would no longer be in part (as in tongues), but it would be completed. He thus spoke of the day, *"when that which is perfect* ("complete" from the Greek word teleios) *is come,"* **1 Corinthians 13:10**.

    d. The completed Bible is *"that which is perfect,"* **1 Corinthians 13:10**. It is *"a more excellent way"* of **1 Corinthians 12:31**.

3. Not long after Paul's statements of **1 Corinthians 12-14**, the last book of the Bible was written and the ministry which supplied the church ceased to be *"in part."* Instead, the Bible is the completed revelation of God and supplies the church with all it needs to serve God acceptably. *"All scripture is given by inspiration of God, and is profitable for doctrine, for reproof, for correction, for instruction in righteousness: That the man of God may be perfect, throughly furnished unto all good works,"* **2 Timothy 3:16-17**.

4. With the completion of the Bible, we have in one book a supply which provides the church all it needs. Tongues alone could never do that. The Bible is *"a more excellent way"* to conduct the services and business of the church.

C. When the Bible (God's completed revelation) was finished, tongues ceased.

    1. **1 Corinthians 13:8** says, *"...whether there be tongues, they shall cease;"* and *"cease"* is from the Greek pauo meaning "come to an end."

2. **1 Corinthians 13:10** locates the time of that *"cease"* to be *"when that which is perfect is come."* When the Bible was finished, the *"in part"* ministry of gifts was terminated.

3. If tongues ceased with the completion of the Bible (and they did), then the gift of tongues is not in effect now. The actions of today's *tongues speakers* prove they do not have the gift of tongues which is seen in the Bible.

Chapter 33

Miracle Healing

Acts 3:1-11

We believe God heals people. If we didn't, we would neither pray for the sick nor ask others to do so. We do pray for sick people believing God will heal as He has promised in His Word. We do not believe that the *miracle healing* claimed by many today is bona-fide. We believe the miracle healers of today are really fake healers preying upon the psychologically weak and unlearned. The Apostles did have the *"gift of healing,"* however, since the completion of the Apostolic Ministry, there has been neither divine healers nor miraculous healings performed by them.

Since the gift of healing was one of the gifts of the Spirit which we believe were limited to the Apostolic Age, therefore we believe the gift of miracle healing ceased when its purpose was fulfilled. Thus we believe that since the completion of that Apostolic Ministry, no one has that gift. Consult the chapters on *The Completion of the Apostolic Ministry*. They show why we believe the gift of healing has ceased. Since those chapters are in this book, this chapter will focus on fraudulent healing practices, the limitations of the healing promises, and Scriptures on healing. The focus will not be on proof that the gift of healing has ceased.

SECTION ONE

THE BIBLE PROMISES OF HEALING ARE NOT WITHOUT LIMITATIONS

A. God can heal anyone of anything.

1. *"With God all things are possible,"* **Matthew 19:26**.

2. He, who created the universe, designed the human body and spirit, and has *"All power ... in heaven and in earth,"* **Matthew 28:18**, proved while He was on earth that He can heal any and all kinds of infirmities. He can even raise the dead.

3. There has never been a question of whether or not God can heal. He can, but He doesn't always see fit to heal.

B. Those who claim to have the gift of healing and those who profess to believe in healing by "miracle healers" use **James 5:13-18** to support their belief. They say that if you have enough faith when a healer prays for you, you will be healed.

1. It is noteworthy that in the case of the real healers (the Apostles) failure to heal a lunatic, **Matthew 17:14-16**, their own unbelief, not the unbelief of the lunatic, was the cause, **Matthew 17:17, 20**.

    a. Note that whether or not the sick man had faith had nothing to do with it.

    b. The big loophole used by modern fake healers is "The person to be healed didn't have enough faith."

2. The truth is that some of the Bible people, who had the greatest of faith and who prayed for healing, never were healed. This is evidence that the promises of healing are not for everyone who has faith and prays.

    a. Who could argue the fact that the Apostle Paul was a man of faith and faithfulness? He was filled with the Spirit; yet, in spite of his prayers and faith, Paul continued to have a *"thorn in the flesh,"* **2 Corinthians 12:4-9**.

Miracle Healing

    b. Trophimus was a man of faith, **Acts 20:4, Acts 21:24**, yet he was *"left at Miletum sick,"* **2 Timothy 4:20.**

    c. Timothy is an example of Godliness, **1 Timothy 4:12**, yet he was not healed of his stomach disorders and various other *"infirmities,"* **1 Timothy 5:23.**

    d. The book of **3 John** will tell you what a faithful man Gaius was, yet he was not *"in health,"* **verse 2.**

    e. Epaphroditus was another Godly man of faith who continued to be sick, **Philippians 2:25-30.**

3. Scripture supports the position that the promise of healing is not general to anyone who may be sick. To the contrary, it is limited to the people and circumstances indicated in the Scriptures.

SECTION TWO

MODERN FAKE HEALERS AND SUPPORTERS OF MIRACLE HEALING MAKE NO ATTEMPT TO OPERATE AND ACT WITHIN THE LIMITATIONS OF HOLY SCRIPTURES

A. Fake healers are dishonest.

    1. If they have the power to heal the sick, then they ought to have enough human compassion to walk through the hospitals, clearing the rooms of their patients. They ought to go over this world and restore the handicapped and amputees.

    2. If they have the power, then who would say they shouldn't use it? Furthermore, if they can't do what we propose, then they lie when they claim to be healers.

    3. In spite of a currently large number of these Pentecostal type *healers,* hospitals worldwide (physical and mental) are running over and more are being built. Every doctor seems to have more patients than he can handle. One has to ask, "Where are the healers?"

B. Today's miracle healers make their mileage by dealing with psychosomatic problems.

   1. It is a medically provable fact that a large majority of all ailments (perhaps in excess of 80%) are brought on by stresses. These can cause all sorts of mental and physical disorders including ulcers, gout, arthritis, headache, high blood pressure, etc.

   2. If a fake healer can get a person with psychological problems to believe strongly that he is healed and all is well, generally the problems will decrease or even vanish completely. Once the stress is gone and the nerves settle down and the patient feels better.

   3. It is easy to see that the healer's power was really only "imaginary" and his supposed healing only a lying wonder.

   4. It is not difficult to see why fake healers always seem to deal with internal functions which an observer cannot see. They make no attempt to deal with such things as broken bones protruding through the skin, chain saw gashes or skin cancers.

   5. You seem to always hear of these *healings* second hand; never are they documented. They are not independent of psychological disturbances.

   6. Since these healers (and often those who claim they were healed) diagnose the cases themselves, it is easy to see how *miraculous recoveries from incurable diseases* occur. These *healings* are characterized by the fact that the patient really never had the disease. The recovery of some who really did have a malady was natural; people often simply *get better*. The body has a marvelous way of recovery.

SECTION THREE

CONSIDER THE HEALING WHICH IS PROMISED US IN GOD'S WORD

A. By faith we can avoid or be healed of those ailments which we bring on ourselves by carelessness, neglect, worry, overindulgence and stress in general.

Miracle Healing

1. Remember that faith is not a matter of doing things blindly, **Hebrews 11:1-2**. Faith is a matter of obeying the counsel of God's Word, **Romans 10:17**.

2. By obeying the counsel of God's Word (exercising faith), many sicknesses will clear up.

    a. The Word of God says, *"But now ye also put off all these; anger, wrath, malice, blasphemy, filthy communication out of your mouth,"* **Colossians 3:8**. These conditions cause a host of maladies in the body. See **1 Peter 2:1, Ephesians 4:31, Titus 3:3**.

    b. God's Word teaches against worry, **Luke 12:22**, hate and resentfulness, **Matthew 18:21-22**, fear, **Matthew 10:28**, greed, **Ephesians 5:3, 1 Timothy 6:10**, and many other such things. These conditions bring on high blood pressure, heart diseases, apoplexy, gastric disorders and countless other maladies.

    c. **1 Corinthians 3:16-17** teaches against abusing the body. It is medically documented that such practices as smoking, drinking, overworking, being overweight and having an improper diet are extremely harmful to the body.

3. Most people having high blood pressure or back trouble due to being overweight could improve their health immensely by exercising faith in God's Word and losing 25 or 30 pounds.

4. When a person has an ailment brought on by disobedience to the teachings of God's Word, he need not go presumptuously to some fake healer hoping for healing in spite of his disobedience. (It's for certain that there is no healer who can override God's consequences for disobedience.) What that man should do is heed (exercise faith in) God's Holy Word. When he does, he will eliminate the thing which was causing his ailment. Chances are the ailment will clear up.

5. Since *"Every good gift and every perfect gift is from above, and cometh down from the Father of lights...,"* **James 1:17**, we know that such recoveries are of God.

6. Such healing as this is real faith healing. It results from hearing and heeding God's Word about good health.

B. Furthermore, God's Word teaches us to cooperate with medicine in bringing about healing.

1. There are ailments which are not related to God's chastening nor to some foolish practice of the victim: allergies, infections, and injuries, plus many other such problems.

2. According to God's counsel, we are to get knowledge and to use wisdom and understanding.

    a. The Bible extols wisdom and understanding, **Proverbs 3:18-23**, and exhorts us to get it, **Proverbs 4:5-13**.

    b. Notice that one of the results is, *"the years of thy life shall be many,"* **Proverbs 4:10**.

3. The Bible gives us examples of using medicine for illnesses.

    a. Timothy was told, *"...use a little wine for thy stomach's sake and thine often infirmities,"* **1 Timothy 5:23**.

    b. The teaching in James about the use of *"oil"* on the sick man seems to be symbolic of using medicine, **James 5:14**.

    c. Christ himself spoke approvingly of using *"oil and wine"* on the wounds of the man who was beaten and wounded on the road to Jericho, **Luke 10:33-34**. This illustrates God's sanction of the use of medicines.

4. Obedience to God's counsel is a matter of faith. The cures that follow are the result of such faith.

5. It should be noted that God does not promise that every use of medicine, however wise, will result in a cure. All men must eventually die, **Hebrews 9:27**. Through sickness, God may be working out a divine purpose in one's life as He did with Job, and with the blind man of **John 9:1-3**. Since we do not know which the case may be, we can simply use what understanding we have and depend upon God to heal, if He sees fit. (The faith is in using understanding as we are told.)

C. Providing the Bible plan is followed, God's Word teaches we can be healed from those illnesses brought on by reason of chastening.

1. Unconfessed sin will bring the chastening of God upon a person who is a child of God.

   a. **Hebrews 12:5-11** shows chastening can be very *"grievous,"* **verse 11**.

   b. Some of the Corinthians were sick, and some dead as a result of their misuse of the Lord's Supper, **1 Corinthians 11:28-32**.

   c. Old Testament Israel illustrates this truth. For their disobedience, they were repeatedly plagued with sickness, disease and pestilence, **Exodus 15:26, Deuteronomy 28:15, 21-22, 27**.

   d. God's chastening is particularly hard on a man who has brought public reproach upon a church, **1 Corinthians 5:1-13**.

   e. If the guilty person does not follow God's plan for removing the cause of his sickness, he will very likely be guilty of a *"sin unto death,"* **1 John 5:16. James 1:15** says, *"sin, when it is finished, bringeth forth death."*

2. **James 5:13-20** outlines the plan for healing from sicknesses stemming from unconfessed sin.

   a. Notice that James is definitely considering this kind of sicknesses.

   (1) He said *"death"* would occur if the person were not healed, **verse 20**.

   (2) That the sick must *"confess,"* **verse 16**, which is exactly what Christians guilty of sin are told to do, **1 John 1:9**.

   b. Such ones are to call the elders of the church, **James 5:14**. This especially applies to cases where public harm to a church has occurred and church action has been taken, **Matthew 18:18**. That was the case in **1 Corinthians 5:1-13**.

    c. The sick man is to *"confess"* his faults both to other church members and to God, **James 5:16**. As he does, the church is to pray for him, **James 5:14-15**. The result will be healing.

    d. When the cause of this sickness (unconfessed sin) is removed, God will remove the effect, which is the sickness itself.

    e. As the case of Elijah illustrates, a person who is sick due to sin in his life cannot expect his prayer for healing to be positively answered apart from his confession of his sin, **James 5:17-18**.

        (1) Elijah prayed there would be no rain, **verse 17**, and was answered because of the wickedness of Israel and Ahab's house, **1 Kings 18:17-18**.

        (2) Elijah prayed again that it would rain, **verse 18**, but he could only expect his prayer to be answered because Israel had repented. In so doing, Israel met the conditions necessary to remove God's chastening from them, **1 Kings 18:39-45**.

3. The use of oil, **James 5:14**, involves primarily the house of Israel.

    a. James addressed his book to the *"twelve tribes which are scattered abroad,"* **James 1:1**. These were his Jewish brethren both nationally and spiritually.

    b. Christ sent the twelve Apostles among the twelve tribes of Israel telling them to anoint with oil, **Mark 6:13**, but he limited this to the *"lost sheep of the house of Israel,"* **Matthew 10:6**. He forbade them to go *"into the way of the Gentiles, and into any city of the Samaritans,"* **Matthew 10:5**.

    c. Christ limited this teaching to Israel because they needed to turn away from the meaningless ceremonial use of oil and start using oil for the healing of everyone. Most Jews believed that strict adherence to Levitical practices and rituals made them right with God. They were constantly at odds with Jesus over ceremonial practices.

Anointing with oil was one of those practices. When used properly for medicinal purposes, oil served a good purpose. When used ceremonially, it served no physical purpose. We believe the teaching of James to mean that oil and other substances with medicinal powers should be used to bring about healing, and that the oil mentioned here is symbolic of the need to use medicines as they are available. We do not believe the passage promotes the ceremonial use of oil or the practice of any other empty rituals.

D. We believe *miracle healing* outside of these methods set forth in the Scriptures is fraudulent, fake and counterfeit.

  1. We believe God continues to heal sick people, but not through the miraculous gift that was operable during the Apostolic Ministry.

  2. We believe God can directly intervene in any sickness or injury, but it will not be upon the strength of a *healer*.

  3. We conclude that the *miracle healers* of today are not true healers, but frauds. We believe that those who believe in them are deceived.

  4. This is not to say there have never been miracle healers. The Bible speaks of several authentic miracle healers. The account of two people and a miraculous healing by them is recorded in **Acts 3:11**.

  5. Since the Apostolic Ministry, there have been no more miracle healers.

  6. Consult our chapters on the completion of the Apostolic Ministry.

Chapter 34

The Lord's Return

Acts 1:11

We believe in a literal Second Coming of Jesus Christ. His appearance is our hope, and we believe His appearance will be soon. His coming will greatly alter the complexion of this whole world.

SECTION ONE

WE BELIEVE IN A PERSONAL VISIBLE, BODILY RETURN OF OUR LORD TO THIS EARTH

A. Jesus Himself said He would return.

  1. While on earth, He spoke of coming again, **Matthew 16:27**.

  2. Note that *"Son of man"* is used. This identifies Him, **Matthew 25:31-32**.

  3. **John 14:2-3** is a reference to His going to Calvary to prepare the way of salvation; it also establishes His Second Coming.

  4. As if the Second Coming was a foregone conclusion, Jesus told His disciples that He would return, **John 21:22-23**.

- **B.** Heavenly beings testified of His Second Coming.
    1. Angels told the disciples that He would return, **Acts 1:10-11**.
    2. Notice that they said *"this same Jesus."* The Christ of Calvary will return.
- **C.** The inspired Apostles were sure of Christ's return.
    1. Paul wrote of the return.
        a. He looked for the Savior from Heaven, **Philippians 3:20**.
        b. He looked for Him who gave Himself for us, **Titus 2:13-14**.
        c. Hebrews 9:28 says Jesus shall appear.
    2. James said be patient in waiting for His coming, **James 5:7**.
    3. Peter looked for His return, **2 Peter 1:16-17**. (He pointed attention back to the transfiguration which foreshadows the Second Coming.)
    4. Jude prophesied of His coming, **Jude 14-15**.
    5. John looked forward to His return.
        a. He said be ready at His coming, **1 John 2:28**.
        b. **Revelation 1:7** announces the return.
- **D.** His coming shall be a very literal, visible one.
    1. Note well that all shall see Him, **Revelation 1:7**. (His coming is not imaginary).
    2. He will return *"in like manner"* as he left. His was a very visible, bodily ascension, **Acts 1:10-11**.
    3. Zechariah 14:1-4 established the literalness of His Second Coming.
    4. There can be little doubt about how literal this is, **Revelation 19:11-21**.
- **E.** All speculation that the Second Coming is figurative, symbolic, etc. is nonsense and without scriptural support.

SECTION TWO

THE LITERAL RETURN IS THE BLESSED HOPE OF THE SAVED

A. **Titus 2:12-13** calls it a blessed hope and says it causes us to live soberly.

B. **1 Peter 1:3-5** says His resurrection and Second Coming gives every believer hope of resurrection. At His return, Jesus will reward those who have served Him.

C. The hope of His Second Coming motivates believers to keep themselves pure, **1 John 3:1-3**.

D. The hope of His return gives us the ability to be patient, **James 5:7-8**.

SECTION THREE

THE SECOND COMING OF CHRIST IS IMMINENT

A. The fact that it is imminent means it could occur at any time.

1. We know that it shall occur; we do not know just when.

2. It is impossible for us to date the appearance, **Matthew 24:36**. This being true, we cannot rule out any date.

B. The Bible shows us that the Second Coming could be at any time.

1. Jesus warned the disciples that His appearance could be at any time, **Matthew 24:42-44**. (He warned us to not grow confident by thinking His return would be a long way off.

2. The seven mystery parables of **Matthew 13** show that sooner or later a climax to the earth will occur. No one can say when the harvest will be, but it will be, **verse 30**.

3. Jesus spoke of His return. See **Matthew 25:14-30**. The servants in the story knew the master would return; they didn't know exactly when, **verse 19**. The point is obvious; Jesus will return, and He could return at any moment.

4. Jesus warned, *"Behold, I come as a thief. Blessed is he that watcheth, and keepeth his garments...,"* **Revelation 16:15**.

5. In a very excellent passage by Paul on the return of Christ, he said the appearance will be sudden, but it should not overtake us unawares, **1 Thessalonians 5:1-4**. We have warnings that the time is near and Jesus will soon appear. Let us, therefore, watch.

In view of the testimony of God's Word, we look for the soon visible, personal, literal Second Coming of our Lord. We can say with Paul in **Philippians 3:20**, *"For our conversation is in heaven; from whence also we look for the Saviour, the Lord Jesus Christ."*

Chapter 35

Resurrection and Judgment

John 5:28-29

We believe the Bible reveals many certain truths about the future. Among these truths is the fact that the day is coming when all men shall rise from the dead and stand before God in judgment. We believe the coming resurrection and coming judgment are both literal.

SECTION ONE

ACCORDING TO THE BIBLE, ALL MEN SHALL RESURRECT

A. The Bible speaks of two main resurrections.

    1. There is the resurrection of *"the just"* and the resurrection of the *"unjust."*

        a. **Acts 24:15** specifically names the two resurrections.

        b. **John 5:29** makes clear that there will be two resurrections.

    2. Every man shall come forth in one or the other of these resurrections.

        a. Jesus said, *"The hour is coming, in the which all that are in the graves shall hear his voice,"* **John 5:28**.

  b. **1 Corinthians 15:22** says, *"For as in Adam all die, even so in Christ shall all be made alive."*

 3. Each of these two major resurrections has several stages.

  a. As to the resurrection of the just, Christ was raised after He was crucified, **Luke 24:5-6**, and several ancient saints arose at His death, **Matthew 27:52-53**. The main resurrection of the just shall happen at Christ's Second Coming, **1 Thessalonians 4:16-17**, and those saved during the tribulation shall rise at the end of the tribulation, **Revelation 20:4-6**. These various stages of the resurrection of the just are called *"orders,"* **1 Corinthians 15:23**.

  b. Apparently all the wicked dead will rise at once as seen in **Revelation 20:5, 13**. **John 5:29** and **Acts 24:15** also mention this resurrection.

B. At the resurrection of the just, the bodies of believers will be changed into heavenly bodies.

 1. This change is described in **1 Corinthians 15:39-44, 51-54**.

 2. We will be changed into bodies like Christ's resurrected body, **Philippians 3:21**.

C. This resurrection will be literal and personal.

 1. One could hardly read the previous Scriptures and fail to see those facts.

  a. Jesus said those *"in the graves shall hear his voice,"* **John 5:28**.

  b. Paul spoke of our recognizing Christ on a personal level, **1 Thessalonians 4:13-17**.

 2. Job looked forward to this resurrection. He said he would see God *"for myself, and mine eyes shall behold, and not another; though my reins be consumed within me,"* **Job 19:25-27**.

D. We believe in a coming, literal resurrection for all men.

SECTION TWO

THE COMING JUDGMENTS ARE VERY DIFFERENT

A. Every man must sooner or later face a day of judgment.

  1. Whether a person is lost or saved, judgment is certain.

  2. Listen to the Scriptures.

     a. *"And as it is appointed unto men once to die, but after this the judgment,"* **Hebrews 9:27.**

     b. **Numbers 32:23** says, *"...be sure your sin will find you out."*

     c. Paul warned, *"Be not deceived; God is not mocked: for whatsoever a man soweth, that shall he also reap,"* **Galatians 6:7.**

     d. **Hebrews 2:2** says, *"...every transgression and disobedience received a just recompence of reward."*

     e. **Romans 14:11-12** shows that everyone shall be judged.

     f. *"For God shall bring every work into judgment, with every secret thing, whether it be good, or whether it be evil,"* **Ecclesiastes 12:14.**

  3. Judgment for all is certain; it cannot be escaped.

B. Though all shall appear before God in judgment, not all will appear at the same time.

  1. Believers will appear in a judgment exclusively for believers.

     a. It is called the Judgment seat of Christ, **2 Corinthians 5:10.**

     b. This judgment will occur before the millennium. By the time of the millennium, the saints will have been already judged and reigning with Christ, **Revelation 20:6.**

  2. Lost sinners will appear in a judgment exclusively for them.

     a. **2 Peter 3:7** calls it a judgment of *"ungodly men."*

     b. It is called the Great White Throne Judgment. It occurs after the millennium, **Revelation 20:11-15.**

C. Furthermore, the basis of these two judgments is altogether different.

   1. The saved will be judged to determine their rewards.

   a. Paul said we walk as one that would receive a crown, **1 Corinthians 9:23-27**.

   b. **1 Corinthians 3:12-15** describes the judgment of believers as one which will reveal true good works from counterfeit. Rewards will be given for good works.

   2. **Revelation 20:11-15** shows lost sinners will be judged to determine the degree of their eternal punishment. At that time, their punishment will be formally pronounced by God.

In light of the Word of God, we believe in a coming literal resurrection and judgment for every man.

Chapter 36

Tribulation and Millennium

Matthew 24:14-22

We believe the Bible reveals the future. We believe that in the future there will be a great time of tribulation on the earth followed by a thousand year reign of Christ on this earth. This chapter is designed to show why we believe these truths.

SECTION ONE

WE BELIEVE THAT THE DAY WILL SOON COME WHEN THIS EARTH WILL BE CAUGHT UP IN A GREAT TIME OF TRIBULATION THAT WILL FAR SURPASS ANY AWFUL PERIODS OF UPHEAVAL AND TRAVAIL THIS WORLD HAS EVER SEEN

A. **Matthew 24:21-22** specifically speaks of this awful coming time.

    1. Note that this is not a figurative, spiritual occurrence.

    2. **Matthew 24:9-22** speaks of it as an awful time unparalleled in all human history.

        a. The reference to wars and earthquakes place these events into a category of literal occurrences.

        b. **Matthew 24:22** specifically refers to *"flesh,"* which points to a literal tribulation.

B. Consider a sampling of Old Testament prophecies of this coming tribulation.

    1. **Jeremiah 30:4-7** calls it Jacob's troubles.

    2. **Ezekiel 20:34-38** says it is a time when Israel shall pass under the rod.

    3. **Ezekiel 22:19-22** sees it as a time of Israel in the melting pot.

    4. Malachi spoke of it as Israel's cleansing by *"fullers' soap,"* **Malachi 3:1-3.**

    5. **Zechariah 13:9** prophecies the tribulation.

    6. **Daniel 12:1** calls it a time of unequalled troubles.

    7. Notice that it is seen mostly as being a time of troubles for the Jews.

        a. It is a refining process to bring them to God.

        b. Even so, the Gentiles will also suffer beyond measure. The side effects of God's wrath upon Israel will devastate the entire earth.

C. **Revelation 6:1** to **Revelation 19:21** is a detailed survey of this awful tribulation.

D. These are only a few of the Scriptures which make us look for a tribulation and an Antichrist who will rule throughout its duration.

SECTION TWO

WE BELIEVE THE END OF THE TRIBULATION WILL BE THE BEGINNING OF A THOUSAND YEAR REIGN BY THE LORD JESUS CHRIST ON THE EARTH. THIS IS COMMONLY KNOWN AS THE MILLENNIAL REIGN OF CHRIST.

A. We believe the event that shall end the tribulation and initiate the millennium will be Armageddon.

1. **Joel 3:9-16** and **Revelation 16:16** both speak of that awful battle.

2. It will be a battle between God and His saints, **Joel 3:16**, and Antichrist and his wicked gentile followers, **Zechariah 14:3, Revelation 19:19, Micah 4:11-12, Revelation 16:14.**

3. The result of the battle will be the destruction of Antichrist and Gentile supremacy, **Daniel 2:31-35** and **Revelation 19:17-21.**

B. Armageddon will usher in the Lord, and He will set up His kingdom.

1. **Zechariah 14:1-4** foretells the Lord coming to earth at the battle.

2. **Daniel 2:35** saw the Lord's kingdom (fifth in a line of five world kingdoms) taking the place of the destroyed Roman (fourth) Gentile kingdom.

3. **Revelation 20:1-7** says specifically that Christ shall rule for a thousand years.

C. Note a few points regarding the kingdom reign.

1. The Lord shall rule out of Zion, **Micah 4:1-7.**

2. Many physical changes shall take place on the earth, **Zechariah 14:4, 10-11.**

3. The land of Palestine will produce profusely, **Joel 3:18, Isaiah 35:1, Isaiah 55:13, Amos 9:13.**

4. Satan will be bound and off the scene, **Revelation 20:1-3.**

5. The animal kingdom shall change, **Isaiah 11:6-9.**

6. During this time, Israel will be the chief nation on earth, **Isaiah 60:11-12.**

7. The saints will rule with the Lord throughout those thousand years, **1 Thessalonians 4:13-17, Revelation 19:11-16, Revelation 2:19.**

Chapter 37

What a Church Is and When It Was Founded

Matthew 16:18

When we speak here of the church, we speak of the Lord's church. We realize there are many churches, but not all are the Lord's. We believe the Lord Jesus Christ established a particular kind of institution which He called "My church."

SECTION ONE

THE NEW TESTAMENT DEFINES WHAT THE LORD'S CHURCH IS

A. The word *"church"* is translated from the Greek word ecclesia.

    1. The literal meaning of the word is "assembly."

    2. Ecclesia stems from two Greek words

        a. ek meaning "out of."

        b. kaleo meaning "to call."

    3. The word ecclesia refers to "an assembly of called out ones," or literally a group called out for a particular purpose.

B. The word <u>ecclesia</u> refers to three different types of groups in the New Testament.

   1. In **Acts 19:32, 39, 41** it refers to the self-governing Greek state.

   2. In **Acts 7:38** it is used to refer to the Old Testament people of Israel.

   3. In **Matthew 16:18** and many other places, it refers to the Lord's church; *"my church."*

C. Of 115 definite uses of <u>ecclesia</u> in the King James Bible, 111 of them refer in one way or another to *"my church"* or <u>ecclesia</u>.

D. Each of these uses refers to one of two aspects of the Lord's church.

   1. The general assembly in glory.

   a. This will consist of all the members of the Lord's churches in a glorious heavenly assembly.

   b. The church in this sense does not exist now, except in prospect. It appears in God's plans for the future.

   2. The particular assembly.

   a. The church today exists only in this sense.

   b. The word employed in this sense refers simply to a local group of baptized believers in common assembly.

   c. The word <u>ecclesia</u> is used 92 times in the New Testament in this common, ordinary sense.

E. The word <u>ecclesia</u> referring to a current, particular assembly is used in two ways.

   1. Like all nouns, it can be used in the concrete sense.

   a. *"The church of God which is at Corinth,"* **1 Corinthians 1:2**.

   b. *"The church that was at Antioch,"* **Acts 13:1**.

   c. *"The church of Ephesus,"* **Revelation 2:1**.

2. Like all nouns, it can be used in the abstract sense.

   a. **Ephesians 3:10, 21** uses the word in the abstract sense.

   b. Both **Matthew 16:18** and **Matthew 18:17** use church in the abstract sense.

   c. Like all nouns, <u>ecclesia</u> can only be applied in a concrete or particular sense. The *"church"* is referred to in the abstract so the truth may be understood as equally applicable to all churches.

   d. **Ephesians 5:23** says, *"The husband is the head of the wife."* Here the nouns *"husband"* and *"wife"* are used in the abstract sense. Everyone understands this is the relationship which should exist between every particular husband and wife.

F. An understanding of the word church as used in the Bible will show that the Lord's church is a particular kind of group. The word *church* cannot legitimately be applied to groups that do not conform to the biblical idea of a Christian church.

1. Though this chapter is not designed to identify the distinctive earmarks of a New Testament church, other chapters do so.

2. Among those earmarks is the fact that those within a true New Testament church are baptized believers, and the group preaches salvation by grace through faith alone.

SECTION TWO

WHILE HE WAS BODILY ON THIS EARTH, THE LORD ESTABLISHED HIS CHURCH

A. There is widespread but erroneous belief that the church was established and originated on the day of Pentecost.

B. The Bible teaches that Christ organized His church while He was on earth. It was already in existence before the day of Pentecost, referred to in **Acts 2**, ever arrived.

1. John the Baptist prepared the material for the Lord's church.

    a. John was not the founder of the church, **John 1:6-8**, but a witness for Christ, **John 1:26-34**.

    b. His purpose was to prepare the materials for Christ, **Matthew 3:3, Luke 1:17**.

2. Jesus Christ organized and continues to build up the church.

    a. He said in **Matthew 16:18** *"I will build my church."* The word *"build"* means to edify or build up.

    b. From His disciples, Jesus took some who had been baptized of John. These He put into His church, **Acts 1:22, John 4:1-2**.

C. The first ones He put into His church were the Apostles, **1 Corinthians 12:28**.

1. Since He ascended to Heaven before the Day of Pentecost, **Acts 1:9-14**, His founding of His church had already occurred.

    a. Long before Pentecost, He had a large group of disciples, **John 1:33-51**.

    b. Before Pentecost, He chose the twelve Apostles, and they were organized. They had a treasurer, **Luke 6:12-16** and **Mark 3:13-19**.

    c. While on earth, He taught and trained them for three years, **Matthew 5, 6, 7, Luke 24:27**.

    d. He sent out at least seventy to work, **Matthew 10:1-16**. See **Luke 10:1**.

    e. He instituted the Lord's Supper while on earth, **Luke 22:19-20** and **Mark 14:22-25**. This was prior to Pentecost. All denominations agree the Lord's Supper is a church ordinance.

    f. He gave the great commission before Pentecost, **Matthew 28:18-20**.

    g. The church assembled together, **Acts 1:4**, received other commandments, **Acts 1:8**, saw Him ascend, **Acts 1:11**, continued in prayer, **Acts 1:14**, and there were about 120 of them, **Acts 1:15**, all before Pentecost.

    h. Before Pentecost, they conducted a business meeting, **Acts 1:15-26**.

2. Other facts also show that the church was organized before and not on the Day of Pentecost.

    a. Jesus said, *"I will build my church,"* **Matthew 16:18,** and **Acts 2:1-4** shows that the Holy Spirit *"filled"* it. How could the Spirit fill that which didn't yet exist?

    b. If the church was not already in existence, how could Christ have said, *"...tell it unto the church,"* **Matthew 18:17?** It is impossible to tell something to an entity that doesn't yet exist.

    c. **Acts 2:41** says that on the day of Pentecost, about 3000 were *"added to"* the church. It would have been impossible to add to what did not already exist.

We believe that Christ organized His church while He was on earth. The Christian church was not organized by Peter or any other man.

Chapter 38

The Lord's Church Is Local

Ephesians 3:21

We believe that the Lord's church is a local congregation of baptized believers. We flatly reject the idea of a universal church. The church is not made up of believers from many different congregations; each congregation is the Lord's church.

SECTION ONE

THROUGH THE AGES, MANY HAVE HELD TO THE COMMON BUT FALSE IDEA THAT ALL BELIEVERS CONSTITUTE THE UNIVERSAL CHURCH

A. There are two major variations of this concept.

1. Some (mainly Roman Catholics) believe in a universal visible church. They say Roman Catholics all over the world make up one true church.

2. Many who reject the Roman Catholic idea hold to a concept that is equally unscriptural; it is the idea that all believers make up one true invisible church.

3. We believe these concepts are not taught in the Bible.

B. The Bible does teach that all the members of God's local churches shall eventually be gathered together into one great congregation in the presence of the Lord.

  1. This is the church in its future glorified state.

   a. Both **Revelation 7:9** and **21:1-2** refer to this future congregation.

   b. This future church will be a congregation of perfected men. This is obviously not a reference to current congregations, **Hebrews 12:22-23**.

   c. Ephesians 5:23-25, 27-29, 32, refer to this glorified congregation.

  2. This is a congregation in prospect and not one that is presently in existence.

   a. Today's church is no more the glorified church than a bride is a wife before the marriage.

   b. There must be a redemption of bodies before this future church can exist.

  3. Many Scriptures speak of the church in the future. Misunderstandings occur when those Scriptures are applied to churches today.

  4. It should be noted from the previous Scriptures that the future glorified church will be one local congregation. It will not be an uncoordinated arrangement of believers in different locations.

C. The Bible also uses the word church in an abstract sense, which some conclude there is a mystical universal church.

  1. Ephesians 3:10 and **21** both use the word *church* in the abstract sense. The abstract use of any noun can only be seen when it is reduced to the concrete. Obviously the only kind of church which exists in the concrete is a local one.

2. Christ said He would build His church, **Matthew 16:18**. He did and it was the church at Jerusalem. He originated it by first making the Apostles members of it, **1 Corinthians 12:28**.

SECTION TWO

THE ONLY CHURCH WHICH EXISTS TODAY IS LOCAL AND VISIBLE

A. In most of the places where the church is mentioned, it is obvious that one particular congregation is under consideration.

1. *"To the church in thy house,"* **Philemon 2**.

2. *"Casteth them out of the church,"* **3 John 10**.

3. *"I teach every where in every church,"* **1 Corinthians 4:17**.

4. **Acts 14:27** speaks of gathering the church together.

5. The church gave to Paul, **Philippians 4:15**.

6. *"I wrote unto the church,"* **3 John 9**.

B. On many occasions the particular church is called by name.

1. *"The church which is at Cenchrea,"* **Romans 16:1**.

2. *"The church which was at Jerusalem,"* **Acts 11:22**.

3. *"The church of the Laodiceans,"* **Colossians 4:16**.

4. Many, many times several different churches are under consideration. Thus, the word *"churches"* is used, **1 Corinthians 7:17, Revelation 1:4, Galatians 1:2**.

C. There is no legitimate way to gather from the Scriptures the idea of a universal church.

1. The Bible is consistent as to what the church is. It consistently uses the word *church* in either the concrete or the abstract sense. The use of the word *church* in another sense by modern theologians is very confusing.

2. The only way the idea of a universal church can be deduced from the Scriptures is by misapplying them.

SECTION THREE

THE IDEA OF AN UNIVERSAL CHURCH CREATES IMPOSSIBLE THEOLOGICAL DIFFICULTIES

A. If the church is universal, there are commands it cannot obey.

1. It cannot assemble, **Hebrews 10:25**, each Lord's day, **Acts 20:7**.

2. It cannot observe the Lord's Supper, **1 Corinthians 11:23-26**.

3. Church discipline is impossible, **Matthew 18:15-18**.

4. The pastor cannot *"feed the church,"* **Acts 20:28**.

B. If the church is universal, who is the real pastor, and who are the deacons? **Ephesians 4:11**.

C. How can a universal church possibly operate as a coordinated body with all suffering and rejoicing together? **1 Corinthians 12:26**.

D. How could a universal church have gotten into Philemon's house? **Philemon 2**.

E. How could Paul have persecuted a universal church? **Philippians 3:6**.

F. This all sounds somewhat preposterous and ridiculous.

1. That is precisely the point. The idea of a universal church is ridiculous and that fact becomes obvious when the idea is pursued to its logical conclusions.

2. The kind of church the Bible discusses is a local church. It is not illogical. Instead it is sensible and charged with the responsibility of carrying out God's work.

3. It is that institution which every believer should be a part.

Chapter 39

Worshipping in the Church

Matthew 18:15-20

We believe that saved men should worship God. Formal worship is primarily to be done weekly when the church comes together. We believe God has a prescribed way to worship Him and that activities in the name of worship which do not meet His standard are not true worship.

SECTION ONE

GOD PRESCRIBED THAT HIS PEOPLE REGULARLY WORSHIP HIM

A. Listen to God's Word which exhorts people to worship God.

1. *"The LORD ... shall ye fear, and him shall ye worship,"* **2 Kings 17:36**.

2. God commanded Moses to *"worship ye,"* **Exodus 24:1**.

3. *"Give unto the LORD, O ye mighty, give unto the LORD glory and strength. Give unto the LORD the glory due unto his name; worship the LORD in the beauty of holiness,"* **Psalm 29:1-2**.

4. David said, *"O come, let us worship and bow down: let us kneel before the LORD our maker. For he is our God; and we are the people of his pasture, and the sheep of his hand...,"* **Psalm 95:6-7**.

5. You find Paul worshipping in **Acts 24:11**, and John in **Revelation 19:10**.

6. The importance of worshipping God is stressed over and over in the Scriptures.

B. It is possible for a man to offer up praise and worship to God even when not assembled with a church.

1. The wise men worshipped in a house, **Matthew 2:11**.

2. The man among the tombs worshipped at a graveyard, **Mark 5:6**.

3. Long before there was a church, many men already worshipped God, **Genesis 24:26, Exodus 4:31, Judges 7:15, Job 1:20**.

4. **Zephaniah 2:11** speaks of a day when men shall *"worship him, every one from his place."*

5. Prayer is worship and the primary place of prayer is in *"thy closet,"* **Matthew 6:5-6**.

C. Let us hasten to strongly emphasize that today God's number one place of formal worship is in His church.

1. That's where God has promised to meet with His people, **Matthew 18:15-20**.

2. The church is the place where God said He desired glory to Himself, **Ephesians 3:21**.

3. God has long had an appointed place for men to formally worship Him, **1 Samuel 1:3, 2 Kings 18:22, Acts 8:27** and **Acts 24:11**. Today that place of formal worship is His church, **Ephesians 3:21** and **Matthew 18:15-20**.

4. A person may worship Him with a family prayer, on the lakeside or at a singing convention. That's fine, but these are not the Lord's church. These should never be considered an acceptable substitute for formal worship in the church.

D. Men are to worship God upon the first day of each week.
1. The church in Troas met on Sunday, **Acts 20:7**.
2. The church in Corinth met on Sunday and worshipped by giving the rightful portion of their money to God, **1 Corinthians 16:2**.
3. **Hebrews 10:25** says members should be present when the church meets.

E. The Scriptures make it clear that the saved are to regularly worship God in His church.

SECTION TWO

THE BIBLE SPEAKS OF FIVE FORMAL ACTS OF WORSHIP IN THE CHURCH

A. God is to be formally worshipped through ***PRAYER***.
1. The believers in the early Jerusalem church practiced prayer, **Acts 2:42**.
2. Paul exhorted the Ephesian believers to pray, **Ephesians 6:18**.
3. James speaks of the church coming together and praying while together, **James 5:13-16**.
4. Jesus said, *"My house shall be called the house of prayer,"* **Matthew 21:13**.

B. God is to be formally worshipped through ***SINGING***.
1. Paul exhorted the Colossians to sing praises to God, **Colossians 3:16**.
2. Paul gave the same exhortation to the Ephesians, **Ephesians 5:19**.

3. When Christ met with His disciples and instituted the Lord's Supper, they sang together, **Matthew 26:30**.

C. God is to be formally worshipped by **PREACHING**.

1. God ordained preaching as His chief means of reaching the lost, **1 Corinthians 1:21**.

2. Paul preached to the assembled church at Troas, **Acts 20:7**.

3. Peter preached to the assembly at Jerusalem, **Acts 2:1-36**.

D. God is to be formally worshipped by **GIVING**

1. God commands believers to give regularly as they come together, **1 Corinthians 16:2**.

2. The giving of tithes and offerings is God's method of financing His work, **1 Corinthians 9:14** and **Nehemiah 13:10-12**.

3. Giving honors God, **Proverbs 3:9**.

E. God is to be formally worshipped with **THE LORD'S SUPPER**.

1. The Lord assembled the early church and instituted the Supper, **Matthew 26:26-29**.

2. The Supper points attention to Jesus, **1 Corinthians 11:23-32**.

3. The early churches at Jerusalem and Troas assembled and kept the Lord's Supper, **Acts 2:42**, **Acts 20:7**.

4. Apart from assembly by the members, it would be impossible to corporately worship God, **1 Corinthians 10:16-17**.

F. Formal, corporate worship in the church is not ambiguous. It consists of prayer, singing, preaching, giving and the Lord's Supper. Much else has been added, but these are the activities that count with God.

SECTION THREE

FOR GOD TO BE HONORED, WORSHIP MUST BE CONDUCTED IN SPIRIT AND IN TRUTH

A. In **John 4:23-24**, Jesus makes this unquestionably clear.

B. A right *"spirit"* means right motives and attitudes.

  1. If a man's attitude is unclean, selfish, cocky, proud and in any way fleshly, he cannot offer up acceptable worship to God, **Romans 8:8**.

  2. In order for worship to be acceptable to God, it must be offered out of a free heart of love for God, **1 Corinthians 13:1-3, 1 Corinthians 10:31**.

C. *"In spirit"* means worship must be according to God's prescribed plans.

  1. What *seems* right to man is not necessarily what pleases God, **Proverbs 14:12**.

  2. Since Adam, people have worshipped God in one way or another. Some worship He accepted and some He didn't.

     a. Consider Cain and Able, **Genesis 4:1-5**.

     b. Some men actually sacrificed their children in worship. However sincere they might have been, the practice was an abomination to God, **2 Kings 17:29-33**.

  3. God's object has not been merely to get men to worship Him. He wants men to worship Him in a right way, **1 Samuel 15:22**.

It is our conclusion that men ought to worship God in His church according to the truths He has set forth in His Word.

Chapter 40

Financing the Lord's Church

1 Corinthians 16:1-2

We believe that God's spiritual work is to be done by His church and His church is to be financed by the tithes and offerings of its members.

SECTION ONE

THE TITHE IS GOD'S BASIC WAY OF FINANCING HIS WORK

A. A tithe is defined in the dictionary as being one tenth. God expects a man to place one tenth of all his increases into the Lord's treasury.

    1. The Bible specifically commands believers to tithe.

        a. *"All the tithe of the land ... is the LORD's: it is holy unto the LORD ... the tenth shall be holy unto the LORD,"* **Leviticus 27:30-32.**

        b. *"Thou shalt truly tithe all the increase,"* **Deuteronomy 14:22.**

    2. The tithe is not limited to the children of Israel who were under Moses' Law.

      a. The tithe was instituted and practiced before Moses was born.

          (1) Jacob said to God, *"Of all that thou shalt give me I will surely give the tenth unto thee,"* **Genesis 28:22.**

          (2) As early as **Genesis 14:20**, the Bible says that Abraham paid tithes unto the Lord's priest. God was well pleased with the tithes of Abraham, **Hebrews 7:5-6, 8-9.**

          (3) Do not think that tithing originate only when God gave the Law.

      b. The tithe was practiced by those under the Law.

          (1) Tithing was a very important part of Moses' Law, **Leviticus 27:30-32.**

          (2) The Israelites practiced tithing, **Numbers 18:28, 2 Chronicles 31:5, 6, 12** and **Nehemiah 10:37-38.**

          (3) God's command to tithe is restated several times, **Deuteronomy 12:6, 11, Deuteronomy 14:22, 23, 28, Deuteronomy 26:12, Malachi 3:10.**

      c. The tithe is to be practiced after the Law.

          (1) Jesus told the Pharisees they ought not to leave off tithing, **Matthew 23:23** and **Luke 11:42.**

          (2) The type of giving being taught here was definitely proportionate. It could only be obeyed by the use of a percentage, **1 Corinthians 16:2.**

   3. The Lord expects believers to tithe. He said, *"Honour the LORD with thy substance, and with the firstfruits of all thine increase,"* **Proverbs 3:9.**

B. When God's people do not tithe, the work of God suffers.

   1. Nehemiah pointed out that when Israel failed to bring in the tithe, the Lord's work virtually came to a halt, **Nehemiah 13:10.**

a. When God's people neglect the tithe, the Lord's work always suffers.

   b. It is a modern reality that generally only a small percentage of the Lord's people support His work with their tithes. Undoubtedly if all of God's people tithed, His work would be far stronger with far greater outreach.

   2. *"They which preach the gospel should live of the gospel,"* can only be carried out when God's people practice God's method of finance, **1 Corinthians 9:13-14**.

C. God's anger is quickly aroused whenever His people do not tithe, and His work suffers.

   1. **Leviticus 27:30** says that the tithe is *"holy"* unto the Lord. **Proverbs 20:25** then says, *"It is a snare to the man who devoureth that which is holy."*

   2. **Malachi 3:8-9** calls neglecting to tithe robbery in the grossest sense.

   3. Tithing is the fairest, most equitable way of giving ever devised. When a man disregards tithing, he is disregarding God. God will hold him accountable for this failure.

SECTION TWO

GOD'S WORD ALSO TEACHES HOW TO TITHE

A. The tithe is to be placed into the Lord's central treasury.

   1. Abraham paid his tithe to the Lord's priest, **Genesis 14:19-20**.

   2. Israel brought the tithe to God's house, **2 Chronicles 31:5-10**.

   3. God told Israel to bring the tithe to the *"storehouse,"* **Malachi 3:10**.

   4. Paul said, *"lay by ... in store,"* **1 Corinthians 16:2**.

   5. Giving was to the church at Jerusalem, **Acts 5:1-10**.

6. The church has the charge today of carrying on God's spiritual work, **Matthew 28:19-20**. God wants glory to come to Him through His saints in church capacity, **Ephesians 3:21**.

7. Since the church today is the only institution God has on earth for carrying on His spiritual work, His treasury or storehouse today must of necessity be His church.

   a. His treasury is not your bank account or a TV/radio preacher.

   b. The tithe is to be placed in the Lord's church.

B. Tithing is to be done regularly.

1. The time to tithe is *"The first day of the week,"* **1 Corinthians 16:2**.

2. The tithe is due on *"all the increase,"* **Deuteronomy 14:22**, or *"as God hath prospered"* you, **1 Corinthians 16:2**.

3. The tithe is due in the Lord's house upon the next first day of the week after you have received the increase.

4. The tithe should be set aside first; not paid after all else is paid.

   a. **Proverbs 3:9** says we should give God *"the firstfruits of all thine increase."*

   b. **Leviticus 23:15-17** teaches giving of our first fruits unto God.

C. Tithing is to be done by all of God's people.

1. *"Let every one of you lay by him in store,"* **1 Corinthians 16:2**.

2. God never intended that only a few carry on His work while all the others enjoy the benefits. All should share.

3. God's plan is clear. If you have not been *"prospered"* or *"increased,"* then you don't give.

D. The tithe is to be given cheerfully; never grudgingly.

1. **2 Corinthians 9:7** says never give of duty or necessity.

2. Giving should always be joyful and liberal, **2 Corinthians 9:6** and **Proverbs 11:24-25**.

3. Those who give stingily and grudgingly to the Lord miss God's intent.

It is our firm conviction that tithing should be joyfully and enthusiastically practiced by every believer.

Chapter 41

The Treatment and Office of the Pastor of the Church

1 Timothy 3:1

We believe the office of *"Pastor"* to be a permanent office of the church of the Living God. We believe it is the highest office of the church, and that the office should be highly respected. Though he is not to be considered infallible or supernatural, a man who faithfully performs the responsibilities of a pastor is to be respected and honored above other men. We also believe it is a grave offense for anyone except he, who is the pastor, to attempt to perform the duties of the pastor.

We shall use the words pastor and bishop interchangeably. Although they do not originate from the same Greek word (poimen = pastor, shepherd and episkopos = bishop, overseer), the two words have very similar meanings. Sometimes the word minister, from the Greek word diakonos meaning servant, also refers to this special sanctified office.

SECTION ONE
CONCERNING PLACEMENT INTO THIS OFFICE

A. We believe a man should only enter the ministry if God wills it for his life.

The Treatment and Office of the Pastor of the Church

1. Though it is not His will for all, God does specifically will that some men take the oversight of His churches and serve as Pastors.

   a. He specifically commanded the Apostle Peter to *"Feed my sheep* (lambs),*"* **John 21:15-17.**

   b. **Acts 20:28** says that *"the Holy Ghost"* makes *"overseers"* of some men.

   c. Though the gospel ministry was not God's will for Cornelius, **Acts 10**, Aquila, **Acts 18:26**, or the Philippian jailor, **Acts 16:33**, it was His will for the apostle Paul who said, *"And I thank Christ Jesus our Lord, who hath enabled me, for that he counted me faithful, putting me into the ministry,"* **1 Timothy 1:12.**

   d. **Colossians 4:17** indicates this ministry was not a self-willed matter, but rather God's will for Archippus. Paul told him, *"Take heed to the ministry which thou hast received in the Lord, that thou fulfil it."*

2. We believe God will reveal His will to those whom He selects to be in the ministry.

   a. This chapter does not address in detail how a man is called into the ministry, but we believe that God can make His call clear to a saved man who is fully yielded to Him. One of His avenues is providence, which is always in harmony with His written Word.

   b. The number one act of God is to put an unquestionable desire in the heart of a man that He calls to be a Pastor. God does this through providence.

      (1) Paul referred to this when he said, *"This is a true saying, If a man desire the office of a bishop, he desireth a good work,"* **1 Timothy 3:1.**

      (2) Jeremiah, who is an Old Testament type of a God chosen minister, illustrates this inescapable burden and desire of the heart by saying, *"Then I said, I will not make mention of him, nor speak any more in his name. But his word was in mine heart as a burning fire shut up in*

my bones, and I was weary with forbearing, and I could not stay," **Jeremiah 20:9**.

    c. The working of God through providence is not merely strange occurrences such as cloud formations, which seem to spell "G.P." (interpreted by some to mean "Go Preach"), nor imagined voices in the night saying, "Preach."

        (1) Providence is the opening or closing of doors of opportunity for you. Paul spoke of this Godly working in **1 Corinthians 16:9, 2 Corinthians 2:12** and **Colossians 4:3**.

        (2) God speaks of this process, *"I have set before thee an open door, and no man can shut it,"* **Revelation 3:8**.

        (3) The divine will of God is largely brought about by the fact that *"things work together for good to them that love God."* **Romans 8:28**.

3. Those who have entered the ministry because they have perceived that it is God's will for their lives are the ones we consider God-called. Not in some strange mysterious way, but in the clear-cut, spiritual sense as explained above that God calls men into the gospel ministry. Only those who are sure it is God's will for them should enter the ministry. All who recognize His call should obey it.

B. We believe that men who do not meet His qualifications should not enter the gospel ministry.

  1. The qualifications are clearly set forth in God's Word.

    a. A minister must have a good testimony before unconverted men, **1 Timothy 3:7**.

    b. A minister must be blameless (not sinless) as a steward of God.

        (1) This includes money, time, talents, conduct and much more, **Titus 1:7-10**.

        (2) A minister must not misuse God's Word, **2 Corinthians 4:1-2**.

> (3) A minister's life must not be a reproach to the ministry, **2 Corinthians 6:3-4**.
>
> c. A minister must be a provider of things honestly.
>
> > (1) He must be honest in the sight of God and man, **2 Corinthians 8:21**. The Bible takes the position that a man who is dishonest with God will automatically be dishonest with other men. Likewise men who are dishonest with other men will be dishonest with God.
> >
> > (2) A minister must think honestly, **Philippians 4:8**, walk honestly, **Romans 13:13**, provide honestly, **Romans 12:17**, speak honestly, **1 Peter 2:12**, and be generally honest.
>
> d. He must also be willing to endure afflictions, **2 Corinthians 6:4-10**.

2. Women cannot legitimately be ministers. They are told to keep silent in the church, **1 Timothy 2:12**, and to *"learn in silence with all subjection,"* **1 Timothy 2:11**.

3. God expressed His will for ministers in His written Word God.

   a. We do not believe that the will of God is ever in contradiction. He is not fickle and does not contradict Himself. His standards as seen in the Bible are still His standards.

   b. In His Word, God has spoken on issues such as women in the ministry, ministers with two or more living wives, ministers of poor character and other matters that have become modern controversies. We do not believe over time and because of cultural changes that God has changed His standards on anything including qualifications for ministers.

   c. Those in the ministry who do not meet God's qualifications are there by their own will, not God's.

C. We believe those who surrender to God's call to the ministry should be ordained by a church.

1. Ordination of overseers was the practice in Bible days.

    a. *"For this cause left I thee in Crete, that thou shouldest set in order the things that are wanting, and ordain elders in every city, as I had appointed thee,"* **Titus 1:5.**

    b. Paul and Barnabas did it. *"And when they had ordained them elders in every church, and had prayed with fasting, they commended them to the Lord, on whom they believed,"* **Acts 14:23.**

2. The practice of *the laying on of hands* at present day ordinations does not confer the gifts of the spirit as it did when the Apostles laid on the hands, **1 Timothy 4:14, 2 Timothy 1:6.** It does symbolize the sanctity and gravity of the office of a bishop or minister. (Only the Apostles confer spiritual gifts; however, men other than the Apostles *laid hands* on men they ordained into the gospel ministry. Timothy is a case in point, **1 Timothy 5:22.** He conferred no gift, but he did confirm the gravity of ordination into the ministry. We thus believe that the symbolic *laying on of the hands* is appropriate at current ordinations.

3. No church should ordain anyone into the ministry without exercising extreme caution. Paul cautioned, *"Lay hands suddenly on no man,"* **1 Timothy 5:22.**

SECTION TWO

THE HIGH OFFICE AND RESPONSIBILITY OF THE PASTOR OF THE CHURCH

A. The office of pastor is an office over the whole church.

1. It is the pastor whom God first holds accountable for the beliefs and practices of the church.

    a. It is common for pastors to blame deacons and other church members for carnality, apathy, lack of concern and other deterioration in the church. Others may indeed be a part of the problem, but it is to commit the sin of Pilate for a pastor to consider himself unaccountable and guiltless in the matter, **Matthew 27:24.**

b. The pastor is the overseer, the person whom God first and directly expects to take the initiative and leadership to correct whatever danger might threaten the church. When a church fails, the finger must first point to the pastor. He is God's man responsible for leading the church to victory. Others may be implicated, but the pastor has the greatest accountability.

2. The Scriptures are clear on pastoral accountability.

   a. The pastor is called *"overseer,"* **Acts 20:28**. He is not a self-made overseer; he was made an overseer by *"The Holy Ghost."* Consider again **1 Timothy 1:12** and **Colossians 4:17**.

   b. Six times the New Testament refers to the pastor as bishop or bishops, which also means superintendent as well as overseer. See **1 Timothy 3:1-2, Titus 1:7**, and **Philippians 1:1**.

   c. Paul specifically declared this truth, *"And we beseech you, brethren, to know them which labour among you, and are over you in the Lord, and admonish you,"* **1 Thessalonians 5:12**.

   d. God even assigned the pastor the responsibility of rebuking, exhorting, and correcting.

      (1) Read **2 Timothy 3:16 - 2 Timothy 4:2** where this strong authority is given.

      (2) If he deems it in the best interest of the work of the church, the pastor has the God given authority to rebuke a transgressor openly, **1 Timothy 5:19-21**.

3. Attempts at oversight by those who are not pastors constitute a very serious offense against God and against the office of the pastor.

   a. The inspired Word of God tells the church, *"Obey them that have the rule over you, and submit yourselves: for they watch for your souls, as they that must give account, that they may do it with joy, and not with grief,"* **Hebrews 13:17**.

b. **1 Timothy 5:17** refers to *"the elders that rule"* and **Hebrews 13:7** says, *"Remember them which have the rule over you, who have spoken unto you the word of God."* These Scriptures speak of pastors for they are the ones who speak the Word of God to the churches.

c. In many churches, an older or charter member, someone who is bold and speaks in a domineering way, the deacons, someone with lots of money or a *busybody* is the real overseer of the church. They *run the show* and it is their leadership which prevails. What a violation of scriptural policy! The pastor is to be the overseer or leader.

d. Two Old Testament examples foreshadow the terrible sin of inserting yourself into an office which is not yours. These examples are great warnings to those who would illegitimately intrude into the oversight of a church.

   (1) Consider **Numbers 16:35**. Korah and a large group of Israelite followers who were already Levites and active in God's service, **verse 9**, thought God's priests (Moses and Aaron who foreshadow pastors) had too much authority, **verse 3**. Korah and his followers thought they should have just as much to say in matters as these priests, **verse 10**. God was so vexed with them that He threatened to destroy the whole congregation, **verse 21**. He did destroy the leaders of this effort to usurp authority by swallowing them up in a great hole in the ground, **verse 31-35**. (It is note-worthy that the Holy Spirit pointed out that this case does have present-day application, **Jude 11**.)

   (2) Consider how God was displeased with King Saul who intruded into the priest's office. Even a king had no business in that office, **1 Samuel 13:1-13**. This case also foreshadows the pastoral office.

B. The office of pastor carries great responsibilities.

   1. As already indicated, the pastor has the oversight of the whole church.

- a. He is the one who is to look ahead, plan and lead for the well-being of the whole church.
- b. He has the responsibility of seeing that people are visited, the music is right, widows and orphans receive proper care, the church has a competent teaching ministry, carnality and dissension are kept down, the church is reputable in its dealings and that a host of other responsibilities are properly attended.

2. A pastor's chief responsibility is to administer God's Word.
   - a. Jesus told his minister, Peter to *"Feed my sheep (lambs),"* **John 21:15-17**.
   - b. Paul told pastors to *"Take heed therefore unto yourselves, and to all the flock, over the which the Holy Ghost hath made you overseers, to feed the church of God, which he hath purchased with his own blood,"* **Acts 20:28**.
   - c. The number one charge to the young preacher Timothy was *"Preach the word; be instant in season, out of season; reprove, rebuke, exhort with all longsuffering and doctrine,"* **2 Timothy 4:2**.
   - d. The Spirit's commission to pastors through Paul is *"If thou put the brethren in remembrance of these things, thou shalt be a good minister of Jesus Christ, nourished up in the words of faith and of good doctrine, whereunto thou hast attained,"* **1 Timothy 4:6**.

3. Though the pastor has the oversight of the church, he is not to do the entire work of the church singlehandedly. The church is a spiritual *body*, and every member of the body should seriously contribute to the welfare of the whole.
   - a. The Bible teaches that every member should share in accomplishing the work.
     - **(1) Ephesians 4:16** speaks of *"the whole body fitly joined together and compacted by that which every joint supplieth, according to the effectual working in the measure of every part, maketh increase of the body unto the edifying of itself in love."*

        (2) **1 Corinthians 12:14-22** ends by saying all the members are *"necessary."*

  b. It is a full time job to keep the church healthy by overseeing and directing of the work of the church.

        (1) This is illustrated in **Numbers 16:1-10**. Though Moses and Aaron were responsible for all that went on in Israel, they did not actually do every task. Instead, they set up certain Levites to care for the various works: the sacrifices, the offerings, the moving of the tabernacle and its furniture plus much more.

        (2) The Apostles emphasized this truth was in effect by saying, *"It is not reason that we should leave the word of God, and serve tables,"* **Acts 6:2**.

  c. Too many times pastors become so burdened down with the work of the church that they cannot get nearly all of it done.

        (1) This is sometimes because other members will not help, but often it is because the pastor shirks his responsibility to offer pastoral leadership. His lack of leadership allows problems to grow, which can cause breakdowns in the church. Too many pastors are excessively passive and reactive.

        (2) **Exodus 17:8-12** illustrates how other workers should hold up the hands of the pastor by sharing and supporting the work.

SECTION THREE

A MAN WHO FAITHFULLY PERFORMS THE OFFICE OF PASTOR IS TO BE HIGHLY RESPECTED AND HONORED

A. He should be treated as one with authority.

  1. God's Word teaches members of a church to be in subjection unto him. *"Remember them which have the rule over you, who have* spoken unto you the word of God: whose faith follow, considering the end of their conversation," **Hebrews 13:7**.

    2. "Obey them that have the rule over you, and submit yourselves," **Hebrews 13:17**.

B. He should be highly respected.

    1. Keep in mind that he has the charge and responsibilities of holy, divine things. *"Let a man so account of us, as of the ministers of Christ, and stewards of the mysteries of God,"* **1 Corinthians 4:1**.

    2. The Holy Spirit inspired Paul to say, *"Let the elders that rule well be counted worthy of double honour, especially they who labour in the word and doctrine,"* **1 Timothy 5:17**. Double means twice.

    3. Listen to Paul's admonition about how church members should feel about their pastor. *"And we beseech you, brethren, to know them which labour among you, and are over you in the Lord, and admonish you; And to esteem them very highly in love for their work's sake,"* **1 Thessalonians 5:12-13**.

    4. God's people should be cautious with the fine line between familiarity and disrespect.

C. A pastor should be fully financially cared for by the church.

    1. When Paul used the word *"communicate,"* he spoke of financial support. *"Let him that is taught in the word communicate unto him that teacheth in all good things,"* **Galatians 6:6**.

    2. The Bible states, *"the workman is worthy of his meat,"* **Matthew 10:10**, and **1 Timothy 5:17-18** says a pastor is worthy of *"double"* honor. That seems to include material help.

    3. **1 Corinthians 9:13-14** draws an analogy between pastors and Old Testament priests. Those priests were supported by the tithes and offerings of the people. Likewise, God's pastors are to be supported by the tithes and offerings of the people.

    4. **Nehemiah 13:10-11** makes it very clear that God is highly displeased when His overseers are not financially supported.

Chapter 42

The Testimony Shown by the Lord's Supper

1 Corinthians 11:20-34

We believe that the Lord's Supper is one of the sacred ordinances of the church, by which His finished work on Calvary is portrayed. This chapter is a general look at some of the specific points regarding the Lord's Supper.

SECTION ONE

THE LORD'S SUPPER IS A PICTURE OF THE DEATH OF CHRIST

A. It is beyond dispute that the Lord's Supper shows the death of Christ. **1 Corinthians 11:26** says, *"As often as ye eat this bread, and drink this cup, ye do shew the Lord's death till he come."*

B. The bread is symbolic, representative and a reminder of the body of Christ that was broken for us.

   1. The Bible emphasizes the fact that He was bodily broken for us.

   a. He bore our sins in His body on the tree, **1 Peter 2:24**.

spoken unto you the word of God: whose faith follow, considering the end of their conversation," **Hebrews 13:7**.

2. *"Obey them that have the rule over you, and submit yourselves,"* **Hebrews 13:17**.

B. He should be highly respected.

1. Keep in mind that he has the charge and responsibilities of holy, divine things. *"Let a man so account of us, as of the ministers of Christ, and stewards of the mysteries of God,"* **1 Corinthians 4:1**.

2. The Holy Spirit inspired Paul to say, *"Let the elders that rule well be counted worthy of double honour, especially they who labour in the word and doctrine,"* **1 Timothy 5:17**. Double means twice.

3. Listen to Paul's admonition about how church members should feel about their pastor. *"And we beseech you, brethren, to know them which labour among you, and are over you in the Lord, and admonish you; And to esteem them very highly in love for their work's sake,"* **1 Thessalonians 5:12-13**.

4. God's people should be cautious with the fine line between familiarity and disrespect.

C. A pastor should be fully financially cared for by the church.

1. When Paul used the word *"communicate,"* he spoke of financial support. *"Let him that is taught in the word communicate unto him that teacheth in all good things,"* **Galatians 6:6**.

2. The Bible states, *"the workman is worthy of his meat,"* **Matthew 10:10**, and **1 Timothy 5:17-18** says a pastor is worthy of *"double"* honor. That seems to include material help.

3. **1 Corinthians 9:13-14** draws an analogy between pastors and Old Testament priests. Those priests were supported by the tithes and offerings of the people. Likewise, God's pastors are to be supported by the tithes and offerings of the people.

4. **Nehemiah 13:10-11** makes it very clear that God is highly displeased when His overseers are not financially supported.

Chapter 42

The Testimony Shown by the Lord's Supper

1 Corinthians 11:20-34

We believe that the Lord's Supper is one of the sacred ordinances of the church, by which His finished work on Calvary is portrayed. This chapter is a general look at some of the specific points regarding the Lord's Supper.

SECTION ONE

THE LORD'S SUPPER IS A PICTURE OF THE DEATH OF CHRIST

A. It is beyond dispute that the Lord's Supper shows the death of Christ. **1 Corinthians 11:26** says, *"As often as ye eat this bread, and drink this cup, ye do shew the Lord's death till he come."*

B. The bread is symbolic, representative and a reminder of the body of Christ that was broken for us.

  1. The Bible emphasizes the fact that He was bodily broken for us.

   a. He bore our sins in His body on the tree, **1 Peter 2:24**.

The Testimony Shown by the Lord's Supper

   b. **Matthew 27** and **Luke 23** describe how they broke Him bodily.

   c. **Isaiah 53** is an extremely vivid description of His sacrifice on our behalf. Especially note **verse 5**.

2. Every time the bread of the Lord's Supper is taken, it stands as a reminder and testimony of Christ's broken body.

   a. Paul quoted Christ, *"The Lord Jesus the same night in which he was betrayed took bread: And when he had given thanks, he brake it, and said, Take, eat: this is my body, which is broken for you: this do in remembrance of me,"* **1 Corinthians 11:23-24**.

   b. **Matthew 26:26, Mark 14:22, Luke 22:19** all record the very words of Christ regarding the Lord's Supper bread.

   c. Every taking of the Lord's Supper bread is a reminder of Christ's awful suffering.

3. The wine is symbolic, representative and a reminder of Christ's shed blood.

   a. His blood was shed, **John 19:34,** for us, **1 Peter 2:24**.

   b. *"Neither by the blood of goats and calves, but by his own blood he entered in once into the holy place, having obtained eternal redemption for us,"* **Hebrews 9:12**.

   c. Paul said, *"He took the cup, when he had supped, saying, This cup is the new testament in my blood: this do ye, as oft as ye drink it, in remembrance of me,"* **1 Corinthians 11:25**.

   d. **Matthew 26:27-28, Mark 14:23-24, Luke 22:20** all prove this truth.

4. The breaking of His body and the shedding of His blood are the two elements that brought about His death for us.

5. The bread and wine symbolize the body and blood of Christ. They are not literally the body and blood of Christ.

   a. As **1 Corinthians 11:26** says, the bread and wine *"Do shew the Lord's death."* They typify, symbolize and represent His death.

b. Some who heard Him speak of eating His broken body and drinking His shed blood, misunderstood His words to mean literal eating of His flesh and blood, **John 6:51-53**. He immediately corrected them by saying, *"The words that I speak unto you, they are spirit, and they are life,"* **John 6:63**.

c. It is not true that in taking the Lord's Supper (communion) one literally eats the flesh and drinks the blood of Christ and in so-doing appropriates salvation. Salvation comes by believing the truth (words) pertaining to Christ and His sacrifice of Himself for sinners, **John 3:36**.

SECTION TWO

THE LORD'S SUPPER ALSO TESTIFIES OF THE PRESENT PRIESTLY WORK OF CHRIST FOR BELIEVERS AND OF THE BELIEVER'S FELLOWSHIP WITH HIM

A. The believer is reminded that this memorial is *"in remembrance of me,"* **1 Corinthians 11:24**.

B. In connection with remembrance of Him at the Lord's Supper, believers are to carefully examine their hearts. They are to make sure their hearts are right with God.

1. This is clearly stated in **1 Corinthians 11:27-28** and **31-32**.

2. The only way that a believer can get his heart right with God is through repentant confession to God, **1 John 1:8-9**.

3. Believers have this right only through Him who is their High Priest, **Hebrews 4:14-16**.

4. Whenever believers confess their sins, they have fellowship, concord or communion with the Lord. They can then honestly typify that communion by the Lord's Supper.

C. Before each Lord's Supper, believers are commanded to *"examine"* themselves. They are thus reminded of Christ who is their High Priest.

SECTION THREE

THE LORD'S SUPPER IS A TESTIMONIAL TO THE RETURN OF CHRIST

A. Paul said we are to take this Lord's Supper *"till he come,"* **1 Corinthians 11:26.**

    1. That statement is based on the foregone conclusion that He is coming again.

    2. Jesus said believers will not forever take the Lord's Supper in absenteeism from Him. He announced that at some point in the future the saints and the Lord will be united and take the Lord's Supper together, **Matthew 26:29.**

B. Of course, we know, too, from many other passages, of His return is a certainty.

    1. Jesus personally announced His return, **John 14:1-3.**

    2. **1 Thessalonians 4:13-17** is a detailed account of His return.

C. Every time you eat the Lord's Supper, it should remind you that things will not always continue as they are now.

    1. One day we shall be delivered from this troublesome, sinful life, **Romans 8:23.**

    2. The One who died for us will return for us.

SECTION FOUR

IN VIEW OF THE GREAT TRUTHS AT HAND, A SACRED ATMOSPHERE SHOULD PREVAIL EACH TIME THE LORD'S SUPPER IS TAKEN

A. There should never be a disrespectful, irreverent atmosphere at the Lord's Supper.

    1. When a common meal approach was taken by the Corinthians, Paul soundly rebuked them, **1 Corinthians 11:20-22, 34.**

2. Talking, passing notes, shifting around noisily, walking in and out while the Lord's Supper is in progress are disgraceful to the Lord's table.

B. Every Lord's Supper should be a holy, heart-breaking reminder of Christ's supreme sacrifice.

1. In **1 Corinthians 11:23-33**, Paul emphasized the sacredness of this event.

2. Who could question the seriousness of the occasion which is recorded in **Matthew 26:26-30**?

SECTION FIVE

THE LORD'S SUPPER IS TO BE OBSERVED WEEKLY

A. Worship is to be done on the first day of the week when the church comes together.

1. Jesus arose from the dead on the first day of the week, **John 20:19** and **Luke 24:1-6**.

2. The early Christians met to worship on the first day of the week, **1 Corinthians 16:2, Acts 20:7**.

B. It is almost universally accepted that **1 Corinthians 16:2** teaches that giving is to be done on the first day of *every* week. In order to be consistent in our interpretation of Scripture, we must interpret **Acts 20:7** to mean the Lord's Supper is to be taken on the first day of *every* week. The wording is identical in both texts.

1. It should be noted from **1 Corinthians** that only the breaking of physical bread, which is to be done in worship, is part of the Lord's Supper.

2. Also, note that **Acts 20:7** is not talking about the breaking spiritual bread (preaching or teaching). The verse already mentions *preaching*. The breaking of bread on this occasion was different from the preaching.

C. The argument that weekly observance of the Lord's Supper will lead to a lack of appreciation for the Lord's Supper is neither scriptural nor reasonable.

1. There simply is no Bible evidence to support such a contention.

2. Furthermore, if weekly observance of the Lord's Supper will make it become humdrum and ritualistic to the participants, then weekly preaching, praying, singing and giving must also make them humdrum and ritualistic to the participants. If the Lord's Supper should only be observed monthly, quarterly, or yearly, then so should these. The argument that weekly observance of the Lord's Supper will cause participants to lose appreciation for it is not valid.

D. Weekly observance is designed to build an ever greater realization and appreciation of the great truths of Jesus' great sacrifice for sinners. There is Bible evidence for weekly observance; there is none for any other frequency.

SECTION SIX

BELIEVERS ARE TO ALWAYS CONFESS THEIR SINS BEFORE PARTAKING OF THE LORD'S SUPPER

A. This is clearly set forth in **1 Corinthians 11:27-28**.

B. Confession produces a clean heart, **1 John 1:9**, which is the thing God wants from each of us, **2 Timothy 2:19-22**. True, repentant confession is the only way to fellowship with Him, **1 John 1:7**.

C. God has instituted weekly communion (Lord's Supper) as a safeguard. Failure to face our sins and confess them to God before taking the Lord's Supper can be disastrous. For this failure, some of the believers in the church in Corinth became very sick and others died, **1 Corinthians 11:27-30**. The Lord's Supper keeps us from ignoring the sins in our lives; it puts us on the spot to get right with God.

Chapter 43

Why We Use Wine in the Lord's Supper

1 Corinthians 11:20-34

We believe wine is to be used in the observance of the Lord's Supper. Although there is more evidence to support the validity of this position than will be offered here, there are three simple Bible reasons why we believe wine is the correct drink to be used in the Lord's Supper.

SECTION ONE

WHEN CHRIST INSTITUTED THE LORD'S SUPPER, HE USED WINE

A. The Bible teaches we should follow Christ's example.

   1. **1 Peter 2:21** teaches us to follow in His steps.

   2. **Luke 9:23** teaches us to follow Him.

B. In our observances of the Lord's Supper, it is scriptural to use the same drink Jesus used.

C. It is a fact that Christ used the same ingredients to institute the Lord's Supper that had been used for centuries in observing the Passover.

1. On the night Jesus initiated the Lord's Supper, He and His Apostles came together specifically to eat the Passover, **Matthew 26:17**. At the beginning of their meeting, they observed the Passover, **Matthew 26:19-21**.

2. Matthew 26:26 says that *"as they were eating,"* Jesus instituted a new order, which was a memorial feast called *"The Lord's Supper."*

3. Note well that the same food and beverage that had been used in the Passover were used in the Lord's Supper. For Christians today who observe the Lord's Supper, nothing could be more scriptural than to use the same food and beverage Jesus used, **Matthew 26:26-27**.

D. Wine and unleavened bread were always used in the Passover.

1. When the Passover originated in Egypt, God commanded His people to prepare for it using *"only"* unleavened foods and beverages, **Exodus 12:18-20**. Leaven is symbolic of sin, which is why it is not used in the Passover.

2. God told them to remember the Passover by keeping an annual memorial feast, **Exodus 12:18-24**.

3. This feast became known as *"the feast of unleavened bread,"* **Leviticus 23:5-8**.

4. During this feast, all leaven was to be put off them personally, **Exodus 13:7**; even out of their dwelling places, **Exodus 12:15, 19**.

5. Wine is the only unleavened state of the fruit of the vine. Thus when Christ observed the Passover and during the institution of the Lord's Supper, it is not difficult to see that He used unleavened bread and wine. That's what Jews had been doing since Moses. For them to have used leavened food or drink would have been a direct violation of the Law of Moses.

   a. Grape juice (the ingredient used by many today) is full of leaven. The impurities and leaven are only removed by the process of fermentation.

    b. For centuries B.C., during Christ's day and currently, orthodox Jews always use wine when they keep the Passover.

    c. Had Christ not used this God-ordained ingredient, He would have violated Jewish tradition and God's mandate on the subject.

    d. Failure to see what Jesus used in the cup is to ignore the evidence.

E. Since we believe Christ used wine when He instituted the Lord's Supper, we believe that we too must use wine when we observe the Lord's Supper.

SECTION TWO

WHEN EARLY BIBLE CHURCHES OBSERVED THE LORD'S SUPPER, THEY USED WINE

A. The question arises, "Did the Bible day churches practice using wine in their observance of the Lord's Supper?"

  1. There is one Bible case that mentions the beverage the church used in its observance of the Lord's Supper cup. The church was in Corinth, **1 Corinthians 11:20-34**.

    a. Notice that this church assembled and made a common meal of the Lord's Supper ingredients, **verse 20**.

    b. Paul reprimanded them for this and told them to eat common meals at home, **verse 34**. He also instructed them as to how to properly observe the Lord's Supper.

    c. Bear in mind that Paul did not reprimand them for the ingredients being used, but rather for the way they were using them.

    d. Note well that the beverage they were using in the cup was capable of making them *"drunken,"* **verse 21**. Grape juice will not make one *"drunken."*

  2. It is noteworthy that the pages of history on the subject of the Lord's Supper always record early churches using wine. For the most part, wine in the Lord's Supper cup was standard practice in churches prior to the Temperance Movement of the 19th and 20th centuries.

B. We believe we should follow Christ's example, and we also believe the favorable examples of early churches are precedents we should follow.

   1. Timothy was to be an example, **1 Timothy 4:12**.
   2. Early Israel was an example, **1 Corinthians 10:6**.
   3. The Thessalonians serve as examples for us, **1 Thessalonians 1:7**.
   4. The Bible can teach by commandment or example.

SECTION THREE

ONLY WINE CAN ACCURATELY CONVEY THE TRUTHS OF THE LORD'S SUPPER

A. The cup represents Jesus' blood, **1 Corinthians 11:25, Matthew 26:27-28**.

B. Jesus' blood was perfect, without blemish or spot, **1 Peter 1:19**.

C. Scientifically, grape juice is a mass of impurities. Only through fermentation does it purge itself and throw off the impurities. That which is left after fermentation removes the impurities is called wine, or *"the pure blood of the grape,"* **Deuteronomy 32:14**. Wine above the purged impurities is called *"wines on the lees,"* **Isaiah 25:6**. The truth of these points can be proven by a simple household chemical experiment of uncooked grape juice. Squeeze the grapes and leave it unrefrigerated for a few days. The process of fermentation will manifest itself and wine on the lees will appear. If the wine is not quickly separated from the lees, the whole product will sour.

D. Why should we use such an impure ingredient as grape juice to represent the blood of Jesus? Why not use the pure state of the fruit of the vine?

E. We believe the pure fruit of the vine should be used to represent the pure blood of the Lamb.

Chapter 44

God's Call for Unity in the Church Demands Closed Communion

1 Corinthians 10:16-17

The body of Christ is the church, and the church is a local assembly of baptized believers. The *church* is not a mystical, universal entity made up of all saved people. When the church is told to take the bread, it is a local assembly or church that is to do it. The scriptural semblance and significance of the Lord's Supper is destroyed if members of two or more bodies jointly participate in the Lord's Supper.

This chapter is intended to show the picture of unity that is inherent in the Lord's Supper. It will also show why only closed communion can properly paint that picture.

SECTION ONE

THE FALSE ASSUMPTION OF OPEN COMMUNION

A. Open communion is the idea that the Lord's Supper should always be open to all saved people.

1. This means a person who claims to be saved should be allowed to take the Lord's Supper with any congregation regardless of local church status or denomination.

2. This position also means that people who claim to be saved but who have not experienced a valid water baptism should be allowed to partake of the Lord's Supper. The argument is that they have been *Spirit baptized* and are thus in the *true church*.

B. Most who embrace the universal church concept find closed communion to be very offensive.

1. They see *being saved* and *being a member of the church* as one and the same. They conclude that a church which excludes all but its members from the Lord's Supper is judging all others to be unsaved.

2. That contention is not true.

   a. When a church practices closed communion, it says nothing about the salvation of others. It simply says other people are not members of that particular church or body.

   b. Being saved and being a member of the church are not one and the same. A person can be saved and not a member of any church.

   c. If all believers did constitute one giant church or body of Christ, then all believers could jointly take of the Lord's Supper without violating the sense of the Scriptures; however, all believers do not constitute one giant universal church.

C. To be honest and consistent, those who advocate open communion must also accept all types of water baptisms to be valid, like immersion, pouring and sprinkling by any authority.

1. The baptism may be by a Baptist, a Catholic, a Presbyterian, a Jehovah's Witness or an individual with no church authority. According to the universal church position, all who claim to be saved have been *spirit baptized* into the true

universal church. In their minds, authority to administer the ordinances of communion and baptism does not come from a local assembly; it automatically comes by being a part of the universal church.

2. The argument for a universal church and open communion is that at faith a spiritual *baptism of the Holy Ghost* makes a person a member of the one *true church* (universal). That *spirit baptism* into the *true church* makes that person eligible to jointly take of the Lord's Supper with all other believers. Membership in the assembly where the Lord's Supper is served in not necessary. In fact, membership in any local assembly is not necessary. If the argument is valid, then that person (Methodist, Catholic, Pentecostal, etc.) can come together with any local assembly and have full participation in the assembly's affairs. Without a valid water baptism or membership in the local assembly, a total stranger who claimed to be saved could vote on a pastor or budget, serve in any office of the church and participate in all church affairs. According to this theory, denying a person such participation would be an accusation that he was not saved. Such a charge is simply unfounded, but that can be said only because each church is a local, indigenous assembly with the authority and responsibility to attend its own affairs, including communion and baptism.

3. The logical end of this whole line of unscriptural thinking is ecumenical inter-denominationalism. Those who embrace one part of the ecumenical stance must embrace all of it. It is self-contradictory to practice an open stance on communion and baptism while practicing a closed stance on other church affairs.

SECTION TWO

THE LORD'S SUPPER IS AN EXPRESSION OF UNITY IN THE CHURCH

A. **Ephesians 4:3-6** is an excellent testimonial of the unity that should be known and existing in the Lord's churches.

1. Notice that *"one body"* is being addressed, **verse 4**. The *"body"* is a local church. See the chapter: *The Church of Christ and the Body of Christ Are the Same.*

2. According to **verse 3**, the *"body"* is to always endeavor to keep a very high degree of unity.

3. Members are to bear in mind that they are *one body*. They are not to forget that they all believe in one Lord, exercise one faith, were baptized by one baptism and are kept by one Spirit, while serving one God.

4. Each church should shine as an example of the unity that runs through the whole system of spiritual things.

B. **1 Corinthians 10:16-17** shows that this unity is expressed when the body observes the Lord's Supper.

1. Note well that Paul said that many members may partake of the bread, but only *"one body"* is involved, **verse 17**. The body always refers to a local church; in this case to the one in Corinth, **1 Corinthians 1:2**.

2. In observing the Lord's Supper, the church testifies of communion both with Christ and with each other.

C. The church in Jerusalem serves as an illustration of this principle.

1. **Acts 1:14** says they *"all continued with one accord."*

2. **Acts 2:1** says, *"They were all with one accord in one place."*

3. **Acts 2:46** shows them continuing *"daily with one accord in the temple."*

4. And notice from **Acts 2:42** that all this was done in connection with *"breaking of bread."*

D. The observance of the Lord's Supper by a church is a great testimonial.

1. It's a testimonial to the death of Christ.

2. It is also a testimonial of the unity of the church and the faith.

3. Furthermore it testifies that the members of the church are in unity with each other and with the Lord.

SECTION THREE

THIS PICTURE OF UNITY CAN ONLY EXIST WHERE MEMBERS OF THE SAME BODY JOINTLY PARTAKE OF THE LORD'S SUPPER

A. When members of two or more bodies or churches jointly take the Lord's Supper, the picture of one unified body or church is not possible.

   1. Instead of there being *"one body"* as both **1 Corinthians 10:17** and **Ephesians 4:4** testify, there are two or more *bodies*.
   2. **1 Corinthians 10:17** said, *"For we being many are one bread, and one body."* It does not say we are *many bodies*.
   3. It would be impossible for the kind of *"communion,"* of which **1 Corinthians 10:16-17** speaks to exist among members of two or more bodies or churches.
      a. They have not all been baptized into the same body, **1 Corinthians 12:13**.
      b. They are not members of the same body, and thus are not able to function or suffer together, **1 Corinthians 12:14-31**.
   4. If members of one body partake of the Lord's Supper with members of another body, the picture of unity for which the Lord's Supper stands is simply not there. The same is true when members of one church invite members of another church to take the Lord's Supper with them.

B. Furthermore, God's requirements for church purity and discipline prior to the Lord's Supper are impossible except for local churches.

   1. Every organization which proposes to work smoothly yet efficiently must have certain rules and regulations to be followed. It must also have the authority to enforce those rules.

2. God gave responsibility and authority to His churches to keep themselves pure.

   a. **Matthew 18:17** talks about bringing an unrepentant sinning brother before the church.

   b. *"Now we command you, brethren, in the name of our Lord Jesus Christ, that ye withdraw yourselves from every brother that walketh disorderly, and not after the tradition which he received of us,"* **2 Thessalonians 3:6**.

   c. The Bible teaches, *"A man that is an heretick after the first and second admonition reject,"* **Titus 3:10**.

   d. *"For the time is come that judgment must begin at the house of God,"* **1 Peter 4:17**.

   e. Listen to the lengthy discussion of this matter in **1 Corinthians 5:9-13**.

3. It is clear that a church has the responsibility of enforcing certain standards of conduct among the membership.

   a. Particularly note **1 Corinthians 5:12** which says, *"judge them that are within."*

   b. Almost all thinking people recognize and admit that only a local assembly is capable of this responsibility.

4. This enforcing of godly standards by the local church is essential to maintaining the unity with which the church is to take the Lord's Supper.

   a. Paul made this point to the Corinthians, *"Ye cannot drink the cup of the Lord, and the cup of devils: ye cannot be partakers of the Lord's table, and of the table of devils,"* **1 Corinthians 10:21**.

   b. The church is told *"not to eat"* with those in such rebellion against God, **1 Corinthians 5:11**.

5. Such exhortations as these can only be carried out by those practicing closed communion.

a. Those who advocate open communion have no way of bringing non-member participants into judgment before the church. Churches have jurisdiction only over their own members. Long ago, most churches rejected and deserted the Bible's teachings on church discipline.

b. Unrepentant church members who take the Lord's Supper heap damnation upon themselves, **1 Corinthians 11:29**.

c. Each local church can discipline its own wayward members, and thereby be in a position to observe the Lord's Supper. No church has jurisdiction over these who are not members, and it does not have the right to serve the Lord's Supper to them.

There is more to be said on this issue, but already the picture takes shape. The arguments for open communion crumble under the light of God's Word. If there is no universal church, then all believers cannot be a part of it. It is impossible to be a part of something that doesn't exist. If the Scriptures do not teach a universal church, then the only kind of church that exists is a local, visible church. When the church assembles to take the Lord's Supper, vote, baptize, ordain or attend other church business, it is the members of that church which must do it.

Chapter 45

The Church of Christ and the Body of Christ Are the Same

Colossians 1:18, 24

This chapter is a continuation of reasons why we believe in closed communion.

This text speaks of one bread for one body. The previous chapter showed that the church is a local body of baptized believers, and not a universal body of all believers. In this chapter, we will show that the *"church"* of Christ and the *"body"* of Christ are one and the same. Since this is true, the bread of the Lord' Supper is not for all believers in joint assembly, but only for those who constitute the body of Christ which is one church in particular, a specific group of baptized believers in covenant relationship. We will now consider what the Bible says on this subject.

SECTION ONE

CONSIDER THESE BIBLE TEACHINGS REGARDING THE CHURCH

A. Members enter it by baptism.

   1. It is said of the Jerusalem church in **Acts 2:41**, *"Then they that gladly received his word were baptized: and the same day there were added unto them about three thousand souls."*

2. This agrees with the commission of **Matthew 28:19** to *"Teach all nations, baptizing them."* It also agrees with the order established by Jesus Christ as seen in **John 4:1**, *"Jesus made and baptized .... disciples."*

3. It was by this means that, *"God hath set some in the church* (at Jerusalem), *first apostles,"* **1 Corinthians 12:28**.

4. How did members get in the Bible churches?

   a. **1 Corinthians 12:28** says they were *"set"* in.

   b. This was done when the saved were baptized, **Acts 2:41, 47**.

B. Furthermore, one church is composed of many members.

1. **1 Timothy 3:5, 12** say it has deacons.

2. By comparing **1 Corinthians 5:13** and **1 Corinthians 6:4**, you will see that the plural *"yourselves"* is used to describe the church in Corinth.

   a. Note that this letter was addressed directly to one specific church (Corinth). Believers beyond the Church in Corinth were baptized, but they did become members of the Church in Corinth. They became members of the church that baptized them.

   b. This one church had many members.

3. According to **Acts 2:41**, three thousand members were added to the Jerusalem church in one single day.

4. **1 Corinthians 12:28** shows *"one body"* has *"many members."*

C. The church has many responsibilities.

1. It is to win people to Christ, then baptize and teach them, **Matthew 28:19**.

2. It is to observe communion, **1 Corinthians 11:28**.

3. It is to purge its own ranks, **1 Corinthians 6:4** and **1 Corinthians 5:5**.

The Church of Christ and the Body of Christ Are the Same

D. All concrete references to the church speak of a specific church.

1. *"Unto the church of God which is at Corinth,"* **1 Corinthians 1:2.**
2. *"The church which was at Jerusalem,"* **Acts 8:1-3.**
3. *"Then had the churches rest...,"* **Acts 9:31.**
4. *"The church that was at Antioch,"* **Acts 13:1.**

E. Bear in mind that the above points speak of the church.

SECTION TWO

ALSO CONSIDER THESE BIBLE TEACHINGS REGARDING THE BODY

A. Members enter it by baptism.

1. **1 Corinthians 12:13** says that those *"by* (eis translates "by" or "in") *one Spirit are ... all baptized into one body:"*

    a. Those who believe are in the Spirit of God.

    (1) Paul said, *"...he that is joined unto the Lord is one spirit,"* **1 Corinthians 6:17.**

    (2) *"Ye are ... in the Spirit, if so be that the Spirit of God dwell in you,"* **Romans 8:9.**

    b. Those who receive the Spirit by faith are not yet water baptized, but they are candidates or fit subjects for water baptism, **Galatians 3:2.**

    c. Notice that the same is true for those who would enter the church.

2. By comparing **Ephesians 4:4-5** and **1 Corinthians 12:13**, you will note that there is but one baptism.

    a. If believers are automatically baptized at faith by the Holy Spirit, thus placing them in a universal spiritual body, then what about water baptism and the local body?

The Bible says there is *"one baptism"* and *"one body"* of **Ephesians 4:4-5**.

    b. The fact is that the *"one faith"* places believers into *"one Spirit,"* and these by obedience to *"one baptism,"* which is in water, are placed into *"one body,"* which is a local body or church.

B. Furthermore, the one body is composed of many members.

    1. **1 Corinthians 12:12, 14** says this is true. If the church or body is made up of everyone who is saved (the Universal Church concept), imagine the absurdness of the analogy in **1 Corinthians 12**. Obviously a local church or body is in clear view.

    2. The whole body is composed of many parts which are bonded together by joints, **Ephesians 4:16**.

C. The body has many responsibilities.

    1. To obey the commandments, **1 John 5:3**.

    2. To observe communion, **1 Corinthians 10:17** and **1 Corinthians 11:24-25**.

    3. To purge its own ranks, **1 Corinthians 11:31** and **1 Corinthians 12:25**.

D. All references to the body speak of a specific group.

    1. *"For we being many are one bread, and one body,"* **1 Corinthians 10:17**.

    2. The *"one body"* of **1 Corinthians 12:20** speaks specifically of the Corinthians. To them Paul said, *"...ye are the body of Christ,"* **1 Corinthians 12:27**.

    3. **Ephesians 4:16** is addressed specifically to the Ephesians, one local church or body.

E. Note well that all these references have been about the body.

SECTION THREE

NOW COMPARE *"THE CHURCH"* AND *"THE BODY"*

A. By comparison:

1. *"God set the members every one of them in the body,"* **1 Corinthians 12:18.**

2. *"God hath set some in the church,"* **1 Corinthians 12:28.**

3. To the church at Corinth He said, *"Ye are the body of Christ,"* **1 Corinthians 12:27.** The whole church was the body of Christ at Corinth. Obviously the *church* and the *body* at Corinth were one and the same. Members were set into it by water baptism.

B. We thus say that the two terms *"body"* and *"church"* are identical.

1. This is the clear assertion of the Apostle Paul. *"And he is the head of the body, the church: who is the beginning, the firstborn from the dead; that in all things he might have the preeminence,"* **Colossians 1:18.** *"Who now rejoice in my sufferings for you, and fill up that which is behind of the afflictions of Christ in my flesh for his body's sake, which is the church,"* **Colossians 1:24.** Note well that in both verses Paul equated *"the body"* with *"the church."*

2. Those who are not water baptized are no more the members of the body of Christ than they are of the church of God. He who is added to one, **Acts 2:47,** has been set in the other, **1 Corinthians 12:18.** This is done at water baptism.

3. If the church is local and the body is the same as the church, then the body is also local.

4. If the body is local, then each body is the body of Christ, not merely a small part of a much bigger universal body. The church in Corinth illustrates this truth, **1 Corinthians 12:27.**

5. *"One baptism"* according to the *"one faith"* in the name of the *"one Lord"* puts those who are in the *"one Spirit"* into the *"one body."* Only those in the *"one body"* can eat the *"one bread"* in the *"one place"* and still maintain the picture of the *"one faith."*

Chapter 46

The Biblical Definition of the Word *Church* Answers Many Questions

Matthew 16:18

Before people can intelligently discuss issues, the terms used must be defined. Mixed metaphors and signals produce confusion. And, often anger! *"For if the trumpet give an uncertain sound, who shall prepare himself to the battle? So likewise ye, except ye utter by the tongue words easy to be understood, how shall it be known what is spoken? for ye shall speak into the air,"* **1 Corinthians 14:8-9**. With this in mind we shall now look at the word *"church"* as used in the Bible. Our particular emphasis will be on the word as used in reference to Jesus' church.

SECTION ONE

THE TRUTH IS THAT THE ONLY KIND OF CHURCH THE LORD EVER BUILT WAS A TANGIBLE ASSEMBLY CAPABLE OF MEETING IN ONE LOCATION ON A WEEKLY BASIS

    A. The word church comes from the Greek word <u>ecclesia</u> and literally means "an assembly of called out ones."

The Biblical Definition of the Word Church Answers Many Questions

    1. Three times the word is used to describe the self-governing Greek state, **Acts 19:32, 39, 41**, and once it is used in reference to Old Testament Israel, **Acts 7:38**.

    2. In every other case, the Bible refers to the kind of church personally established by Jesus Christ, **Matthew 16:18**.

        a. 19 times it refers to the church as it will be in glory, (Prospective).

        b. 92 times it refers to a particular assembly.

            (1) The word is used in both the concrete or abstract senses, but in every one of these cases, the word denotes some particular assembly.

            (2) There is not one case in the Bible where the Lord's church is under consideration that the word *church* applies to any institution other than a particular assembly of water baptized believers.

            (3) The idea that Jesus' church is something bigger than a local assembly is not founded in the Scriptures.

B. Jesus built the first local church and said that kind of church would continue until His return.

    1. The first church was not built by Peter or Paul, but by Christ Himself, **Matthew 16:18**.

    2. Since that Jerusalem church, there has been a continuous line of churches embracing those same doctrines which Jesus taught.

    3. These have constituted the churches of the living God.

C. There are many Bible references which denote these local churches, but not one which denotes a mystical body made up of all saved people.

    1. **Revelation 1-3** speaks of seven local congregations.

    2. Time after time, the Bible refers to local bodies or churches, **1 Corinthians 1:2, 1 Thessalonians 1:1, 3 John 9, Romans 16:1, Galatians 1:2**, etc.

3. Surely if there exists a mystical body (church) of which all believers are members, the Scriptures would have mentioned it at least once.

D. Only a local church could possibly obey the Lord's command to assemble regularly, **Hebrews 10:25**, discipline its members, **Matthew 18:15-18** and suffer and rejoice together, **1 Corinthians 12:26**.

SECTION TWO

THE NON-BIBLICAL IDEA THAT JESUS' CHURCH IS UNIVERSAL

A. Many who profess Christ mistakenly assume that all believers are members of one true body or church. The concept is mystical in that the membership is not identifiable and only God knows who is in it. This mystical body is commonly called the universal or catholic church. The word catholic means universal. The concept falls into two main views.

1. A universal visible church. This is the Catholic Church idea, both Roman and Eastern. It's the idea that all Roman Catholics compose one true visible church. The Eastern Orthodox Catholic Church similarly believe that their membership constitutes one universal visible church. Though weekly assembly for a church of this sort is impossible, the members can be mentally identified as all members within the ranks of the given church. For both Roman and Eastern Catholic Churches, a personal faith in Jesus Christ is not necessary for membership. What is necessary is identification with the given church.

2. A universal invisible church. This is the idea that when a person believes in Jesus Christ as personal Savior, that person is spiritually baptized by the Holy Spirit into an imaginary spiritual body which is commonly known as the Universal Invisible Church. It is then believed that all saved people are members of this church, which they believe to be *the true church*.

B. The concept of a universal church not a valid biblical concept.

1. The concept is self-contradictory. *Universal* speaks of something that exists in all times at all places. *Church* speaks of assembly which demands locality. A church is a local assembly; it cannot be universal. Furthermore, that which is *invisible* is not *visible*. How could an invisible church visibly meet? Even the shallowest of critical looks exposes the weakness of such a self-contradictory concept. A universal church is really doubletalk.

2. The idea of a universal church is unfounded in the Scriptures and such an organization does not exist.

SECTION THREE

COMMUNION IN LIGHT OF THE TRUE CONCEPT OF JESUS' CHURCH

A. Since communion or the Lord's Supper is for the church and the church is a visible, identifiable assembly of baptized believers, it is not difficult to see that communion is an ordinance for the members of each visible, identifiable assembly or church.

1. From the Bible, it is impossible to get the idea of members of two or more churches jointly observing the Lord's Supper. Each Bible church of Jesus Christ was a complete, self-contained entity under the headship of Jesus Christ. Each met in its own location, had its own pastors and deacons, met on Sundays, conducted worship services, engaged directly in missionary work and kept the ordinances of baptism and the Lord's Supper.

2. The idea of members of two or more churches jointly observing the Lord's Supper contradicts the very concept, nature and definition of a true church of Jesus Christ.

B. The practice of all saved people being able to participate in communion or the Lord's Supper any time it is observed in any assembly or church is generally known as *Open Communion*.

1. It is obviously based upon a misconception of what a church of Jesus Christ is. The idea is based upon the misconception that all saved people make up one universal church. Since persons view themselves as saved and a member of the true universal church, they think they should be able to take communion. Thus members of multiple Baptist Churches along with Lutherans, Pentecostals, Catholics, Methodists and others have no problem joining together for a *"Communion Service."*

2. The whole practice is based upon a false or mistaken concept of what the Lord's church is and the fact that the ordinances (baptism and the Lord's Supper) are to be kept by each church.

C. Communion that is consistent with the Bible definition of Jesus' church and with the practice seen in the Scriptures is *Closed Communion*.

1. Members of one and only one church or assembly take the Lord's Supper or communion.

2. Each church is viewed as autonomous and conducts its own internal affairs. Each has its own location, members, pastor(s), deacons, treasury and constitution and bylaws. Members of other churches are not allowed to vote on internal affairs such as the church budget, the calling of a pastor and the buying or selling of property. Even in a court of law, only members have a voice. A lawsuit against a church is against a specific identifiable entity, not against all who claim to be saved people. In the legal world, the idea of a universal invisible church is a myth. As the Bible teaches, all true churches are visible and identifiable.

3. This is the only practice we see in the New Testament. As evidenced by the church in Corinth, each church attended its own business, including keeping the ordinances. Each church, not a mixture of churches, baptized and kept the Lord's Supper. The New Testament churches were not isolationists. They worked and cooperated in many ways, but each church was an autonomous, separate entity from each other church.

4. We believe the biblical definition of *church* and the practice we see in the New Testament demand an approach toward communion and baptism that is consistent therewith.

5. Those of us who practice closed communion are not trying to be offensive. We are not sitting in judgment of anyone's salvation. We highly value friendship and fellowship with other believers, and seek cooperation in the work of our great God. We genuinely believe communion is for the members of each assembly or church. Obviously there are solid biblical grounds for our convictions and practices.

The word church is clearly defined as a local assembly of people called out for a special purpose. All concepts and ideas that fail to conform to God's definition of *church* are proven false. That includes ideas such as a Universal Church and open communion. Staying true to the Scriptures demands conformity to scriptural definitions, **2 Timothy 2:15**, and a scriptural definition of Jesus' church demands closed communion and a local assembly of people.

Chapter 47

The Make Up and Structure of an Autonomous Church

Exodus 25:40 - Acts 7:42-45

It is granted that these text verses do not refer to the church. They do talk about doing God's work the way He said to do it. We believe that whatever God tells you to do, from building a tabernacle to operating His church, it should be done according to His instructions or after the pattern which He has given. We believe that once God has shown us the way on anything, we have no right to alter it in any way.

Regarding church association or affiliation with other churches, God has shown us the way. Since we find that our pattern churches (the Bible churches) were autonomous and independent of each other, then in following their pattern, we too must be autonomous.

This is the first of four chapters dealing with the autonomy of each local church. This chapter shows that an autonomous church is structurally different from all other forms of interaction between churches.

A. An autonomous church is built after the pattern of the New Testament churches.

    1. Its foremost concern is following the leadership of the Lord.

- a. Christ alone is recognized as the head of the church. He was unquestionably recognized at the head of churches during Bible days, **Ephesians 5:23**.
- b. The Scriptures prove that the church should always be free to follow the leadership of God.
  - (1) *"For as many as are led by the Spirit of God, they are the sons of God,"* **Romans 8:14**.
  - (2) *"But if ye be led of the Spirit, ye are not under the law,"* **Galatians 5:18**.
  - (3) Regardless of what other men or churches do, each church is to walk in truth before God, **2 John 4**.
  - (4) The church through God's Word is to function as God's final, sovereign and authoritative institution for propagating the truth on earth, **Matthew 16:19** and **Matthew 18:18**.
  - (5) The church is never in any way to be tied to another party which has the capacity to over-rule it and divert its attention from following the leadership of God, **2 Corinthians 6:14**.

2. An autonomous church cooperates, but never becomes allied with other churches.
   - a. The Bible churches cooperated to do missionary work.
     - (1) The Antioch church sent out Paul, **Acts 13:2-3**, but other churches helped in various ways, **1 Corinthians 16:2, 1 Corinthians 16:15-17, Philippians 1:5, Philippians 4:14-16**.
     - (2) Note that each church directly assisted Paul. They did not do so indirectly through any sort of parachurch organization.
   - b. The Bible churches cooperated together in the asking and giving of advice and recommendations.
     - (1) **1 Corinthians 16:3** speaks of letters of recommendation.

(2) **Acts 15:1-6** is an example of requested advice.

c. There are not any Bible examples where one or a group of churches had jurisdiction or control over a sister church. No church could boss, reprimand or censor another church. The Apostles had jurisdiction over those early churches, but when they died, that jurisdiction ceased.

3. An autonomous church believes the Lord's Great Commission rests squarely on the shoulders of the church and the church alone, **Matthew 28:19-20**.

4. An autonomous church would be diagrammed as one church tied solely to God and not in any way subject to the authority of another church or ecclesiastical organization.

B. Churches that are not fully autonomous are structurally different.

1. In all cases, the church is only a small part of something bigger; the structure generally is as follows:

    a. The local church is one of many in a local area organization.

    b. The local area organization is one of several local organizations in a state or area organization.

    c. The state organization is one of many state organizations.

    d. These are a part of the parent or national organization. There may even be an international organization.

    e. The local church becomes a very small part with very limited voice in a big, big machine.

2. Upon affiliation with the organization of churches, the local church largely loses its identity and relinquishes to some degree its sovereignty, autonomy and independence.

    a. Whether its cooperation is voluntary or involuntary is irrelevant; the end result is the same.

        (1) The local church voice is swallowed up by the organization.

(2) The church finds itself like a chained man; he may be chained voluntarily or involuntarily, but he is still chained.

b. Local church policy is not solely influenced by the leadership of the Lord, but it is largely determined by the denomination, board of directors or majority vote of the churches of the organization.

c. In name, the head of the church is the Lord, but in effect and practice, the head is the person or persons running the organization of churches.

d. The church cannot answer to God alone for its actions and convictions. The church must abide by the standards of the organization. Furthermore, as a part of the organization, the church becomes a partaker in all the deeds of the organization.

e. In church organizations such as conventions, associations and denominations, functions that should be exclusively those of the local church are passed to the organization for administration.

(1) Generally the organization assumes the role of approving, sending and administering missionaries.

(2) Often organization officials set themselves up as spokesmen for the churches.

(3) The organization assumes the role of policy leadership for its local churches. All churches within the organization are expected to follow that leadership.

f. If one local church strays too far from the policies and programs of the parent organization, it is either reprimanded, sanctioned or removed.

g. The organization churches interpret the great commission to be the responsibility of the combined churches and not the responsibility of each local church.

3. The diagram of organization churches is very different from that of autonomous churches.

C. It is up to those who would terminate the autonomy of the church by bringing it into an organization of churches to justify their action in the Scriptures.

    1. It is really not up to churches that are autonomous to prove that parachurch ecclesiastical organizations are wrong. It is up to those parachurch organizations to justify their existence on biblical grounds.

    2. Let them show from the Bible that such an organization ever existed.

    3. Let them show from the Bible that a *Missions Board* ever existed. Outside of a church, let someone produce a Bible example of a president, vice president, treasurer, secretary or board of directors for a parachurch organization.

    4. Let them give us one Bible case where any institution on earth other than a church ever approved or sent out a Christian missionary.

    5. Let them show us from the Bible where a group of churches ever got together and voted anything binding on a sister church.

    6. Let them point out in the Scriptures one parachurch central treasury to which two or more churches sent money.

    7. Let them show us in the Bible where the churches ever held an organizational meeting and what business they conducted.

    8. If there was ever an organization of churches, which churches were in it? If they can produce such an organization, what was that organization designed to accomplish?

D. The fact is that when you look into the Bible (the only book that really counts when it comes to pleasing God, **Romans 10:17** and **Hebrews 11:6**) you can see plenty of autonomous churches that cooperated but were independent of each other. You will not see even one example of any other kind.

Chapter 48

The Bible Churches Were Autonomous

Exodus 25:40 - Acts 7:42-45

These text verses were chosen because they show that when God gives a pattern or plan, He expects that plan or pattern followed without variance. This being true, God wants every one of His churches to follow the pattern and examples of the New Testament churches. Since all the pattern churches were autonomous, then all churches in every age should also be autonomous.

The previous chapter compared and contrasted the differences in the structure of an autonomous church and the structure of churches which entangle themselves in ecclesiastical organizations. This chapter will focus on some of the autonomous church models that abound in the Scriptures.

SECTION ONE

IN THE NEW TESTAMENT, GOD ESTABLISHED A PATTERN OR MODEL CHURCH

A. The only God-given models for churches which we have to follow are the ones seen in the New Testament. In them we see only models of autonomous churches.

1. As the Scriptures are examined, no ecclesiastical organizations of churches are found. None!

2. It is a historical fact that ecclesiastical organizations originated long after the completion of the New Testament.

B. Look at the Bible churches.

1. Consider the very first church that ever existed.

    a. It was built personally by Jesus Christ.

        (1) To His Apostles, Jesus said He would build His church, **Matthew 16:17-18**.

        (2) These Apostles were the first members of that first church, **1 Corinthians 12:28**.

        (3) When that church began to function, those Apostles were named as being part of it, **Acts 1:13**. There were other members bringing the number to about 120 people or members, **Acts 1:14-15**.

        (4) This church met in Jerusalem, **Acts 1:12**. They were a church, **Acts 2:47**, which soon became known as *"the church which was at Jerusalem,"* **Acts 8:1**.

    b. Surely the church built personally by Jesus Christ is the ultimate pattern for all churches.

        (1) No one knows more than Jesus about how to set up and run a church.

        (2) If the pattern established by Jesus is not the right pattern, who could say what the right pattern is or how a church should be set up and governed?

        (3) Unquestionably, the church which Jesus built is the pattern to be followed.

    c. Let it be carefully noted that no church existed before Jesus built the Jerusalem church.

        (1) That church was the very first one that ever existed upon the face of the earth.

(2) Later other churches sprang up, but all of them resulted from efforts put forth by the Jerusalem church. In the process of time, these baby churches grew up and established other churches, but all of them stemmed from the Jerusalem church.

(3) The scriptural record confirms that from the beginning of the Jerusalem church, it was several days, weeks, and probably months, before there was a second church. Obviously, the Jerusalem church was autonomous. It was the only church in existence.

d. The conclusion is evident: it had to be an autonomous church.

(1) There were no other churches with which it could affiliate.

(2) It would be irrelevant to speculate about whether or not it would have if it could have joined an ecclesiastical organization.

(3) An examination of the original, God ordained pattern for scriptural light about how a church is to be structured and operated says churches must remain autonomous.

2. Furthermore, all churches which later sprang up in the New Testament were autonomous and unaffiliated with ecclesiastical organizations.

a. As time passed, churches were formed in Antioch, **Acts 13:1**; Corinth, **1 Corinthians 1:2**; Ephesus, **Revelation 2:1**; Philippi, **Philippians 4:15**; Galatia, **1 Corinthians 16:1**; Rome, **Romans 16:1-27**; and in many other places.

b. They preached, prayed, sang, sent and supported missionaries, gave and did many things, but they never formed an ecclesiastical organization of churches.

c. There's no evidence to support any position except that each church solely ran its own affairs. They followed the leadership of the Lord strictly, separately and apart from all the other churches.

    d. Only the autonomous church model is seen in the Scriptures.

SECTION TWO

WE BELIEVE THAT WE SHOULD FOLLOW THE BIBLE PATTERN AND EXAMPLES SHOULD BE FOLLOWED BY CHURCHES

A. It is God who gives the orders about churches and how they should function. All churches are to follow His leadership.

    1. In **Matthew 4:19, Mark 2:14, Luke 5:27, Matthew 16:24, Matthew 19:21** and many other passages, Jesus said *"follow me."* Listen to Jesus' words, *"if any man serve me, let him follow me,"* **John 12:26**.

    2. **Ephesians 5:23** calls Him *"the head of the church"* and it is a fact that the head tells the body what to do; not vice-versa.

    3. The Bible calls Him *"captain"* of our salvation, **Hebrews 2:10**, *"The author and finisher of our faith,"* **Hebrews 12:2**.

    4. Too often men and churches assume they have the right to enter into the realm of command.

        a. They take it upon themselves to change God's plans and methods.

        b. They are not content to follow; they want to help God run His business.

B. In all we do, the Bible often admonishes us to follow God's pattern or instructions.

    1. **Exodus 25:40** is one of many passages which clearly establishes God's thinking on the subject. To paraphrase, God said *Do it just like I told you to do it.*

2. *"God is a Spirit: and they that worship him must worship him in spirit and in truth,"* **John 4:24**. *"My little children, let us not love in word, neither in tongue; but in deed and in truth,"* **1 John 3:18**.

   a. *"In truth,"* not just however you see fit! Follow God's pattern.

   b. Do it God's way. That means acting in accord with what God has said in His Word. His Word is truth, **John 17:17**.

3. Jesus said, *"If any man will come after me, let him deny himself, and take up his cross daily, and follow me,"* **Luke 9:23**. The scriptural principle is denial of our ways and submission to His ways.

4. Peter left no doubt about how we're to do it. He said, *"For even hereunto were ye called: because Christ also suffered for us, leaving us an example, that ye should follow his steps,"* **1 Peter 2:21**.

C. The Bible argument speaks: In all things follow the Scriptural patterns. When it comes to an internal church structure and the matter of ecclesiastical entanglements, every church must be autonomous. Otherwise it violates the Scriptural pattern.

Chapter 49

No One Is at Liberty to Violate the God-Ordained Pattern for Church Organization and Operations

Exodus 25:40 - Acts 7:42-45

These chapters are designed to show you that every church should be patterned after the church which Jesus built. Since that church and the ones which came from it were fully autonomous, we believe that all churches should be autonomous. We do not believe that anyone is at liberty to alter, change or forsake God's pattern.

A. The great God whom we serve is a jealous God and He is very much opposed to any man altering His methods or plans even in a small way. Listen to His warnings.

   1. The divine attitude of God on changing His plans is illustrated in King Darius, **Ezra 6:10-12**. Failure to do things His way is a most serious offense to God.

   2. God warned about changing His Book, **Revelation 22:18-19**. The Bible contains the methods and plans of God including those about His churches and how they are to function.

   3. In light of these two passages, what do you suppose God thinks of a church which violates or turns from His methods and plans of operation?

4. Listen to these other passages which lead us to believe God wants things done exactly as He prescribes.

   a. God said, *"Remove not the ancient landmark, which thy fathers have set,"* **Proverbs 22:28**.

   b. God told Joshua, *"Be strong and of a good courage: for unto this people shalt thou divide for an inheritance the land, which I sware unto their fathers to give them. Only be thou strong and very courageous, that thou mayest observe to do according to all the law, which Moses my servant commanded thee: turn not from it to the right hand or to the left, that thou mayest prosper whithersoever thou goest,"* **Joshua 1:6-7**.

   c. *"Ye shall observe to do therefore as the LORD your God hath commanded you: ye shall not turn aside to the right hand or to the left,"* **Deuteronomy 5:32**.

   d. *"And thou shalt not go aside from any of the words which I command thee this day...,"* **Deuteronomy 28:14**.

   e. Through his prophet Jeremiah, God said, *"But this thing commanded I them, saying, Obey my voice, and I will be your God, and ye shall be my people: and walk ye in all the ways that I have commanded you, that it may be well unto you,"* **Jeremiah 7:23**.

   f. *"Ye shall walk in all the ways which the LORD your God hath commanded you, that ye may live, and that it may be well with you, and that ye may prolong your days in the land which ye shall possess,"* **Deuteronomy 5:33**.

   g. Because the Ephesus church altered God's pattern, He said to them, *"Nevertheless I have somewhat against thee, because thou hast left thy first love,"* **Revelation 2:4**.

   h. To let it be known that he was following God's pattern to the letter, Paul was careful to point out, *"I delivered unto you first of all that which I also received,"* **1 Corinthians 15:3** and **1 Corinthians 11:23**.

5. It is with scriptural authority that we say that no person is at liberty to vary, alter, and attempt to improve God's methods.

    a. To the contrary, we are to follow His plans and leadership precisely, realizing and acknowledging Him and Him alone as the boss and the one who establishes policy.

    b. Churches that practice unscriptural ecclesiastical affiliation and fail to remain autonomous would do well to consider God's attitude about their activities.

B. The Scriptures provide a host of examples which illustrate that God would have us follow His instructions precisely.

    1. By comparing **Hebrews 11:4** with **Romans 10:17**, it can be seen that Abel followed God's instructions while Cain didn't. The result is that Abel's sacrifice satisfied God, while Cain's disgusted Him, **Genesis 4:1-15**.

    2. Noah built an ark *"according to all that God commanded him, so did he,"* **Genesis 6:22**. Only he and his family survived the flood, **Genesis 7:23**.

    3. The righteous man David, **Romans 4:6**, chose to do a good thing in a slightly different manner than God had prescribed. To his sorrow, he found that his misdeed kindled the wrath of God.

        a. He decided to move the Ark of the Covenant from the city of Baale to Jerusalem, **2 Samuel 6:2**. The thing he proposed to do was good and according to the will of God, **1 Chronicles 13:1-4**.

        b. Earlier, God established rules for moving the Ark of the Covenant. Any time that Ark was to be moved, it was to be carried on foot by priests on their shoulders, **Exodus 25:14**.

        c. Furthermore the Ark could only be carried upon the shoulders of the priests who were the sons of Kohath, **Numbers 7:9**.

        d. However, David proceeded to move the Ark on an oxen drawn cart, **1 Chronicles 13:7-9** and **2 Samuel 6:3**.

      e. The result was the death of Uzzah, a great soldier of David, **2 Samuel 6:7**. This dramatic intervention by God halted the moving of the Ark for three months, **1 Chronicles 13:13-14**. The fear of God fell on David who asked, *"How shall I bring the ark of God home to me?"* **1 Chronicles 13:12**.

      f. When later David moved that Ark on to Jerusalem, the priests *"bare the ark of the LORD,"* **2 Samuel 6:13**. The sons of Kohath carried it by foot, **1 Chronicles 15:5**, and bore it upon their shoulders as they walked, **1 Chronicles 15:15**. This is exactly how God originally commanded the Ark to be transported. David acknowledged that if he had done it God's way the first time, God would not have been angered, **1 Chronicles 15:2, 12-13**. Doing what God said from the start would have prevented enormous grief and embarrassment.

4. King Saul also took upon himself to do a thing reserved for God's priests, **Leviticus 1:7-9**. He intruded into the office of the priest, **1 Samuel 13:8-10**. To his great sorrow, Saul learned that his foolish failure to follow God's method highly displeased God. Saul paid a very high price, **1 Samuel 13:13-14, 1 Samuel 15:11**.

5. Consider what happened to Moses when he disobeyed God in what appeared to be a small matter. In an effort to get water, God told Moses to *"speak"* to a rock, **Numbers 20:8**. Instead Moses *"smote"* the rock, **Numbers 20:11**. The sad result is recorded in **Numbers 20:12**.

6. There are many other fine examples in the Bible which teach us to stick closely to God's plans in all things.

C. In light of what we see in the Bible on this subject, we conclude that no man or church has the liberty to depart from the patterns which God has given us to follow.

    1. There is not one case in the Bible where God approved of departure from His way.

2. If God wants people to follow His patterns in all things, then it must be true that His people should follow His church pattern.

3. The first church and all the churches in the Bible were autonomous.

   a. These churches are God's pattern for all churches to follow.

   b. Since they were autonomous, every church should be autonomous.

Chapter 50

The Sin of Failing to Exactly Follow God's Pattern in Church Organization

Exodus 25:40 - Acts 7:42-45

The Scriptures prove that God requires compliance with His patterns and examples. We believe that we should obey God and follow His example in all things, even in determining what kind of relations one church can have with another. The majority of modern churches do not think that taking a strict interpretation of Scripture is important. We believe it is important to do what God said in the way He said to do it. This applies to church matters. Our argument simply is that we are autonomous because church autonomy is taught in the Scriptures.

A. Much Bible evidence has already been presented proving that what God thinks it is very important.

B. However, many modern church people rationalize.

    1. They rationalize that the good accomplished by big organizations far offsets the evils and shortcomings.

        a. In effect, this says the end justifies the means.

    b. If this line of argument is sound, then why can't we rob banks to feed the hungry? Why don't we take the blood of whole men to save those in need of blood?

2. They rationalize that the organizational method is the only really effective way to accomplish the Lord's work in this century.

    a. In effect, this says that Bible methods won't work anymore.

    b. The fact is that God never has given us reason to believe His methods will become outdated and unworkable.

3. They also rationalize that variations from God's plan are acceptable as long as a person is sincere in what he is doing.

    a. It has already been shown that God expects far more than sincerity, **John 4:24**.

    b. *"There is a way which seemeth right unto a man, but the end thereof are the ways of death,"* **Proverbs 14:12**.

4. Men and churches cannot accurately guide their lives by the map of human reasoning (rationalization). God said through Jeremiah, *"O LORD, I know that the way of man is not in himself: it is not in man that walketh to direct his steps,"* **Jeremiah 10:23**.

C. In spite of this, churches by the thousands have felt at complete liberty to change God's plan for local church autonomy by a multitude of ecclesiastical entanglements.

    1. If a church is at liberty to change God's instructions about His church, then why not alter God's instructions on other matters?

        a. Why tithe? Why not give as you please: a fifteenth or 25th?

        b. Why have church services on Sunday; why not Thursday? Why not drop all services on holidays and meet just once a month?

  c. Why not just drop preaching and giving, and just have a music event?

  d. Why obey God's laws about marriage? Why not have 5 or 6 wives? Why marry at all? Why not just live together?

  e. It's not difficult to see the drift in this direction. The slippery slope of compromise is hard to control. Where does it stop? After all, if you can change God's plan on one point, why not on all? Is it any worse to compromise in one area than in another?

  f. The truth is that those who violate church order, yet claim to hold to the truth are inconsistent.

2. No church has any right to rationalize away God's methods as being outdated or unimportant. When they do, they are wrong.

  a. Heresy can be preached or practiced. Desertion of the teachings of God as set forth in the Scriptures is a form of heresy.

  b. **Ephesians 2:10** says we should *"walk"* in truth.

D. The result of walking in error is corruption and trouble just as Saul, David and Moses learned.

1. All ecclesiastical organizations outside the church run into inequities and corruptions.

  a. Most all of them provide a political ladder for their young preachers to climb. This diverts attention from God and appeals to pride, self-exaltation and vain-glory. It has been the ruin of many young preachers.

  b. Members of ecclesiastically entangled churches lose their voices. To keep peace, they must go along with the big organization of churches. That often means violation of their own consciences.

  c. Individual churches within the big organization find themselves disapproving many things, but not quite disgusted enough to quit.

d. Many ecclesiastical churches funnel the Lord's money into activities that are not remotely related to the Great Commission.

2. Inequities arise because the whole system is an unholy alliance. The Bible says, *"If the root be holy, so are the branches,"* **Romans 11:16**.

3. There is a day of reckoning to God for churches that depart from God's pattern.

   a. *"Every transgression and disobedience received a just recommence of reward,"* **Hebrews 2:2**.

   b. Churches that refuse to align themselves with God's methods will perish under God's chastening hand.

We conclude that to be scriptural, churches must be autonomous.

Chapter 51

The Lord's Church Should Be Missionary

Mark 16:15

We believe the number one responsibility of every saved person is to evangelize; to reach out with all zeal to bring others into the family of God. That responsibility rests upon us, not only as individuals, but collectively as a church.

SECTION ONE

THE NECESSITY OF BEING EVANGELISTIC IS CLEARLY UPON US

A. A large number of Scriptures teach us to be constant witnesses.

1. The text teaches us to *"go,"* **Mark 16:15**.

2. The heart of the Great Commission is evangelism, **Matthew 28:19-20**.

3. The last thing Christ told the apostles was to be missionaries, **Acts 1:8**.

4. **Luke 24:46-48** teaches us to be witnesses.

5. Jesus said, *"As my Father hath sent me, even so send I you,"* **John 20:21**.

6. Jesus said in **Matthew 4:19** *"I will make you fishers of men."*

7. Our purpose as believers is to bring others to the knowledge of Christ.

   a. Jesus said, *"I have chosen you, and ordained you, that ye should go and bring forth fruit,"* **John 15:16**.

   b. God told Paul that he was saved for the purpose of winning souls, **Acts 26:16-18**.

8. The example which the church is to follow is seen in **Acts 5:42** where *"daily in the temple, and in every house, they ceased not to teach and preach Jesus Christ."*

B. We conclude that neither individuals nor churches can be obedient to God without being actively engaged in missions.

   1. Missions and evangelism are the heart and core of our business.

   2. Nowhere do the Scriptures teach us to wait for men to come; we are to go after them.

SECTION TWO

THE PROSPERITY AND INCREASE OF THE LORD'S WORK DEPENDS HEAVILY ON HOW ENGAGED HIS PEOPLE ARE IN MISSIONARY WORK

A. The Bible teaches that if we are faithful to evangelize, God will bless our efforts.

   1. If we go, we will win some, **Psalm 126:5-6**.

   2. *"Cast thy bread upon the waters: for thou shalt find it after many days,"* **Ecclesiastes 11:1**.

   3. *"To him that soweth righteousness shall be a sure reward,"* **Proverbs 11:18**.

4. Evangelism is an essential prerequisite to building churches, winning souls and developing dedicated workers.

B. Nothing of spiritual value is accomplished when Christians cease to be evangelistic.

   1. Unless someone tells them the gospel, souls will not be won, **Romans 10:14-15**.

   2. Fulltime ministers should live of the gospel, **1 Corinthians 9:14**. Without adequate support, the work pastors and missionaries is greatly hampered, **Nehemiah 13:10**. Evangelism diminishes, which does not please God.

   3. When God's people quit sowing, there is no legitimate reason to expect a bountiful harvest of souls. Consider **Proverbs 6:6-11**.

      a. Without evangelism, the number of people won to Christ goes down, pews grow empty, coffers grow empty, a shortage of laborers develops and the work of God suffers.

      b. Missionizing is what perpetuates and enlarges the Lord's work.

   4. The Bible thus warns, *"Woe to them that are at ease in Zion,"* **Amos 6:1**.

SECTION THREE

THERE ARE THREE WAYS TO PARTICIPATE IN MISSIONS

A. Every person can be a witness wherever he goes. God calls some to special fulltime service. The Christian most likely to be called to broader service is the one who is faithful where he is.

   1. Our personal testimony should be in effect daily, **Matthew 5:16, Philippians 2:15**.

   2. As He did with Isaiah, on occasion God sets some men wholly into His ministry, **Isaiah 6:8**.

B. Every person can directly participate in missions by praying for missionaries and the furtherance of God's work.

    1. The Bible teaches us to *"Pray one for another,"* **James 5:16**, and particularly for missionaries and the prosperity of His work, **Hebrews 13:18**.

    2. Prayer is a means of sustaining missionaries and missionary work, **Philippians 1:19-20**.

    3. We believe that every believer should pray for the furtherance of God's work and kingdom.

C. People can also directly participate in evangelism by giving of their substance to missionary work.

    1. Giving pays the bills and feeds the workers, **Nehemiah 13:10-12**.

    2. Giving will produce fruits to the account of the one who gives, **Philippians 4:15-17**.

    3. Churches and individuals should give to the work of evangelism and missions.

D. Evangelism is our main business. It is extremely important that every Christian and church be fully engaged in evangelist and missionary work.

Chapter 52

The Authority to Carry out Missionary Work Rests in the Church

Mark 16:15

We believe that God gave the authority for doing mission work exclusively to the church and that the church alone has the authority to send and supervise missionaries. As individuals participate in missionary work, they are to do so through the church.

SECTION ONE

MISSIONARY WORK IS TO BE CONDUCTED DIRECTLY BY THE CHURCH

A. God gave the Great Commission to the church, not to individuals apart from His church.

1. The Great Commission was given by Jesus, **Matthew 28:19-20**. He gave it to the first members of the church He established in Jerusalem, **1 Corinthians 12:28**.

2. The Commission was reemphasized in **Acts 1:8**.

B. In Bible days, the practice was to conduct missionary work directly through the churches.

   1. The missionaries were directly approved and sent by the local churches.

   a. The Jerusalem church sent Barnabas directly by the church, **Acts 11:22**.

   b. The Antioch church directly sent Paul and Barnabas, **Acts 13:2-3**.

   c. Paul was sent a second time directly by a church, **Acts 15:39-40**.

   2. The Bible missionaries answered to the local church.

   a. Paul and Barnabas answered directly to their home church, **Acts 14:26-28**.

   b. Again Paul answered to a local church, **Acts 15:30-31**.

   c. The same approach is seen in **Acts 18:22-23**.

   3. Bible missionaries were directly supported by the local church.

   a. The Philippians directly supported Paul, **Philippians 4:14-18**.

   b. The Macedonians practiced direct missionary support, **2 Corinthians 8:1-4, 2 Corinthians 11:9**.

   c. Other churches directly supported Paul, **2 Corinthians 11:8**.

C. God wants glory for work in His service to come through His churches: souls saved, new churches established, new believers brought to maturity and the list could go on for a long time.

   1. The church is the institution which Christ *"loved ... and gave himself for,"* **Ephesians 5:25**.

   2. It is primarily through this channel that God wants to glorify Himself, *"Unto him be glory in the church by Christ Jesus throughout all ages, world without end. Amen,"* **Ephesians 3:21**.

D. Keep in mind that God wants His business conducted in His way.

   1. Missionary work is His business and He wants it done by local churches.

   2. No church is at liberty to alter God's method for missionary work.

E. When missionaries are sent directly by the church:

   1. The church knows the missionary and each missionary is supported solely on his own merits. He rises or falls on his own record. Other missionaries may not do their jobs, but each church-sent missionary is accountable to his local church and those who assist only for his own record.

   2. The voice for approving and administering each missionary rests solely in the church. Once the church approves a missionary, no other religious organization has a voice. He is accountable to his church.

   3. Furthermore, by this approach the missionary receives 100% of the money sent by the church to him.

SECTION TWO

THE TREND TODAY IS TO DEPART FROM THE NEW TESTAMENT PLAN FOR MISSIONARY WORK

A. The current tendency is to do missionary work through parachurch organizations. In Bible days, missionary work was always done by local churches.

   1. Such organizations are generally called mission boards or societies.

   2. The board or society is often the arm or sub-organization of a large organization of churches. It is indirectly an organ of the churches.

   3. These boards set standards, approve and administer missionaries.

4. Many large missionary agencies direct funds and financially administer missionaries from a large central money pool financed by the contributing churches. Control is not in the churches; it is in the agency.

5. The missionary is directly accountable to the mission board or agency and only indirectly to the churches.

B. This system is quite different from the *church-sent* missions system which is seen in the Scriptures.

1. The mission board assumes the responsibility of the Great Commission which was given to the church.

2. The mission board takes charge and the church loses most of its voice in the matter.

   a. God calls missionaries, and churches send those missionaries to the mission board for approval.

   b. If the missionary can't pass the physical, is too old, doesn't have sufficient education, hasn't taken the right *missions course* in the college that satisfies the board or in some other way he can't meet muster, the mission board usually will not approve him.

3. Once the missionary is sent, he answers first to his mission board and then to his church. In the larger, more sophisticated mission agencies, a home-church for a missionary is not a consideration. The real power and authority lies in the mission agency or board.

4. Mission board missionaries are only indirectly an extension of a church.

5. Any glory that God gets from that type missionary operation comes through the mission board, not through the church.

C. This system is an alteration of God's plan. We believe God does not approve or sanction it.

1. We believe missionaries should be sent, administered and supported solely and wholly by the Lord's churches.

D. Keep in mind that God wants His business conducted in His way.

1. Missionary work is His business and He wants it done by local churches.

2. No church is at liberty to alter God's method for missionary work.

E. When missionaries are sent directly by the church:

1. The church knows the missionary and each missionary is supported solely on his own merits. He rises or falls on his own record. Other missionaries may not do their jobs, but each church-sent missionary is accountable to his local church and those who assist only for his own record.

2. The voice for approving and administering each missionary rests solely in the church. Once the church approves a missionary, no other religious organization has a voice. He is accountable to his church.

3. Furthermore, by this approach the missionary receives 100% of the money sent by the church to him.

SECTION TWO

THE TREND TODAY IS TO DEPART FROM THE NEW TESTAMENT PLAN FOR MISSIONARY WORK

A. The current tendency is to do missionary work through parachurch organizations. In Bible days, missionary work was always done by local churches.

1. Such organizations are generally called mission boards or societies.

2. The board or society is often the arm or sub-organization of a large organization of churches. It is indirectly an organ of the churches.

3. These boards set standards, approve and administer missionaries.

4. Many large missionary agencies direct funds and financially administer missionaries from a large central money pool financed by the contributing churches. Control is not in the churches; it is in the agency.

5. The missionary is directly accountable to the mission board or agency and only indirectly to the churches.

B. This system is quite different from the *church-sent* missions system which is seen in the Scriptures.

1. The mission board assumes the responsibility of the Great Commission which was given to the church.

2. The mission board takes charge and the church loses most of its voice in the matter.

   a. God calls missionaries, and churches send those missionaries to the mission board for approval.

   b. If the missionary can't pass the physical, is too old, doesn't have sufficient education, hasn't taken the right *missions course* in the college that satisfies the board or in some other way he can't meet muster, the mission board usually will not approve him.

3. Once the missionary is sent, he answers first to his mission board and then to his church. In the larger, more sophisticated mission agencies, a home-church for a missionary is not a consideration. The real power and authority lies in the mission agency or board.

4. Mission board missionaries are only indirectly an extension of a church.

5. Any glory that God gets from that type missionary operation comes through the mission board, not through the church.

C. This system is an alteration of God's plan. We believe God does not approve or sanction it.

1. We believe missionaries should be sent, administered and supported solely and wholly by the Lord's churches.

2. We believe that no person or parachurch organization has any Scriptural right to engage in missionary work independently of local churches.

About the Author

LESTER HUTSON served as a Baptist pastor for over 55 years. He is now Associate Pastor of Northwest Baptist Church in Houston, a field representative for the Christian Law Association, a conference and revival speaker and the author of numerous books including *Basic Bible Truths,* an internationally used soul-winning method.

www.lesterhutson.org